WISCONSIN'S FLYING TREES
IN
WORLD WAR II

A VICTORY FOR AMERICAN FOREST PRODUCTS AND ALLIED AVIATION

Sara W. Connor

SARA WITTER CONNOR

Charleston · London

THE
History
PRESS

Published by The History Press
Charleston, SC 29403
www.historypress.net

Front cover, top: The De Havilland Mosquito or "Wooden Wonder. *Courtesy of Camp 5 Museum Foundation/Wisconsin Forestry Museum, Laona, Wisconsin*; *bottom*: Howard Hughes's H4 Flying Boat, known as the "Spruce Goose," under construction in Culver City, California. *Courtesy of the U.S. Forest Products Laboratory Library, Madison, Wisconsin.*

Back cover, top: Northwestern Aeronautical Corporation CG-4A gliders at Chamberlain Field, St. Paul, Minnesota. *Courtesy of Villaume Corporation, St. Paul, Minnesota*; *bottom, left to right*: Lumber Goes to War. *Courtesy of Northwestern University Library, Evanston, Illinois*; Rosie the Riveter. *Courtesy of the Library of Congress, Washington, D.C.*; More Firepower to Win. *Courtesy of Camp 5 Museum Foundation/Wisconsin Forestry Museum, Laona, Wisconsin.*

First published 2014

Manufactured in the United States

ISBN 978.1.62619.350.5

Library of Congress CIP data applied for.

CONTENTS

This book is dedicated to my family and my grandchildren, Holden, Robert, Libby, George and Henry James, so that they will continue to "connect the past to the present" and learn what it means to have "sawdust in their veins."

ACKNOWLEDGEMENTS

Many 82nd Airborne and 101st Airborne friends have told their stories in this book. I would like to thank the World War II veterans for their service. I would also like to thank the men and women on the homefront for their contribution to the war effort in the forest products industry. Some have gone, and this book is for them in their memory. The people of northern and central Wisconsin—Marshfield, the "women in the barn"; Wisconsin Rapids; Stevens Point; Mellen; Butternut; White Lake; Park Falls; Laona; Phelps; and Goodman—as well as Wakefield, Ironwood and the Upper Peninsula of Michigan and so many forest products communities; this is our story.

This book was assembled through the help of Connor and Roddis family members. Thank you to Bruce and our many journeys, Jim for technology support and Justin for encouragement. Mary provided untold hours of manuscript editing, as well as fact checking. Cate accumulated Mosquito photos and the "War Papers." Thanks to Diane for her work on the title! On the forestry side for resources, I relied on my brother, Gordon. The Hamilton Roddis Foundation supported the "Wisconsin's Flying Trees: Wisconsin Plywood Industry's Contribution to WWII" exhibit through Camp 5 Museum Foundation in Laona, Wisconsin.

There are many people on this journey who deserve thanks for their continued assistance, corporations, libraries, museums, organizations nationally and internationally and individuals included. Thank you to Dr. Mark Schug, University of Wisconsin–Milwaukee (Emeritus), friend and colleague; Kathy Borkowsky for her friendship and the Wisconsin Historical Society; the University of Wisconsin–Department of Forestry, Wildlife and Ecology, particularly Dr. Jeff Stier and Dr. Scott Bowe; and last, but far from least, Dr. Tom Steele, director of UW–Kemp Station, who supported this project from its infancy. Thank you to Charles Day, friend, for his World War II glider expertise. Thanks to Karen Baumgartner for her efforts and the Price County Historical Society.

Research support came from Julie Blankenburg, librarian at Forest Products Laboratory, and my friends Sue Paulson (retired) and John Koning, who sadly died in 2012; his work at and brilliant history of the U.S. Forest Products Laboratory was greatly appreciated. So, too, was the continued research support from Cheryl Oakes, archivist and librarian of the Forest History Society at Duke University in Durham, on my visit and during the writing of this book. T.R. Dellin did research at the National Archives in London. Thanks to Charles Babbage Institute at University of Minnesota, Karen Sughrue, Nicole Jordan, Erika Eichelberger, Maureen Drennan in New York, Steinway & Sons and its LaGuardia & Wagner Archives at CUNY and Gib Endrezzi. Jack, thank you. Again, last but not least, thank you to my forester friends: Miles Benson, Steve Guthrie and Mike Sohasky. The 101st Airborne—you know who you are. Thank you to Vietnam marine veteran Ed Staskiewicz at Northwoods Graphics Display for his tremendous work not only on the "Wisconsin's Flying Trees" exhibit but also for his work on the photos of this book.

CHAPTER 1

WAR!

We wonder what we would have been, if it weren't for World War II.
—Colleen Holloran Austin and Verna Fohrman, February 10, 2006[1]

O n Sunday, December 7, 1941, Wisconsin was shaken to the core, as was
the nation, with the bombing of Pearl Harbor. Until the "Day of Infamy,"
the war seemed remote, and manufacturing jobs were growing after years of
unemployment. The uppermost thought that day for many Wisconsinites was
the potential for a Green Bay Packer playoff game in Green Bay. Playing with
an 11-1 record, the Packers would possibly play on the "frozen tundra" of then
City Field on December 14 for the National Football League Championship
game.[2] The outlook for a Merry Christmas seemed bright.

At the University of Wisconsin men's dormitory, Terrence Hall, a chemical
engineering student from Loyal, a small town in central Wisconsin, Verland
Drake was working his way through school. On the morning of December
7, he was waiting on the tables in the dormitory. He said:

> *Everyone was stunned, as it was announced that Pearl Harbor had been bombed.*
> *It was hard to believe it had happened. There was no television. After breakfast,*
> *everyone gathered around the radio in the Commons to hear the president.*
> *A reaction of ours was realizing the draft would be after us...We had thought*
> *originally, maybe, of going to Pearl Harbor and helping with the reconstruction.*

The United States Navy would subsequently take over the dormitory.[3]

A Wisconsin Pearl Harbor veteran, Ivan Bourguignon, in sick bay on board the *West Virginia*, later reported:

> We couldn't see much of what was going on, but one of the petty officers came down and told us. The noise was terrific. The concussion of exploding bombs and the answer to our own antiaircraft fire…Still, there wasn't any confusion. Every man knew what he was supposed to do, and he did it. Our antiaircraft guns got into action without any loss of life. One bomb hit our ship, and it trembled all over.

Over a dozen men from northeastern Wisconsin alone were on "Battleship Row" in Pearl Harbor and were killed. One American Legion post in Green Bay is named for Earl Wallen, who "with the Japanese planes filling the air…volunteered to man a machine gun in the crow's nest of the battleship [*California*] after the gunner had been killed, climbed under heavy fire to the perilous post, and fired round after round at succeeding waves of enemy aircraft until Jap tracer bullets found their mark."

The University of Wisconsin Badgers football team was also affected by Pearl Harbor and the United States' entry into the war. All-American David Schreiner wrote a letter to his parents on December 11, 1941: "I'm not going to sit here snug as a bug playing Football when others are giving their lives for their country…If everyone tried to stay out of it, what a fine country we would have!"

David Schreiner made the ultimate sacrifice. So did co-captain and B-17 co-pilot Mark "Had" Hoskins after his plane was attacked over Germany on June 27, 1944. Standouts "Crazy Legs" Hirsch and Pat Harder served their country.[4] Bob Baumann, a Badger tackle, fought in Guadalcanal, and Paul Hirsbrunner fought in Saipan, while Bud Seelinger was wounded in Okinawa.[5] The 1942 Badger football team fought on the game field and the battlefield with distinction and valor.

Standout University of Wisconsin football player and All-American Elroy "Crazy Legs" Hirsch was from Wausau in central Wisconsin. He was called "Crazy Legs" because on the football field, "[h]is crazy legs were gyrating in six different directions, all at the same time."[6] Elroy Hirsch joined the U.S. Marine Corps and was stationed at the University of Michigan as part of the United States Navy V-12 program.[7] He became an icon of University of Wisconsin Badger football.

The famed Wisconsin 32nd Red Arrow Division, U.S. Army, had been in training in Louisiana since October 1940. The National Guard unit, in maneuvers in Louisiana, was called up and activated immediately. The 32nd would fight bravely in the Pacific Theater. Joining the 32nd Red Arrow Division at Camp Beauregard in Louisiana and when it left San Francisco for Australia was Marshfield's Company C of the 128th Infantry Regiment. Four officers and 118 soldiers had enlisted and were sworn in on October 15, 1940; 19 members would make the ultimate sacrifice throughout Asian campaigns.[8]

World War II had begun for the United States. For Wisconsin, over 320,000 men and 9,000 women served in the Armed Forces. Of that number, more than 8,000 were casualties and 18,600 were wounded to return home.[9] Thousands more would be civilians participating in Wisconsin's workforces supporting the war effort. No longer were we just an economic participant; the United States was fully engaged in the war effort.

Veterans in Wisconsin's American Legion wanted to keep their homefront safe. The "Commander of the American Legion in Wisconsin appealed for the creation" of an army brigade composed of all Wisconsin deer hunters—a "formidable foe for any attackers."[10] Always the week before Thanksgiving and the week afterward, deer hunting season had just ended in Wisconsin.

The war had begun, and people were nervous about an on-shore attack. Civil defense was a high priority in people's mind: "No hamlet was too isolated and no city too sophisticated to completely escape the post–Pearl Harbor jitters. Americans fretted, tacked black cloth on their windows, and waited half-expecting their Homeland to be tested by the fires of war."[11]

Verna Fohrman had graduated from Marshfield High School in 1941 and decided to leave Marshfield for Chicago. She was hired to "put Tinker Toys together for display windows." When her mother called her after Pearl Harbor, her mother said, "Come home because the Japs are going to bomb Chicago!" Verna responded, "I was so happy to return home. And I had a good excuse to come home, too!"[12] Verna Fohrman returned to Marshfield and was hired by Roddis Lumber and Veneer Company, later Roddis Plywood Corporation

Both young and old understood the significance of the attack. Out of the initial shock came resilience, determination and a unification of purpose. "You could almost hear it click into place," reported Arthur Krock of the *New York Times*.[13] The Great Depression had spawned an insecurity and desperation. When the war began, America's "'can-do' spirit had revived."[14] Women would walk miles to work. "Walk[ing] from Hewitt to Marshfield for a shift…they were happy to have a job. It was after hard times."[15] The "times" would be more difficult after Christmas 1941, with families coping

Courtesy of the U.S. Library of Congress, Washington, D.C.

with deployments. Families and industry would cope with shortages of goods, rationing, manpower and the possibilities of sabotage.

> *The importance of wood and its derivative in the war effort has been recognized not only in the news but in official pronouncements. Draft boards have been notified that forestry, logging, and lumbering are activities necessary to war production, and the heads of the War Manpower Commission, the War Production Board, and the Selective Service System have appealed to woods and mill workers to stick to their jobs because "Lumber has Gone to War."*[16]

The Selective Service Draft had been implemented in October 1940. Some of Wisconsin's young men from Forest County and Connor Lumber and Land Company employees from Laona had joined the army. Darrell Davis had sent a postcard to W.D. Connor Jr. on April 21, 1941: "Just a card to let you know I'm still alive. They sure treat us well here at Camp Shelby. I am in Co. G, 135th Med. Reg. Camp Shelby, Miss. Will write and tell you about the life here when I find time."[17]

Davis wrote a letter to Connor a week later:

> *So far, the grub has been lousy. If the fellows kick on the eats they get at your boarding house I sure don't know what they'd do in the army. I think it is either getting better or else I'm getting used to it. I am fortunate in being able to eat almost anything, but some fellows have to get hungry before they eat much. We get no cake or cookies so far, just doughnuts one day. I sent home for a few things and they sent a box of cookies that Bob made and they sure tasted good. Right now we are eating sausage and rye bread and Coca-Cola. A fellow in the tent got a large box of eats today.*
>
> *Well, thank you for all you did for me. I hope that this letter proves interesting.*

The letter "proves interesting" also because of the postscript: "I forgot to mention that Greske, Trudeau, Collins, Stewart, Wilbur, Bods, and Halasce are here in the 135th."[18] Men marched off to serve and knew that the war was coming. Despite the lack of comforts in the army, they were comforted knowing their friends were with them.

Connor responded to Davis's letter on May 22, 1941:

> *Thank you very much for your letter of April 26th.*
>
> *Certainly glad to hear that you are getting along nicely. Have shown your letter to some of your friends here. It is not every fellow that takes time to write us and we do appreciate your interest.*
>
> *If we can do anything for you back home, let us know. Say "Hello" to the other boys that went with you from Forest County.*[19]

It was Connor's interest and assistance that had already sparked Davis to write to him, but again Connor reached out with an offer to help "back home."

Record numbers of men enlisted in December 1941 with the unified thought of the "American Creed: To Defend Our Country Against All Enemies." Reverend Brendemiehl, the chaplain at the headquarters of the 2nd Cavalry at Fort Riley, Kansas, wrote at the end of December 1941 to the Roddis family in Marshfield about the stress of deployment and the conditions at Fort Riley:

> *We have had a Happy Christmas, in spite of existing conditions…Housing conditions in the vicinity of the Post are impossible so I afraid that she [Mrs. Brendemiehl] will have to return to Marinette after New Years. No acceptable flat can be touched under seventy dollars a month. There is*

also uncertainty of our unit remaining here. We are on the alert and must be able to move out in four hours notice. I work…making calls at hospitals, guard house, and organizations: from one to four, office work, and four to ten consultations…The problems that come to me are the problems of young men everywhere: trouble at home, girl trouble (very prevalent), financial difficulties, persecution complexes, homesickness, occupational adjustments. Many of the boys are unsuited for work with horses, usually because of their fear of them, and must be detailed to clerical work or to motorized units. I also have a class of fifteen men learning to read and write…We have officiated at a military funeral for a Sergeant, thrown from a horse and killed…

At the Christmas service we were singing Christmas Carols. The Congregation numbered about one hundred and fifty, mostly Officers in dress blues and their wives. The majority of them are regular army and have relatives in either the army or navy seeing active service somewhere in the Pacific. That fact makes the war very real here.[20]

Reflecting a young man's worry about leaving his job with Goodyear Tire and Rubber Company and his future in the military, John Holloway, a nephew of Catherine Prindle Roddis of Marshfield, wrote from Childersburg, Alabama:

Dear Aunt Catherine,
I will be inducted into the Army, January the seventh. I have a bonus check coming from Goodyear about January the fifteenth and will be able to pay the dentist bill out of that.
I am glad to hear that Bill didn't have to go to the Army. I don't know where I'll be stationed for my training, but I have to report to Pensacola. With love to you all,[21]

A young man went off to war.

Verland Drake, the young chemical engineering student at the University of Wisconsin, decided not to enlist until June 1942. The idea of "helping with the reconstruction of Pearl Harbor" gave way to enlisting in the U.S. Air Force "because we did not want to be in the Infantry." His buddy, Fred Lakosky from Loyal, "did not want to be in the Navy either because we could not swim very well!" At the University of Wisconsin, there were many "Navy personnel on campus, but there was not a great exodus of boys from school."

Drake said that the "Recruiting Officers came from Chicago...While waiting to be accepted...I had a part-time job with the railroad for awhile. I was very happy to be accepted by the Air Force!" His buddy Lakosky had received his letter in January 1943.

Drake received his letter to report to Lackland Air Force base in San Antonio, Texas, in February 1943. "I went into Navigation Training. I started as an Aviation Cadet, the equivalent of a Private...graduated from Navigation School as a Second Lieutenant." Mr. Drake would become an instructor of navigation at Hondo, Texas Air Force Base before being shipped to New Guinea in the Pacific Theater as a navigator on C-47s. Later, Drake said, "We heard about the Surrender on the camp radio. It was a very happy day in our life."[22]

While men were transitioning from civilian life to the military, transitions were taking place in the forest products industry. Whether fighting the war in the Pacific or Europe, forest products were used or developed during World War II. A partial list was prepared by the director of the United States Forest Products Laboratory in 1942:

Top: Lieutenant Verland Drake in Japan, 1945. *Courtesy of Verland Drake.*

Bottom: Verland Drake in the Philippines in World War II. *Courtesy of Verland Drake.*

Hangars, scaffolding, boats, wharves, bridges, pontoons, railway ties, telephone poles, mine props, antitank barriers, shoring, shipping containers, and air raid shelters, plywood for airplanes, blackout shutters, prefabricated housing, concrete forms, ship patterns, assault boats, ship interiors, truck bodies, army lockers, fuel for gasogenes for trucks and tractors. Pulp and paper for surgical dressings, boxes, cartridge wrappers, buildings, papers, paste boards, gas-mask filters, printing and propaganda distribution; synthetic wood fibers, such as rayon, artificial wool and cotton for clothing, parachute, and other textiles: wood cellulose

Roddis Collection, Wisconsin Historical Society, Madison, Wisconsin.

for explosives: wood charcoal for gas masks, and steel production: rosin for shrapnel and lacquer, cement, and molded articles: wood flour for dynamite, woodbark for insulation, tannin, and dye stuffs; and alcohol from wood for rubber...Army truck bodies shall be built of wood to conserve steel—requiring approximately a Million board feet of hardwood per day...The number of boxes required for the shipment of ammunition alone runs into thousands per day. [23]

Over one hundred uses of wood would contribute to the Allies' victory. Many more were developed before the war was over. "More planes, boats, and truck bodies are wood in this war...This time we have to supply all the required wood from the U.S.

Roddis Collection, Wisconsin Historical Society, Madison, Wisconsin.

Most everything our armed forces eat, wear, and fight with will go overseas in wooden boxes and crates." [24]

Not only were men mobilized, but industries were also converting to war products. The forest products industry in Wisconsin was racing to complete its contract obligations. Forest product companies were all doing business together in a unified effort to win the war. The cash book of the Connor Lumber and Land Company in Laona from January 28, 1942, to September 21, 1944, illustrated the unified effort and the conversion process: [25]

On July 8, 1942, the Connor Lumber and Land Company received $887.50 from the Penokee Veneer Company in Mellen, Wisconsin, to provide lumber for crating.

On July 14, 1942, the Northern Hardwood Veneer Company in Butternut, Wisconsin, ordered lumber in the amount of $6,365 from the Connor Lumber and Land Company for crating and shipping war materiel.

On August 6, 1942, Richardson Brothers in Sheboygan Falls, Wisconsin, a furniture manufacturer, ordered $1,205.15 worth of lumber from the Connor Lumber and Land Company for their conversion making rifle gunstocks for the army.[26]

On August 13, 1942, Lloyd Manufacturing in Marinette, Wisconsin, a subsidiary of Heywood Wakefield Company in Gardner, Massachusetts, ordered $1,706.37 of lumber from the Connor Lumber and Land Company. Lloyd made steel frames for cargo gliders CG-4A and CG13-A, manufactured by Ford in Kingsford, Michigan, and Northwestern Aeronautical Corporation in St. Paul/Minneapolis, a conversion from craft paper, steel tubes, wicker furniture and fine furniture.[27]

On August 15, 1942, Consolidated Power and Paper Company in Wisconsin Rapids, Wisconsin, ordered $1,723.05 of lumber from the Connor Lumber and Land Company; Consolidated with its subsidiary, Consoweld, was making glider floors and ammunition boxes of pressed phenol-resin paper product developed by the Forest Products Laboratory.

On September 9, 1942, an order was received from Pluswood of Oshkosh, Wisconsin, a subsidiary of Lullaby Furniture Company in Stevens Point. It had converted its manufacturing process from baby and juvenile furniture to aircraft veneer and plywood. The Connor Lumber and Land Company was supplying lumber for crating to Northern and Pluswood. Both were subsidiaries of Lullaby Corporation in Stevens Point, Wisconsin.

On September 9, 1942, Hamilton Manufacturing ordered lumber. Connor Lumber and Land Company was supplying lumber for crating.

Ford Motor Company had been converted to manufacture aircraft. In Kingsford, Michigan, the Connor Lumber and Land Company had supplied lumber for the Woody station wagon. The orders for July 20, 1942, Ford Motor Company of $1,858.58 and May 29, 1943, of $2,075.75, respectively to the Connor Lumber and Land Company, were for crating material and lumber for the CG-4A cargo gliders.

The purchases of lumber from the Connor Lumber and Land Company to furniture companies, piano manufacturers, aircraft propeller manufacturers and Ford illustrated the diversity of the conversion process to war products.

Government facilities and industries were on alert; for example, guards and fencing were standard procedure at the United States Forest Products Laboratory. Corporations also fenced their manufacturing plants. At the Roddis Lumber and Veneer Company in Marshfield, Leroy Treutel said: "All of the lunch buckets were checked, and at night, there were spot checks around the plant...One day a man was passing through the gate with a wheelbarrow full of ashes. The guard asked, 'What are you stealing?' The man answered, 'The wheelbarrow!'"[28]

It was not always that lighthearted. Identification badges were required and carefully scrutinized. Dorothy Catlin Schubert worked at Roddis and years later would show her ID badge.[29]

Security increased because of war-related products. Wes Sydow, a former Roddis employee, recalled, "My mother was required to wear an identification badge to the mill because of national security."

Verna Fohrman wore an identification badge and said, "We knew that the plywood was going for aircraft. It was not a secret."[30] In fact, the *Marshfield News Herald* had reported that a female plywood worker wrote her name and a message for Hitler on a shipment going to England.

Dorothy Catlin Schubert's Roddis Lumber and Veneer Company ID badge. *Courtesy of Marshfield Veterans' Museum, Marshfield, Wisconsin.*

Another important defense plant was Penokee Veneer Company in Mellen. John Boettcher worked as a teen for the summer at Penokee in 1943. Nationally, over three million teenagers were a part of the war workforce. John Boettcher's father was a guard at Penokee. It, too, had a defense designation, producing aircraft plywood with a priority rating.

Government inspectors were assigned to sawmills, plywood plants and paper mills. Jim Wirsbinski's father was a millwright at Mosinee Paper Company, which was designated a defense plant. Mosinee was making boxes and packaging materials. Wirsbinski said, "There was only one way to get into the plant. Even before the pulp trucks went through the gate, they were inspected. The cars were too."[31] Security measures were taken to prevent sabotage. The Connor Lumber and Land Company in Laona was

John Boettcher's Penokee Veneer Company ID badge. *Courtesy of John Boettcher, Park Falls, Wisconsin.*

John Boettcher's father, *second from left*, as a guard. *Courtesy of John Boettcher, Park Falls, Wisconsin.*

completely fenced around its sawmill operations.[32] Vigilance would continue throughout the war.

Logging in the Northwoods of Wisconsin was in full swing, producing millions of board feet required in the war effort. "Lumber is a 'critical material,' and logging and lumber manufacture throughout the United States are just as important as the construction of ships, cantonments, planes, gliders, pontoons, etc. for which lumber is needed and to be used."[33]

Donald M. Nelson, chairman of the War Production Board, exhorted the industry to produce as much lumber as possible, particularly the higher grades.

The Roddis Lumber and Veneer Company produced thousands of board feet per day:

> *The roads up north are now frozen solid, and we are in full swing in our logging operations at our various camps. At Camp 15 out of Mercer, we have twenty trucks hauling and expect to handle about 100,000 feet to*

110,000 feet of logs per day. This means about twenty flat cars per day plus what pulpwood is cut.

The pulpwood will average about three cars per day. At Camp 5 near Mellen, we produce popple for core lumber which is used in $^{13}/_{16}$" tops and boat work. Here we get about ⅔ of our requirements, or about 60 cords per day. All of this material is hauled to railroad siding and loaded on cars and hauled over our railroad to connecting points with the Soo Line Railroad or the Chicago & Northwestern.[34]

In pulpwood production, it was estimated that one tree contained enough cellulose for the explosives in five hundred Garand rifle bullets.[35]

Still, the Roddis Plywood Corporation lamented the lack of manpower. "The manpower situation, however, is quite a problem. We have practically all new men in the second shift with the exception of Frank Hastraiter and Frank Drapes, the Head Sawyer."[36] The War Production Board attributed the decrease in lumber production to lack of manpower and equipment shortages.[37]

In the throes of December production, there were thoughts of the GIs who were missed and fighting in the war effort:

The shrill of a postman's whistle on a quiet street here at home, of the call of mail in some mud flanked dugout in the far corners of the world gives the same air of expectancy. Just as the ground man shouts "Contact" to the pilot of the airplane, so also the mail brings contact with our loved ones forced by circumstances to be far from home and friends. It's a privilege to write to you G.I. Joe's and G.I. Jane's and a blessing our times make it possible to bring these letters to you so speedily. Let's not overlook the privilege, but take advantage of the blessings of CONTACT BY MAIL.[38]

CHAPTER 2

THE WISCONSIN HOMEFRONT

Today every American has one and only one major objective: the winning of the war. He is now convinced that the time has come for all-out whole-hearted, sustained, and courageous action.[39]

By 1942, the War Production Board had banned items considered "nonessential to the war effort." That meant consumer goods with metal components were largely eliminated. Refrigerators, bobby pins, can openers, bicycles (because of rubber tires and metal) and even coat hangers made of metal were prohibited for the consumer. New cars were allocated to the military. Gasoline rationing reduced travel. Flashlight batteries were in short supply.

Rubber was in short supply and high demand, despite a June 22, 1940 congressional appropriation of $500,000. With it was a three-year plan to implement the planting and growing of rubber trees in the Western Hemisphere.[40] Also, there was a 1941 Department of Agriculture initiative with the Goodyear Tire Company to move rubber plants from the Philippines to Haiti to secure America's rubber supply.[41] At the beginning of 1942, 90 percent of the United States' rubber supply was cut off when Japan conquered the Dutch East Indies and Malaya. With the United States facing less than a year's supply, rubber was also on the restricted list.[42] The military needed the rubber for airplanes, with one B-17 requiring half a ton and a tank requiring one ton of rubber.[43]

Not only were consumer goods only allocated if a natural disaster had occurred, but food was rationed too. In a letter to her mother and father on June 5, 1942, Mary Roddis Connor wrote about the "potential" rationing of material and clothes: "*The Kiplinger Letter* last Thursday talks of clothes rationing and the tailor told me the other day that if anyone needed clothes to hurry up and get them, as materials were getting shoddy and he had to pay double for his materials than what he had a few months ago."

The Kiplinger Letter also talked about food rationing. Mrs. Connor worried about the impact on her family:

> *Kiplinger also threatens that we may all have a ration on food...That would really hit me. I don't know how to feed my family on a more overall scheme per month. Aren't you lucky to have food lockers in Marshfield, so that you do not have to be dependent on as much usage for canning, and care with your garden produce! I don't see the necessity of only as many qts. of milk per person either, where there is no dehydration here...*
>
> *Gordie and I have a frozen food locker in the basement. I understand that you have to prepare the foods and fruits and vegetables, however. Do you know much about it?...*
>
> *My jam is so low. I don't see how one can make strawberry and raspberry jam and jellies with one cup sugar per 4 qts.*[44]

Freeze canning was new technology with the "frozen food locker."

With ration books, people could only obtain eight to twelve ounces of sugar per week. One pound of coffee was allowed every five weeks. Twelve pounds of butter per year was allocated to each person.[45]

> *Voluntary meat rationing is here, and obligatory meat rationing will be here as soon as the machinery to administer it is working. This plus gasoline rationing and the restriction on all pleasant living, will bring this war home with a sharp smack to every civilian in the United States. We do not yet know exactly how the meat rationing is going to work. We know that it applies now to the "red" meats—beef, veal, pork, and lamb or mutton. We understand that there is to be no rationing of poultry and fish.*[46]

Meat was rationed. Black markets for food became commonplace.[47] Families came together to pool their rations, and "Victory Gardens" were grown to supplement food shortages.

Interestingly, food rationing was not to save the food but to save the tin from the cans for war uses.[48] Bing Crosby's "Junk Will Win the

War" summed up life on the homefront. There were scavenger hunts for rubber, tires and metal. Research accelerated for industry alternatives.

Even women's fashion and the making of women's shoes did not escape the war and rationing:

> *Rayon, a type of "artificial silk" made from wood cellulose, became a popular fashion necessity during the war years. The long-sleeved, rayon crepe dress, worn by Catherine, Mrs. Hamilton Roddis, is embellished with abstract, satin appliqués surrounded with...a type of embroidery developed in France during WWII that utilized leftover cords from passementerie and other recycled trimming materials. The slim lines and narrow seam allowances were dictated by special wartime restrictions.*[49]

Beautiful detail on the bodice made up for the simplicity of design.

Shoes were included in the simplicity of design and style of the war fashion.

> *Modest wedge-heeled shoes reflect*[ed] *the restrained fashion during WWII. Despite deprivation, excessive high platforms were the height of fashion in 1940's. Yet many women favored less fashion forward, but more practicable wedge heels for everyday.*

Dress with bodice worn by Catherine P. Roddis (Mrs. Hamilton Roddis) in 1945. *Photo courtesy of Ms. Jane Bradbury, project manager of the Fractured Atlas: Roddis Dress Collection Project. Photo by Gillian Bostock.*

Don Kircher with his collection of World War II aviation cards, Laona, August 2011. *Author's collection.*

…Using materials that were not rationed, such as wood, straw, and snakeskin, shoemakers were able to create shoes uplifting and playful during darker years of war.[50]

Life on the homefront was a constant challenge.

World War II was a vivid memory for Don Kircher of Laona, who grew up in Barton near West Bend, southeastern Wisconsin. In a bird's-eye view of life on the homefront during the war and as a Korean War veteran, he later recalled:

As I think of it, it is amazing to me how they propagandized kids into World War II…My mom would give me money to go to the grocery store. There would be an extra penny or two for gum, but I would buy the gum for the picture cards. I have over two hundred with ships and airplanes. The cards were collected and were identification cards for airplanes and ships.

24

Don Kircher with his World War II aviation card. *Author's collection.*

I was always interested in aviation and built model airplanes... During World War II, I kept a scrapbook of the cards. My first card was 1939 from Hawaii with lots of airplanes. There were also P-39s, P-40s, Flying Tigers...[51]

As a boy of eleven and in the Cub Scouts and then Boy Scouts, Mr. Kircher went with his troop *to Green Bay and Sturgeon Bay to watch a subchaser launch, and then to Sister Bay and Camp Ledeen for six weeks to pick cherries. We were paid by the gallon, $1.50 per day. They used to kill the bugs on the cherries with pesticides, and we would eat the cherries! The pesticides made you go to the bathroom and sit in the outhouse! Today, at least they don't use ALAR.*

We were also put on a bus to pick beans, one cent per pound for beans. Spinach was paid by the pound too. It was all to help the war effort. I lived near West Bend. Krier Canning Company was out at Random Lake. Fifteen kids would get on a bus early in the morning. We would meet on the corner in Barton. The staked truck would pick you up within twenty miles of West Bend. We were in the Cub Scouts, but it was not a sponsored council activity. We were just trying to help the war effort. They needed the manpower. August (Augie) Homuth was the leader...I was sent a certificate from the President of the United States thanking me for help in the war effort.

Mr. Kircher also spoke of the power of the movies from a young man's perspective. A view of the war was "a pilot bailing out of an airplane and the Japanese shooting down our aircraft. I was twelve years old, and I got angry!" He continued:

I picked milkweed pods for life preservers. There were rubber drives for old tires. We pulled old tires out of the ponds and rivers. We could see them through the ice, ice skating. We were paid one cent per pound. It was a form of recycling, I guess. I even put in my rubber ball!

I sold newspapers. Newspapers were recycled too for making sewer pipes. They were made by Line Material Company, a part of McGraw Edison.

The Germans were sinking all of our ships bringing rubber from Brazil. The first tires were nylon-based tires. Then the rubber to petroleum-based tires.

My dad was part of the Civil Defense in Barton. He would go around town with a flashlight, and everyone had to turn out lights in case of an air raid. If someone didn't, he would remind them.

When I went to the store with my dad, he had stamps for gasoline. You were allowed three gallons per week and had to have the stamps. Doctors got more stamps and farmers had more, too. My uncle, dad, cousin and I and an uncle from Hudson collected enough stamps to go to Little Bear Lake for a fishing trip! That was quite an adventure.

All of the good cigarettes were sent to the troops overseas like Camel, Chesterfields, Pall Malls went too. They were scarce.

Don Kircher's "Ace" Lieutenant Edward H. O'Hare aviation card. *Author's collection.*

Don Kircher's wife, Joyce Dricken Kircher, said, "During the war, I remember picking beans for $1.50 per day, too. My mom worked for West Bend Aluminum. They made 50mm shells. In peacetime, they made pots and pans."

Her sister-in-law, Joan Dricken, remembers a prisoner of war camp at what is now Mitchell Field in Milwaukee: "One day, I walked up to the fence. Some of the men started to talk to me. I did not understand any of it because it was in German. I was just a little girl."

Mrs. Kircher also collected stamps for war bonds. "If you filled a book, it was good for $18.75.[52] The war bond effort was led by America's heroes and celebrities to raise money for the war effort."[53] Mr. Kircher said, "Looking back, it was amazing how they [the government] mobilized the people. I wonder if we could do it again."

The effects of shortages lingered in Europe after the war. In 1949, Augusta D. Roddis returned to England. She later wrote:

> One of my "Bon Voyage" presents…was a beautiful three-pound box of candy. I decided that I would save the bottom for Amy, as I knew that chocolate was rationed in England…She opened it, and said, "Oh, Augusta, it's just beautiful," and she looked at the chocolates as though they were from some another world…She of course asked me about the trip over and I told her…that our food wasn't very good. She said, "All I'd want to know—was there enough?" And this is a comment from someone, who before the war was living in circumstances fully comfortable…And it brought home rather forcibly that just as it seems like fairyland to an American to go to Europe and see all of the wonderful old castles,…it is just like fairyland to Europeans, and more particularly the British, to see a well-dressed, well-fed American, who had been eating all he wants and can buy anything he wants in the way of clothes.[54]

The observation was startling.

War News

The editor of the *Roddis Bulletin*, Gertrude A. Seymour, said that Private First Class Melvin Becker was wounded and had written a poem with his "first gunner" that he wanted published in the bulletin:

War News from Roddis Lumber and Veneer Company Servicemen

To My Pals Who Stayed Home
I'm pulling all my punches, I've flung my week away,
I think it's been two months at least since I drew my pay.

I'm tired of being a dog face, so help me God I am,
Of eating molded biscuits with margarine or spam,
Of fighting dirty Nazis, in the mountains far from Rome,
When I think of dear old America, and my Pals who stayed at home.[55]

Many of the Roddis employees had gone off to war. Knowing war was imminent, photographs had been taken in May 1939 of all the Roddis Lumber and Veneer Company employees in Marshfield.[56] World War II was being fought by 225 employees of the Roddis Plywood Corporation who had joined the military. All of the "pals" who stayed at home were working feverishly to support the troops.

In beginning the *Roddis Bulletin* in November 1944, Gertrude A. Seymour kept track of the many Roddis Plywood Corporation servicemen and -women, including the following: "Sgt. Leroy Behrens, one of our boys from the plant here, recently returned from Pearl Harbor where he was one of a staff of four men appointed as body guard and orderly to Admiral Nimitz." Returning to Marshfield on furlough, he married Corrine Krasin,[57] daughter of a well-known Marshfield architect.

Donovan Barron "recently transferred from the Navy to the Marines." Corporal Ruth Ledger married Patrick Dowd.[58] "Byron Becker...recently returned from New Guinea and is now reassigned to Camp Shelby, Mississippi." Sergeant Clarence F. Seidl, who had worked at Roddis Plywood Corporation, had also been in New Guinea.[59]

The *Roddis Bulletin*'s national and international focus was on the Roddis Company employees who were serving in the war. While the *Roddis Bulletin* reported the scores of the New Year's football bowl games, the most interesting score was the "Spaghetti Bowl IN ITALY. The 5th Army played the 12th Air Force, with the 5th Army winning 20–0. Our hats off to you boys!"

There was some normalcy even with the war in the upper minds, not only in the military but also with the civilians contributing to the war effort. Reported in the *Roddis Bulletin,* John Dishinger sent a postcard from Paris that he had been

promoted to PFC. A letter from Edwin Bores in New Britain says he is getting our bulletin...Russell Faber write from Anchorage, Alaska, that he arrived safely...Godfrey Lautenberg has again been wounded, this time in the Philippine's, Ray Potter has just completed his 50th mission in aerial combat in the Mediterranean theater. Ray is a waist gunner on a B-24.[60]

War action was seen on the seas as well. Roy Bitman was on the USS *Sheridan* in the Pacific.[61] Men from Roddis Plywood Corporation were stationed and fighting all over the world. Augie Frankwick was in France. Harold Brusewitz, the *Roddis Bulletin* continued, "writes from Holland that he is much intrigued by the Dutch windmills…On the other side of the world, John Krall writes from Hawaii that they are giving the 'Sons of the Rising Sun' plenty of hell." Private First Class James Cherney had spent twenty-six months in Alaska. Fighting with valor, Oscar Molter was awarded the Bronze Star.[62] Corporal Robert Binning had just landed in the Philippines.[63]

In New Guinea was Arnold Wallner, who said, "They didn't like the 'back to nature' idea and built themselves shower rooms and a new mess hall."[64] Verlyn Schmidt, a former Roddis Plywood Corporation employee, had been "wounded twice in the Philippines" and was onboard the USS *North Carolina* as an electrician. Donald Becker was stationed in the Marianas. Roman Andres was in New Britain. Bundy Scheer "was a sniper" and had been previously "bringing back comrades under fire, and has received the Silver Star and several other medals."

Some news in the bulletin was "personal," with Sergeant Erwin Fischer a proud new father of a baby boy and Clarence Treml being promoted to corporal. Master Sergeant Charles Ploen, based in Mojave, California, and Private Frank Lahr, stationed in Harvard, Nebraska, had been home on furlough. Some enlistments took place, with Private Louis Boldt being stationed at Camp J.T. Robinson in Arkansas. Other news was from the war front. Private First Class Laura Hustedt was in New Guinea, where she was cooking for the army. Also promoted to corporal and cooking for the U.S. Army Air Corps in India was Fred Yaeger. Private Romaine Rossow had been in the Netherlands East Indies for a year and was looking forward to a furlough. Mike Krall "cooked eggs on the rocks in the Ascension Islands!"[65]

On the European front, Gordon Schmoll had arrived in Germany with the U.S. Army Engineers. Schmoll worked his entire forty-seven-year career at the Roddis Lumber and Veneer Company in the Core Mill in Marshfield. He was the "glue man." He mixed the glue for five machines in the plant with two large mixers. He said, "I used to get full of glue…I took the pans, not too deep ones, like a large cake pan, to the different machines. The men were laying up the blocks for the doors. There was a big long chain, four men were laying up the blocks and gluing them together. At the end, they would cut them off."[66] Corporal "Gordie" Schmoll returned with the Purple Heart to the Roddis glue room after the war.

Gordon Schmoll's (1924–2013) Service Medals. *Courtesy of the* Marshfield Herald, *author's collection.*

Technical Sergeant John Kraemer was a "radio operator on a B-24 Liberator bomber with the 15th Air Force in Italy…He had received the Air Medal with two Oak Leaf Clusters, the Good Conduct Medal, and the Presidential Unit Citation and wears four battle stars."[67]

Late in the war, the B-24s flew out of Italy on the Eastern Front on long missions without any fighter escorts: "The German air defenses were pretty well knocked out and we encountered little resistance. We flew without any fighter escorts. We were on our own."[68] The missions were dangerous.

In the Pacific Theater, Technical Sergeant William Soloski, who had worked in the Marshfield mill, had spent "33 months in the South Pacific," a long tour of duty. Sergeant First Class Cliff Merkel was stationed "somewhere in the Pacific." Loose lips sink ships! The location of where the troops were often was not revealed. Corporal Keith Becker was promoted to sergeant in the Philippines. Al Bores said, "He is in the Netherland East Indies…and there is everything from coconuts to parrots."

In Europe, spending an old English Christmas, F.M. Frank had made friends with an English family. Private Alphonse Weix wrote that he "hoped to drive [his truck], the same truck he had brought from the states…up the main street of Berlin." In Europe, Harold "Haf" Schlafke celebrated New Year's in Lorraine, France. Sergeant Donald Evanson was with Patton's 3rd Army. He said that "he had quite an interesting trip across France from the beaches of Normandy—sometimes too interesting." Wounded in France, "Bob Pacourek…used to work in Spuhler's department on ship doors." Private Armin Walsh was in Italy, and although sunny, he "would much prefer to hear the seven o'clock blast from our steam whistle."

Stateside, Air Cadet Marvin Flink "graduated from Deming Army Air Field in Deming, N.M." Corporal Gertrude Berg reported to Vint Hill Farm Station in Warrenton, Virginia. Also in the Washington, D.C. area was Yeoman Third Class Gladys Craft. Private Constance DeWorth joined the Women's Air Corps and was stationed at Fort Des Moines, Iowa.[69] Also enlisting and stationed at Great Lakes Naval was Airman/Seaman Jim Schulte. Millions of men and women were fighting for our freedom in Europe and in the Pacific.

On the Western Front of Germany was Tippy Allen, who had worked as a Roddis office boy. Clarence Jensen observed the farming methods in North Africa, where the Arabs used "mules, steers, and camels to plow with." Harold Steinmetz in the Philippines observed that the "natives there enjoy such fights [cock fights] as we would a football game or Joe Louis in the ring." The rain in France caused deep mud, according to Fred Harbinger. Harold Becker was in Italy.[70]

The realities of war struck home again in the *Roddis Bulletin*. The reports of the wounded and deaths of the Roddis employees were heartfelt. "We deeply regret to hear of the death of Harold Brusewitz, who was killed in Belgium on Jan. 25th."[71] Private First Class Melvin Becker had written from the "Italian front":

> *North of Rome, near the Arno River, my company was in the attack, every draw, ditch, and hill was completely zeroed in by the enemies' machine guns and artillery. You could hear our men calling for the Medics. Shortly after taking the hill, we were ordered to dig in and ready ourselves for a counter-attack. I had good observation on the enemy, and caught 50 or 60 Jerries leaving a house about 800 yards to my left and with my machine gun and six boxes of ammo, I really played hell with them.*

The editor of the *Roddis Bulletin* said that Becker was wounded.

So many of Private First Class Becker's "pals" were in the Pacific Theater in March. Arnold Wallner was in the Netherlands East Indies, and Lyle Krasin was in New Guinea. He was located in an area with plenty of forests. Walter Hoffman was in the Philippines. Alvin L. Federeit was on Iwo Jima as a carpenter third class mate with the Seabees. Furloughed from thirty-six months in the Pacific, Technical Sergeant Robert May visited the Marshfield plant again. Occasionally, Marshfield friends ran into each other on the front. Johnny Dietel ran into Lou Dillinger in New Guinea. Both had worked at Roddis.

In Europe, Private First Class Becker's "pals" were fighting hard. Sergeant Paul Martin was a paratrooper in Belgium who had worked at Roddis Lumber and Veneer Company on the drag saw in the plant, while his wife worked in the office. Also in Belgium, Harold Groth had extensive wounds and was in the hospital. Herb Wellman was in England looking forward to a furlough. Ray Wilcox was with the U.S. Army Air Corps in England. Leonard Feit was in France, where the weather was cold. Leo Schreiner was enjoying "shooting down the 'Luftwaffe.'" Fred Ogden said, "He doesn't know what the Germans are fighting for," and he wanted more mail. Mail was a precious commodity.

A B-24 bomber group with the 15th Air Force was in Italy. Johnny Kraemer wrote of his Italian experience. By this time in the war, the 15th Air Force in Italy was bombing the Eastern Front.

Leo and Leonard Martin spent their furlough at home together before returning to duty at Fort Meade, Maryland. Home from sixteen months in Iceland, Alvin Sitman was sent to France in an engineering unit.

Men and women were still enlisting; Private Robert Bores was stationed at Fort McClellan in Alabama. Sergeant George Krall married Mildred Jechort. Sergeant Arnold Evanson married a girl from Eau Claire, Wisconsin.[72]

Not only were the women working on the civilian side for Uncle Sam, but women working at Roddis Plywood Corporation also had sons and husbands serving overseas:

> *The women on the second shift of the driers are challenging anyone to show better proof of service to Uncle Sam. Mrs. Upton's husband is serving in the South Pacific, and she also has four brothers in active service; Mrs. Ver Kilen has three sons and a son-in-law overseas, as well as a sister serving in a hospital in France; and Mrs. Pavelski has a brother and brother-in-law in the service. John Darst, the foreman, has two sons overseas.*[73]

They should be added to the 225 Roddis employees serving in the military.

Even if the men were stateside, they wanted to receive word from home. Private First Class Paul Lindekugel requested mail at Camp Cooke in California. Oscar Boehm was stationed in Utah.

In writing from France, Private Harvey K. Hunt reported that "when he sailed from Ireland, he sailed on a boat with Roddis doors and frames and

---

CDA;An

U. S. NAVY RECRUITING STATION
Plankinton   Building
Milwaukee, 3, Wisconsin

Dear   **Mrs. Catherine P. Roddis**

Welcome to the ranks of Navy families!

William Henry Roddis   has taken his

oath as a man-o'-warsman and now is a member of the finest Naval organization in the world. We know that you are proud of him and of the important part he is to play in helping to achieve an early and victorious peace. We want to add that we are also proud to have him as a shipmate.

As you are his closest relative, we are enclosing a booklet titled CLEAR THE DECK FOR ACTION, which we suggest you read carefully. This booklet contains important information concerning the rights and benefits of men serving in the U. S. Navy. If at any time you desire additional information, please feel free to write us.

Sincerely yours,

G. C. ELLICK
Lieut.Comdr.,D-V(S),USNR
Officer in Charge

Induction letter of William H. Roddis II. *Roddis Collection, Wisconsin Historical Society, Madison, Wisconsin.*

that gave him quite a thrill. He is looking forward to the time when he can drink some good old Wisconsin Lager beer."

The *Roddis Bulletin* reported that "George Gillen, our contact in touch with all of our warehouses and distributors, has just returned from the west coast where he was present for the launching of Victory boats installed with Roddis door units."[74] Sailing on Victory boats, the successor to Liberty ships, installed with Roddis door units would have, indeed, been "a thrill."

C.E. Weaver, Roddis Lumber and Veneer Company treasurer, returned from Oregon after visiting fir mills to ensure fir supplies for the Roddis warehouses.

William H. Roddis II as a young enlistee. *Author's family collection.*

Marshfield was well represented in the Pacific. Private Henry Holz was in New Guinea shooting howitzers. Erwin Schmitz was in New Britain and promoted to corporal. Ken Zoller was in the Philippines and sent Japanese money home. Others were in Europe. Peter Thomas had worked for the Roddis Company and was a cook in an air depot in France. Ken Prust was a military policeman (MP) on a transport to America escorting German prisoners of war. He said that the POWs were ages fifteen to fifty-two.[75] Many German prisoners of war came to Wisconsin and worked in the canneries.[76]

Some Roddis employees were stationed stateside. William H. Roddis II, vice-president of the Roddis Plywood Corporation and son of Hamilton Roddis, president, enlisted and was reported as a Navy Third Class radio technician in training in Corpus Christi, Texas.[77] He would later write as part of the "Fleet Air Wing in the Pacific" that he had met up with "Ken Istinski and 'Fritz' Upham."[78] Some men were furloughed before returning to their units. Reuben Ohm was stationed at Camp Myles in Standish, Mississippi.

Staff Sergeant Joe Keller had been in the South Pacific since 1942. He finally returned home on furlough. Al Bores was "somewhere in the

Moluccas." George Pongratz was still in the Philippines, as were Nick Long and Arnold Wallner, wounded at Luzon. Hopes were high for troops that would be returning home. Max Nelles, a "Seaman Second Class on board the USS *Walter Raleigh* says he hopes to have the chance to transport our boys back home."[79] The war went on but finally with an eye to reconversion.

There was always support for the troops. Staff Sergeant Ray Martin was in Belgium with the 7th Armor Division and was awarded the Bronze Star. He was congratulated in the *Roddis Bulletin*. So, too, were Private First Class Ray "Bandy" Scherr on the Western Front in Germany and Corporal Robert Schmelke, who fought at Leyte in the Pacific. Cliff Merkel, sergeant first class, had also been at Leyte and fought in "the battle of the Marianas." Private First Class Norman Pacourek's brother, Robert, who had also worked for Roddis, "was seriously wounded on the Western Front." Also, "Staff Sergeant E.A. Walter…was wounded on the Western Front." Lawrence Bohman wrote that he enjoyed reading the bulletins. "Roy Stizman on the USS *Sheridan* says he has taken part in practically every major operation in the Pacific—Gilbert Ises, Marshall, Sampan, Guam, and Philippines." The island invasions took their toll. Leander Ziegelbauer was wounded at Iwo Jima. Art Kohlbeck had returned from the Pacific after being "among the first group that left Marshfield." Corporal Lloyd Backaus and Corporal Orlin Backaus were home too. Furloughs were cherished. Russell Palmer, who had been a "hot press helper," was shipped to England. Oscar Boehm was wounded in Germany. Others were stateside doing their duty. Private Agnes Boehm was repairing aircraft and became crew chief at Craig Field in Alabama. There were so many contributing so much to the war effort.[80]

April had been a significant month throughout the war for major events. In 1940, Germany had captured Denmark and invaded Norway. In 1942,

> *U.S. planes bombed Tokyo for the first time. In April, 1943, Major Doolittle, stationed in northwest Africa, struck Europe proper with his air force for the first time, raiding Naples; Bolivia declared war. In April, 1944, Soviet Russia captured Odessa; MacArthur's forces land in New Guinea. Now, in April, 1945, there is no question but what the war in Germany will come to a close.*[81]

However, there was foreshadowing at the "world peace conference at San Francisco" on April 25, 1945. The United States had one vote, Britain had six votes and Russia had three votes. The war was not over, but the stage was set for the end-of-the-war division of the spoils.

Private Hunt was looking ahead; there was also optimism in Marshfield. The *Marshfield Herald* reported:[82]

> *34 airline, bus, and trucking companies are seeking to provide Air Service to 101 Wisconsin cities and towns…Marshfield, Stevens Point, Wisconsin Rapids, and Wausau are included in the proposition of Des Moines Flying Service, Mercury Development Company, Parks Air College, Inc., and Milwaukee Boston Store, Inc.*

Interstate transportation was only one component of what could be imagined for the future of aviation. Aviation "air traffic of all types" will include "glider towed passenger and freight service, and helicopter-dropped frozen fish direct from the seaports."[83] Imagine the possibilities coming out of the war!

Looking to the future of the lumber industry, what was in store for the lumber industry in 1945? There was hope for a peacetime economy:

> *Much has transpired since you boys and girls have gone to service. New faces have come and gone, and those of us who have remained here are ever hopeful for the day when calm and peace is again with us; when the drone of the saw in the Core Mill and the "hist" of steam from the hot plates mingles with the satisfying knowledge that the material passing through our hand is peace-time goods. Peace on earth, good will toward men.*[84]

In the meantime, word from the front continued to arrive in letters from the GIs. A New York Roddis warehouse employee, Morris Wolinski was in the Medical Corps. Bob Smith, who had worked in the Marshfield sawmill, was fighting in North Africa. Sometimes, the news was about men with shrapnel wounds. Roy Rogers had worked in the Roddis Glue Room but had shrapnel wounds in Italy. In April, the *Roddis Bulletin* said, "Another one of our boys who fought the battle of Iwo Jima was Leander Ziegelbauer. Word has been received that he was wounded and is now in a hospital in Seattle." The casualty rate and price of war were high for the timber industry.

Enlistments in the military also continued for the Roddis Lumber and Veneer Company. "Lorren Pinney, Apprentice Seaman, Pvt. Elwin Harmann, Pvt. Wm. Hahn, and Pvt. Ray Ampe" were new employee enlistments. They grew the military ranks of Roddis Company employees.

Mobilizing for the war effort in the forest products industry, Roddis Lumber and Veneer Company reported, "The company has just secured a large order

Aerial photo of the Roddis Plywood Corporation, Marshfield, Wisconsin. *Courtesy of Weyerhaeuser Company, Tacoma, Washington.*

for doors to be used in prefabricated hospital units going into the South Sea Isles."[85] The prefabricated units were a new technology of the war effort.

Another new technology was installed at the Roddis Plywood Corporation plant in Marshfield. It had just installed a new "hot-plate veneer re-drier… to take care of our increased capacity due to war production." In mid-December, the company added a new jointer: "Diehl continuous feed veneer jointer in our Center Dept…This is a different type jointer from any previous used in our operations. It joins and glues the edge of the veneers, making the material ready for the tapeless splicers. It has about four times the capacity of any jointer in our plant."[86] The new capacity was needed to meet the war demands.

Insight into the production was provided again by the *Roddis Bulletin.* The Roddis sawmills at Marshfield, Park Falls and Schofield were reported as a "primary critical material and practically our entire output is for Government use. This is true mainly of 5 and 6/4 Birch and Maple, which is used in Army trucks."[87] Not only was Roddis Plywood Corporation shipping material for ships and airplanes, but the Roddis Company was complying with Direction 6 of L-335 for No. 1 common in maple and birch.

> *Last week, we mentioned a few pertinent facts about logs brought into our Log Yard, and this week we take you into our Cutting Dept. under the*

A lathe in the Cutting Department at Roddis Lumber and Veneer Company. *Author's family collection.*

supervision of Ed Wendt. From the Log Yard, the logs are taken to the drag saw and cut to length. Then they are placed in vats and steamed the required length of time, depending on the species. Cold weather also requires longer steaming.

After they are taken out of the vats, the bark is taken off, and the log is hoisted into the lathe. In charge of the lathe set-ups is Fred Mielke, and lathe operators "Snooze" [Herman] Johnson, Rudolph Werner, and Ralph Murphy. Here, veneer is cut to the required length and thickness. In the first instance, only what we call veneer logs are sent to the Cutting Dept., and from these logs the best is taken and <u>used for aircraft purposes.</u>[88]

After the veneer is out it is clipped for size and put in the driers where it is dried to the required moisture content. In this connection we might say that we have all new driers. In charge of drier operations are John Durst and Ken Graff. The veneer is graded for centers or faces and sent to these respective departments.[89]

During World War II, most veneer was rotary cut with a rotary lathe and cut to $\frac{1}{64}$. The Roddis Company veneer was cut at $\frac{1}{90}$ and dried at $\frac{1}{100}$. Larry Wartner worked for Roddis for thirty-two years. He said that

Left: Leroy Treutel, 2006, Marshfield, Wisconsin. *Author's collection.*

Below: Roddis Splicing Department. *Roddis Collection, Wisconsin Historical Society, Madison, Wisconsin.*

the Roddis Lumber and Veneer Company veneer was so thin that they "hung the veneer with clothes pins on the third floor to dry."[90] It could not be kiln dried because it would shatter. Leroy Treutel said, "It was so thin, you could see your hand behind it." He later moved into sales.[91]

Some veneer cut at $\frac{1}{110}$ was considered "specialty veneer."[92] For Roddis, however, it was used in aircraft wing skins.[93] United States veneer today is cut as thin as $\frac{1}{50}$ to $\frac{1}{55}$.[94]

For the civilians at Roddis Plywood Corporation during the war, the responsibility was great in manufacturing aircraft plywood. The *Roddis Bulletin* gave a bird's-eye view of the Splicing Department, headed by Ed "Smiler" Olstinski:

> *Veneers selected in our Cutting Room have only preliminary inspection. When they reach the Splicing Dept., they are subjected to another, more rigid inspection, sorted and clipped for grade to be used for faces or backs as the specifications permit. They are then matched for figure and grain and taped on our tapeless splicers.*
>
> *Centers and crossbanding for panels and tops are made in our Center Dept., which is a subdivision of our Splicing Dept. and is supervised by Bill Schaefer. In charge of clipping rotary veneers in the Basement are Curly Neus, Bob Kliner, and Al Schulte.*
>
> *However, our greatest production thru the Splicing Dept. is of aircraft plywood for which we operate three shifts of 8 hours each. This requires the further assistance of "Red" Zygarlicks and Lawrence Wunrow in supervising these additional shifts.*
>
> *About 80% of the veneers are purchased and consist of Mahogany principally, as well as Poplar, Spruce, and Fir. These veneers, as well*

Barn at the Roddis Lumber and Veneer Company, now Masonite Corporation. *Author's collection.*

as all figured and foreign veneers are under the expert eye of Ted Wendt…After his men have cut the veneer to length, it is sent to the Splicing Dept. to be laid up into aircraft plywood. Three resident government inspectors are stationed at our plant who thoroughly inspect the finished aircraft plywood.[95]

Wes Sydow said, "The women splicing the veneer toiled on the second floor of the barn. Horses were kept on the first floor."

Colleen Holloran Austin, a former Roddis war employee, said that she "only lasted three days in the barn."[96] Colleen said that she did not have the skill necessary to splice the veneer. The precision needed to clip the defects, reinsert a new piece, glue it together and piece the sheets exactly took great manual dexterity and patience. Using the heavy, hot hand irons to seal the glue joints was difficult, so Colleen moved to the company office.

Colleen Austin as a young woman. *Courtesy of Colleen Austin, Marshfield, Wisconsin.*

Many of the women, like Anna Mancl Wunrow, Celia Heselberger, Helen Fiechter and Marion Frederick Polivka, at the Roddis Lumber and Veneer Company in Marshfield worked splicing the veneer together with those hot flat irons in the barn. The shifts at Roddis were 6:00 a.m. to 10:00 a.m. and 2:00 p.m. to 6:00 p.m. The next week, the shifts would be 10:00 a.m. to 2:00 p.m. and 6:00 p.m. to 10:00 p.m. Women could not work more than four hours per shift.

Anna Mancl Wunrow said that during the war, "you worked in four-hour shifts. If you had a family with children, you could only work a four-hour shift. You had to leave and then you could come back after two hours and work the next four-hour shift."[97]

Marion Frederick Polivka worked ironing veneer. She said, "It was easy to iron it [the veneer] if it was straight and hard if it was crooked."[98]

By the end of 1942, over six million women had entered the workforce.[99] At Roddis Lumber and Veneer Company, there were over two hundred women working in the Marshfield plant.

Helen Fiechter as a young woman. *Courtesy of Helen Fiechter, Marshfield, Wisconsin.*

Verna Fohrman (1923–2012) as a young woman. Mrs. Fohrman worked for Roddis Plywood Corporation for thirty-seven years. *Courtesy of Verna Fohrman.*

Courtesy of the Library of Congress, Washington, D.C.

Verna Fohrman recalled that "the barn smelled of horses. It was colder than heck in the winter and hotter than heck in the summer!"[100]

Roddis Plywood Corporation in Marshfield went on strike in 1944. Fohrman said, "We went on strike for a three-cent raise and settled for the most part for one cent." The women received the same maximum wage as unskilled labor and only slightly more than children working at the mill.[101]

Many women had replaced men in the woods as lumberjills, and many were driving heavy equipment. Others working in the sawmills were supporting their families as their husbands went to war.

While the Splicing Department was working on aircraft veneer and plywood, the Core Mill, under Art Reich, was "preparing doors and jams for Liberty and Victory boats." The lumber used for the cores was dried with a 5 percent moisture content in the kilns. The lumber was then cut to length and glued in blocks. The Liberty and Victory ships generally took fifty days to build. Henry Kaiser's Liberty ships used thirty thousand board feet (bdf) of western fir plywood[102] with Roddis Lumber and Veneer Company fireproof doors.

Fireproofing wood was not inexpensive. The cost depended on the class or fire retardant aspect needed. If the wood was to have a slow-burning Class C retardant, it would cost thirty-eight to forty dollars per board foot. If the wood was to be nonflammable, it would cost twenty-eight to thirty dollars per board foot and approximately eighty dollars per thousand board feet in total. The itemization for the wood treatment was a chemical cost of twenty-five dollars, impregnating the wood for ten dollars and kiln drying for eighteen dollars. For ships, it was extremely important to be fire retardant so that the flames would not spread or burn into the wood.[103]

For the door core stock, it was

> necessary for us to buy a considerable quantity of our core stock, and this is sent to us in small core blocks to be built up…pine is most commonly used for door cores, whereas Popple or basswood is generally used for all other materials. We handle approximately two carloads of core stock per day, and operate a day and night shift. In charge of the night shift is Frank Butke. After the cores are laid up, glued and seasoned they are taken to the Putty Room, in charge of Curtis Utter, which is a division of the Core Mill. There cores are thoroughly inspected…The material is then ready for the Glue Room, where it meets faces and backs prepared by "Smiler" in the Splicing Dept…In addition to this, all of the solid Oak doors and jambs for Liberty and Victory boats are cut to size and machined in our Core Mill—ready for assembly.[104]

Roddis Plywood Corporation shipped doors and jambs to Bethlehem's Baltimore yard, where "Bethlehem's wartime built yard at Fairfield near

Roddis Finishing Department. *Roddis Collection, Wisconsin Historical Society, Madison, Wisconsin.*

Baltimore…produced LSTs."[105] The Roddis Company LST Marine plywood was under the trade name "MARINEWOOD."

Shipping troops all over the world, doors for the cargo ships were still needed. The Finishing Department at Roddis was run by Melvin "Ole" Schunk.

> *Since the war, and due to our experience in making jambs for ship doors… doors are fitted and hung and mortised for locks and hinges…Right now we still have considerable ship work to be done…*[106] *Aircraft material also goes thru the Finishing Dept. to be ripped for width and trimmed to length before it is sent to Joe Steger in the Aircraft Inspection Dept.*[107]

The Finishing Department was an active place.

Although the Roddis Plywood Corporation was in the throes of providing aircraft and ship materials, it was also looking ahead to the end of the war. "Plans are underway for the reorganization of our second floor with a view for a straight line production…We expect to increase our production considerably in the post war period for commercial goods over that maintained before the war."[108] The comparison was between the Great Depression and the boost of war production.

The postwar period would bring new products and technologies. A new 106-inch Coe lathe had been installed to boost production 80 percent, and another 92-inch Coe lathe was on order. "It will operate in conjunction with our old clippers, although we have new clippers on order."[109] The plant was redesigned to accommodate new equipment and improve war production.

Back on the homefront, the Office of Price Administration held meetings in Chicago with timber industry representatives. These meetings were followed by the War Production Board meetings with the Hardwood Advisory Committee on April 23 and April 24.[110] Lumber production was lagging and labor issues were ever present, but there were bright spots. On April 30, the "News from U.S. Plywood Corporation" announced the receipt of the "Army-Navy 'E' Award for the high achievement in the production of material." It was awarded to U.S. Plywood's Algoma Plywood and Veneer Company subsidiary in Algoma.[111]

Roddis Plywood Corporation had received the "V" Victory flag from the Maritime Commission for its outstanding production. Roddis Plywood Corporation, with its extensive distribution warehouse system, had partnered with U.S. Plywood Corporation and Algoma distributing plywood throughout the country. With the resultant control of 60 percent of the plywood market going into World War II, Roddis had warehouses in Cambridge, Charlotte, Chicago, Detroit, Kansas City, Los Angeles, Louisville, Milwaukee, New York, Philadelphia, San Francisco and St. Louis.[112] In total, there were almost one hundred warehouses.[113]

Roddiscraft warehouse distribution map. *Author's collection.*

Despite the vast network of distributors and warehouses, the reality of the war situation was that the sawmills and distributors were still under the stringent restrictions of the Office of Price Administration's Limitations Order #L-335[114] and War Production Board controls. It was business but not "business as usual."

Nor was it "business as usual" in the Shipping Room. A description prefaced, "There is not much explicit information we can give you about the operations of the Shipping Room." The Shipping Room was under the direction of Arnie Korth. Shipments were shrouded in secrecy. It was exacting work keeping track of all the shipments and paperwork. All that could be said was that Roddis doors were being shipped to the South Pacific and that "our aircraft [were] being flown all over the world."[115]

The good news was that to accomplish all the war manufacturing, Roddis Lumber and Veneer Company had rebuilt its power plant, generating its own power by recycling sawmill waste. It also "installed new driers, 2 hot plate presses, put in a new basement, erected a new warehouse, and removed some of our smokestacks. At present we are installing a new lathe…Foundations are laid and pillars cast…to hold these huge machines…At the present time, we also have under construction our new office building."[116]

The Maintenance Department was working overtime. Bill Kraschnewski had forty men working with him.[117] All of this was accomplished with severe production and price ceiling restrictions, to say nothing of continued labor issues.

Civilian shortages were increasing: "Points have been increased on meat cuts, and some of the items that have been point free are now on the ration list. There are practically no meats not rationed. Pork especially has become very scarce. By mid-Summer, it is estimated there will be very little meat for civilian use."[118]

There was a tension of war, wariness and weariness.

The War Production Board optimistically reported that of the 1945 lumber production to date, 1 percent had been shipped overseas on Lend-Lease working with the British War Commission. In fact, 5.6 million board feet was bound for Holland for dike repair. Dockworkers in France would benefit from 23.6 million bdf. French war damage would receive 4.7 million bdf. Britain would need 80.0 million bdf to repair bomb damage and 164.0 million bdf for temporary housing for displaced war workers.[119] The over 200.0 million bdf was only part of the billions of board feet of lumber produced during 1945.

The great joy of celebrating the victory in Europe on May 8, 1945, and the formal surrender by Hitler was tempered by the continuation of the war in Japan.

VE Day in Europe! We have come a long way since that fateful day in December 1941 when the U.S. plunged into war, and with the bulldog tenacity that only an American can display we arrested victory from the enemy on one front, and on our terms. With the same farsightedness our leaders are not letting us lose sight of the fact that we still have another front to conquer on the other side of the world. That enemy precipitated our entry into this war, and we have a very grim fight ahead.[120]

Although the war was over in Europe, lumber and plywood production pressed on for the Pacific Theater. At Roddis, three "army officers and two civilian members of the Army Air Force" visited the Marshfield plant: Lieutenant Colonel C.J. Morey, chief of the Inspection Bureau; Captain M.N. Pallotto, materials and processes; and Lieutenant Steneck. "The civilian members are technical advisers for the Air Force on wood products. These men were here for the purpose of investigating our facilities, and they were very much pleased with the quality of our work and our production methods."[121]

Also visiting the Roddis plant in Marshfield at the end of May was Mr. Robert MacLea of MacLea Lumber Company in Baltimore, "our distributors in that territory, with Mr. Glenn Cahill of the Western Hardwood Lumber Co., Los Angeles…and Mr. Bill Gray of our Kansas City, Mo. Office." The visit confirmed MacLea Lumber Company's work with Roddis. MacLea Lumber Company was active in the National Hardwood Lumber Association. D.C. MacLea was its president from 1944 to 1946.[122]

In June 1945, the crystal ball for the future was somber:

On the eve of Memorial Day when we all pause to publicly honor our dead and with the historic San Francisco conference still in session drafting rules and regulations to maintain world peace, with the issues of Poland and Trieste, etc. not yet settled, we are faced with still another uprising between France and the Syrians. It is a pity that the word of man can no longer be counted upon in a world as highly civilized as ours, and that the report of gun fire must be the law by which we live.

There is no doubt but what the U.S. will be looked upon as the mediator in all disputes, both big and small, and it will be to the interest of all red blooded Americans to see not only that men whom we send to public office are capable of the vast responsibilities inflicted upon them, but also that they carry them out to the interest of America and all civilized mankind.[123]

How prophetic.

32nd Red Arrow Division insignia.
Author's collection.

Among those who defended our nation was Harold Dommer, twice wounded at Iwo Jima. "Seven Marshfield men were among the 185,000 of the 8th Air Force congratulated by Gen. Doolittle after V-E Day…Corporal Lawrence Warren in Germany says he is glad the war in Europe is over." For Private First Class Norbert Anderson, the war was never over, as he was wounded and had a "spinal operation."[124]

Many of the National Guard men from Marshfield and throughout Wisconsin and Michigan were part of the famed 32nd Red Arrow Division. The *Marshfield News Herald* had reported and also summarized in the *Roddis Bulletin*:

> *The Red Arrow Division is now starting its 4th year of overseas service, while behind it lies a record any unit of the U.S. Army might well be proud. For 543 days out of the 1095 which have elapsed since the 32nd sailed, its men have been on the line and committed to action. That is more than half the time the Red Arrow Division has been overseas...On this basis the 32nd claims proudly more fighting time than any other U.S. Army outfit in World War II. The 32nd has piled up an impressive list of "firsts": First full Army Division to sail from the U.S. in one convoy; first American ground force to be airborne into combat; first Army to defeat the Japs in Buna; first Division to test and prove Gen. MacArthur's famous "by-passing actions."*

Included in the actions was

> *valiant action on the Villa Verde rail and passage forced thru the Caraballo Mountains, hastening the completion of the Luzon campaign...The C.O. states, "After 120 days of fierce hand to hand combat over terrain more difficult than any yet encountered the Red Arrow again pierced the enemy's line." A recent newspaper article states the Philippines have filed a bill in the Philippines' Congress to change the name of the Villa Verde Trail to the Red Arrow Trail in honor of the Red Arrow Division.*[125]

Fighting in the "face of mortal combat," many of these brave men worked in the forest products industry.

CHAPTER 3

SHIPS

*It was said by military experts that the First World War was won on a sea
of oil. Certainly, the statement is no less true of World War II...ships cannot
deliver troops and materials, land transport cannot operate, tanks cannot move,
planes cannot bomb or deliver atomic missiles.*
—*P.C. Spencer, president of Sinclair Oil Corporation*[126]

The *Roddis Bulletin* reported that George Gillen, "our contact in touch
with all of our warehouses and distributors, has just returned from the
west coast where he was present for the launching of Victory boats installed
with Roddis door units."[127]

"Victory ships" followed the famed Liberty ships. They were designed
by Henry Kaiser's naval architects. Three of his shipyards built LSTs. All
of these ships required hundreds of thousands of board feet of lumber and
plywood. In addition, these "Wartime Emergency Yards" built ships with
workers who had little or no previous experience in shipbuilding. It was on-
the-job training.

Henry Kaiser, a genius with a seventh-grade education and favorite
slogans like "Think big!" would become the everyman and the "Father
of the Shipbuilding Industry." Having only visited a shipyard once in his
life before he became a shipping magnate, he was undaunted by the job.
He had, of course, already built the Hoover Dam, the Grand Coulee, the
Bonneville Dam and the Oakland to San Francisco Bridge. Building ships in
massive quantities did not seem to be a daunting task. In the postwar era, he

Courtesy of the Library of Congress, Washington, D.C.

would be most well known for establishing the Kaiser Permanente Medical Care Program, the nation's largest healthcare organization.

A peripatetic man, Henry Kaiser soon realized that shipbuilding, heretofore, was inefficient and too labor intensive and lacked basic raw

Henry Kaiser. *Courtesy of the Oakland Museum, Oakland, California.*

U.S. Maritime Commission logo. *Courtesy of the Library of Congress.*

materials. He would invent the new shipbuilding process, hire and train laborers on the job and build the newest steel mill in California at Fontana when he ran out of steel.

The Liberty ship was 441 feet in length.[128] The name was derived from Roosevelt's launching of the USS *Patrick Henry*. Patrick Henry's famous "Give me liberty or give me death" was in this case appropriate, as Britain and Europe struggled to survive Germany's advancement on the continent. FDR said, "[T]his new class of ships would bring liberty to Europe."[129]

Using 30,000 feet of fir and 700,000 board feet of lumber per ship, the result was the production of one Liberty ship per month.[130] This unheard-of rate resulted in the production of 1,509 Kaiser Liberty ships. The first Liberty ship launched on September 27, 1941.

During the previous year, President Franklin D. Roosevelt "secretly negotiated the trade of fifty overage destroyers to Great Britain in exchange for leases on six naval air bases in the West Indies."[131] On June 22, 1940, France surrendered. The response by the United States Congress was almost instantaneous. On June 29, 1940, Congress "authorized the United States Navy and Coast Guard to negotiate contracts for the acquisition, construction, repair, or alteration of complete naval vessels or aircraft...including plans, spare parts, and equipment...and also for machine tools and other similar equipment with or without advertising or competitive bidding."

By July 1940, recognizing the outcome of the China/Japanese War, Congress voted in favor of a $37 billion expenditure for a "two-ocean Navy,

Liberty ship. *Courtesy of the Oshkosh Public Museum, Oshkosh, Wisconsin.*

tanks for the Army, aircraft for the United States Army Air Corps, and aircraft for the Navy."[132] Stockpiling for war had begun. Wisconsin shipyards would produce LCTs (Landing Craft, Tank), frigates and submarines.

The shipping industry had risen to the challenge of a war across two oceans, but defending against attacks was difficult. "From January until the end of May, eighty-seven ships were sunk in American waters."[133] The Merchant Marines had the highest casualty rate of any of the services per number of men who served. They were not recognized and entitled to veterans' benefits for their service until 1988.[134] The author's sons' grandfather was among those whose ship was sunk underneath him from a German attack. A Merchant Marine in the Atlantic, J.W. Greer Sr., survived the attack.

America was building ships on both coasts and on the Great Lakes. In Superior, Wisconsin, Walter Butler Shipbuilders and Global Shipbuilding first built N-3 cargo ships for Britain. Later a Maritime Commission shipyard, it built frigates and cargo ships (AKs) for the United States Navy. Leatham D. Smith also built patrol boats, transports and net layers. In Sturgeon Bay, Peterson Boat Works produced subchasers, motor minesweepers, patrol craft and rescue tugs. On November 4, 1940, a story in the *Green Bay Press*

Gazette read, "Subchaser on Way to Coast…the Sub-chaser *SC432* moved out of Green Bay harbor…Aboard were a crew of Green Bay men, Lt. Leo V. Barron, commanding officer…of the 34th Naval Reserve Division." The subchaser was bound for active duty.[135] "To the farewell salutes of harbor tugs, barges, and two good-bye blasts from the paper mill whistles, the Subchaser *SC432* moved out of Green Bay harbor at 2 o'clock this afternoon…A large crowd composed of friends, families…There were little dramatics, outside of the tearful good-byes of wives and mothers of the men." Manitowoc Shipbuilding Company was renowned for its submarines and also built LCTs. Burger Boats in Manitowoc was another shipyard. "Prairie shipyards" in the Midwest seemed incongruous, but frigate escort ASWs were built on the Great Lakes.[136]

Vice-chairman Vickery of the Maritime Commission awarded contracts for an additional 148 Liberty ships on March 7, 1942, part of 922 contracted since January 6, 1942.[137] The doors for the Liberty ships supplied to MacLea Lumber in Baltimore for the Bethlehem-Fairchild Shipyard were made by the Roddis Lumber and Veneer Company in Marshfield, Wisconsin. They utilized the new techniques of laminating plywood to a mineral asbestos core for fireproofing. The process had been developed by George Meyercord

Dennis Kundinger and Sheila Fredrickson pouring the core board mixture. Roddis Lumber and Veneer Company became Weyerhaeuser, then Marshfield Door Systems in 2008; it is now Masonite Corp., Marshfield, Wisconsin. *Author's collection.*

at Haskelite Corporation.[138] The mineral core was made of amorphous silicate, amesite asbestos, crysolite asbestos, water, auto clave and quick lime (eventually, the asbestos would be replaced with a wood binder).[139]

The plywood was laminated with phenolic resins developed by the Roddis Plywood Corporation's own chemists, Joe Schumann and Ken Rapala.

The "door units were manufactured to equip 55 boats and enough plywood bulkheads for 75 boats per month."[140] Ship production was in full swing to counter enemy attacks.

According to Paul Mueller, the Roddis Company had manufactured the doors at the Marshfield plant but rented "another plant from Louis Trosen for the purpose

Jeff Zondlo, sales at Marshfield Door Systems, now Masonite Corporation, showing the mineral core for the fireproof doors to the author in 2007. *Author's collection.*

. . . from the RODDIS
Kansas City warehouse

Roddiscraft
PRICE LIST
No. 1156

Supersedes No. 656

HERE are the latest prices on:

- **PLYWOOD**
- **DOORS**
- **MOLDING**
- **HARDBOARD**
- **PLASTICS**
- **And other Allied Products**

You're assured of Service—when you call on RODDIS

Roddis
LUMBER & VENEER COMPANY, INC.
1016 Southwest Boulevard
Telephone: TAlbot 2-8111 — Teletype KCK 1009
KANSAS CITY 3, KANSAS
DALLAS — SAN ANTONIO — HOUSTON

Roddiscraft price list. *Courtesy of Warren Weaver, Roddis Lumber and Veneer Company, Kansas City, Missouri.*

of assembling the frame and doors. Ron Fulweiler was the supervisor of the operation on east Fourth Street. The hinge side of the Liberty door was two inches shorter than the lock side for the purposes of the lower deck."[141]

The Liberty ships transported war material to England. Many would be sunk by German submarines, spawning Henry Kaiser's idea for the famed "Spruce Goose" (HK-4) "Flying Boat."

"MARINEWOOD" was developed by Roddis Plywood Corporation under its subsidiary called Roddiscraft:

Roddis MARINEWOOD is a trade name used to identify plywood built to specifications to withstand exposure to rain, snow, water, or sun. The glue used Tego Resin film and the bonding is done in a hot plate press producing plywood that will withstand soaking in cold or boiling water, mold, heat or freezing. This dry glue film introduces no liquid into the wood, and permits precise control of the moisture content of all wood plies during the gluing operation.

Plycor 16-Foot Hot Press Installed in the Roddis Factory. Will glue Panels or Doors Up to 50" x 192" RODDISCRAFT MARINEWOOD, resin-bonded plywood up to 16 feet long.[142]

A Plycor sixteen-foot hot plywood press. *The Golden Anniversary Catalogue: 1890–1940: Fifty Years of Service*. Roddis Plywood Corporation, Marshfield, Wisconsin. *Author's collection*.

Roddis Plywood Corporation shipped plywood internationally under tight security. Ironically, the Tego Resin film glue, hot plate press and veneer dryers were German derived. Domestically, under Roddiscraft and Roddis Lumber and Veneer Company, plywood was shipped for battleships and aircraft. Roddis was

> *one of the largest manufacturers of airplane plywood in the United States. It supplied airplane plywood to the governments of France, Great Britain, and the United States; and in World War II Roddis also furnished millions of feet or marine plywood to Hopeman Brothers Manufacturing Company for the building of battleships. There were two or more government inspectors stationed at the Roddis plant throughout the war.* [143]

Roddis had supplied aircraft plywood in World War I and throughout the interwar years. Also, the supply of plywood, doors and bulkheads for battleships was not Roddis Lumber and Veneer Company's first foray into being a sub-contractor for large ship renovation and shipbuilding.

The German imperial flagship *Vaterland* had been constructed by the Hamburg-American Line in 1914. It was a U.S. World War I troop carrier ship, having been confiscated from Germany early in the war. Roddis

Lumber and Veneer Company "supplied panels for the doors and bulkheads on the E, F, and G decks on the renovation of the S.S. *Leviathan*."

The SS *Leviathan* was featured in a 1920s *Roddis Flush & French Doors* catalogue. William Francis Gibbs, the naval architect, utilized Roddis products in the "E-deck first class purser's office, second class dining room, first, second, and third class stateroom corridors, F-deck first class dining room, barbershop, and bank…[and] G-deck the first class 'Pompeian' swimming pool." The ship sailed from 1923 to 1938 as a luxury liner. The renovation project was "the biggest American marine engineering feat of the 1920's."[144]

Roddiscraft MARINEWOOD was a trade name developed by Roddis Lumber and Veneer Company for marine plywood made of mahogany, "Unselected Birch or Sliced Elm."

RESNPREST, fir plywood, was also used for boats with the Tego film glue.[145] Again, the unique characteristics of the Tego Resin film glue meant that the "dry glue-film introduces no liquid into the wood and permits concise control of moisture content of all wood plies during the gluing operation."[146]

The assertion that the glue would not penetrate the wood meant that the wood characteristics would remain. The United States Forest Products Laboratory research demonstrated that the glue would improve the durability of the wood.

"V" award flag, U.S. Maritime Commission. *Courtesy of the Library of Congress, Washington, D.C.*

Roddis would eventually ship "millions of board feet of marine plywood to Hopeman Brothers Manufacturing Company in New York for the building of World War II Battleships."[147] Industries nationally received the coveted "E" Awards more than once for expeditious production and the coveted "V" Eagle Flag from the Maritime Commission during World War II. Hopeman would eventually win the "V" Award from the Maritime Commission for its work. The New York Yard plus New York Shipbuilding, Philadelphia, Norfolk, Bethlehem-

Quincy and Newport News were the battleship builders, as well as builders of aircraft carriers and battle and heavy cruisers during World War II.[148]

Roddis Lumber and Veneer Company, too, won the coveted "V" Award from the Maritime Commission. On Saturday, November 7, 1942, there was a presentation of the Maritime Victory Eagle Flag.

Marshfield Herald, November 6, 1942. *Author's collection.*

A full-page tribute, "Roddis Congratulates Its Employees," by the Roddis Lumber and Veneer Company for "Winning the Coveted Flag," appeared in the *Marshfield News Herald*:

> *Working Together for Victory…celebration marks a new high point in the manufacturing history of Roddis Lumber and Veneer Co. A high point that could only be attained by the combination of the loyalty, skill, efficiency of every worker…in wholehearted cooperation with the efforts of its officers to produce in record time urgently needed materials for the merchant marine.*
>
> *Your efforts are real evidence of practical patriotism. To you has fallen the task of providing our valiant men on the high seas with the equipment to do their job. You, in this great company have been doing your part and doing it splendidly. Your enthusiasm and accomplishments are a grand example and an inspiration to the rest of the country.*
>
> *The Maritime Victory eagle Flag is the highest honor Roddis Lumber and Veneer Co. could receive. It's the nation's tribute to the spirit of patriotism and production effort of the Roddis Lumber and Veneer Co. Bigger tasks and responsibilities lie ahead…we know that with the same cooperation…the same determination, you will continue to carry through on the production line…our fighting front to victory. Roddis Lumber and Veneer Co. is proud of its employees…as is Marshfield and the whole country for the splendid record you have made in producing for victory.*[149]

A tremendous accomplishment and accolade for all forest product employees.

CHAPTER 4

WISCONSIN "WOOD FLIES TO WAR"

The story of Wisconsin's men flying in "Wisconsin's Flying Trees" into battle is remarkable. During World War II, the glider combat missions carried 101st, 82nd and 17th Airborne men who fought valiantly in "the face of mortal combat."[150]

Flying into Normandy and Operation Market Garden in Holland, Frank Parzatka of Armstrong Creek and a "glider rider" said, "We were just doing our job." He was also a veteran of the Battle of the Bulge and Bastogne.

According to Les Schwarm of Wausau, an 82nd Airborne glider rider, "The people of Holland are still thanking us for what we did."

Schwarm continued, "We never got our due." He said, "I always sat in the thirteenth seat to be the first one out. They had told us if we were the first ones out, the Germans couldn't shoot straight and wouldn't hit the first guy out."[151] Schwarm was awarded a Bronze Star Medal for his service.

In Wausau, he was responsible for establishing the Battle of Bulge Monument near the Marathon County Courthouse. Walter Pakulski Jr. was also a World War II glider rider from Stevens Point. Awarded the Bronze Star Medal for his service in Europe, Pakulski was responsible for establishing the 82nd Airborne Bridge Memorial, which serves as reminder of the Wisconsin Airborne's contribution to all wars.

Dr. N.H. Stolp from Wisconsin Rapids fought in Holland. Other Wisconsin glider riders included Bob Herriot, Art Schmitz and Ray Nelson from Beloit. Nelson fought in Normandy and Holland. He said, "I was one

Above: World War II gliders, CG-4As landing in "Zone W" in Normandy during the D-Day invasion. *Author's collection.*

Left: World War II "glider rider" 82nd Airborne Frank Parzatka of Armstrong Creek on Memorial Day, May 2013, at the King home in Waupaca. *Courtesy of Tom Laney, editor of the 82nd Badger Airborne News.*

Above: Glider riders Les Schwarm, 325th GIR 82nd in the foreground, beside Walter Pakulski, 326th GIR 82nd with Herb Huebschen in the co-pilot seat, Iron Mountain, 2010, Glider Restoration Dedication. Schwarm constructed the restored glider floor. *Courtesy of Tom Laney, editor of the* 82nd Badger Airborne News.

Right: Les Schwarm, 325th GIR 82nd, with Lieutenant General Caldwell. *Courtesy of Tom Laney, editor of the* 82nd Badger Airborne News.

Les Schwarm (1924–2012) at the Wausau World War II Memorial. *Courtesy of Les Schwarm.*

of the lucky ones who came back." So was Gene Strutzenberg, who fought in Africa, Italy, France and Germany. He liked to remember

> *how well we were treated in France and even by some of the German conscripted soldiers…We were taken into a farmhouse. We had dinner. When it was time for bed, we were told to take off our uniforms and throw them down the ladder. We were a little skeptical, but we did it. The next*

morning our uniforms were clean, our boots had been polished to the highest shine. We were grateful and stunned that they had done that for us. [152]

The 82nd Airborne had a "rendezvous with destiny" and fought heroically. General William Westmoreland (Retired) would say of the glider pilots:

The intrepid pilots who flew the gliders were as unique as their motor-less flying machines. Never before in history had any nation produced aviators whose duty it was deliberately to crash-land, and then go on to fight as combat infantrymen. They were no ordinary fighters. Their battlefield was behind enemy lines. Every landing was a do-or-die situation for the glider pilots. It was their awesome responsibility of repeatedly risking their lives by landing heavily laden aircraft containing combat soldiers and equipment in unfamiliar fields deep within enemy-held territory, often in total darkness. They were the only aviators during World War II who had no motors, no parachutes, and no second chances. [153]

From the beginning of aviation until 1940, the United States had manufactured seventy-five thousand airplanes. However, America was caught short on a stunning German glider raid in Belgium to capture Fort Eben Emael. In early 1941, the United States Army Air Corps (USAAC) had no glider designs, no gliders and no glider pilots. The army had no real experience in conducting a glider program.

The war effort was aptly illustrated by the World War II development of CG-4A cargo gliders. The conversion of manufacturing plants from automobiles and pianos to aircraft carrying small jeeps, howitzers and the men of the 101st and 82nd Airborne into battle was an incredible feat. The magnitude of the scale for forest products conversion to war is almost unfathomable today. Wisconsin was called on to supply aircraft plywood for "Wisconsin's Flying Trees." Beginning in 1939, Wisconsin had its own Civilian Pilot Training programs for training single-engine power pilots. In 1942, the Badger State would have its own glider pilot training school in Janesville led by a famous Wisconsin barnstorming aviation pioneer. America acted quickly![154]

The most famous Wisconsin-trained glider pilot and the most decorated 82nd Airborne soldier in its history is Lieutenant Colonel James "Maggie" Megellas.

Maggie left the Glider Corps for "more excitement"[155] and became a paratrooper. His heroism as he fought from "the beaches of Anzio to… Field Marshall Montgomery's vainglorious Operation Market Garden

Lieutenant Colonel James "Maggie" Megellas is holding a paddle the 504th Paratrooper Infantry Regiment men gave him in Afghanistan because they knew that he had used his Thompson .45-caliber sub-machine gun as a paddle crossing the Waal River during the famous battle in World War II. The paddle has a static line connected to it. Behind Maggie are his 1945 jump jacket and his many awards and decorations. *Photo and description courtesy of Tom Laney, editor of the* Wisconsin Badger Airborne News, *taken 2007.*

in Holland," and at the Battle of Herresbach, has been written about in his own *All the Way to Berlin* and recorded in the documentary *Maggie's War* (released in 2012).[156] Lieutenant Colonel Megellas lectures on "Leadership in the Face of Mortal Combat," conducting training for the Department of Defense. "On the night of 28–29 January 1945, Lieutenant James Megellas of H Company, 3/504 parachute Infantry Regiment 82nd Airborne Division led an attack on the town of Herresbach, Belgium that has been called, by those who witnessed it, 'the perfect battle.'"[157]

Later, Colonel George Heib, World War II paratrooper H/504 PIR, Special Forces Vietnam, said of his experience at the Herresbach battle with Maggie: "We were catching hell from a Panzer when I saw someone charging the tank with a Thompson sub-machine gun! I asked myself, 'Who in the hell is that crazy sonofabitch?!' I saw him knock that tank out with a couple of grenades and found out later that it was Maggie. He saved us all!"

Reaffirming Colonel Heib's opinion, SSG Bill Hannigan, 504 PIR paratrooper and "a squad leader in Maggie's platoon," said:

> *Maggie was the bravest man I ever saw. He cared about each one of us. He appreciated us all so much! He would do anything for us, and we would follow him anywhere. It wasn't just that he was a paratrooper and a heroic combat leader. He was the best at that, of course. But he is more. He is a good man. He's done good things for people all his life.*

Lieutenant Colonel James Megellas was recommended for the Congressional Medal of Honor.

> *The government thought this "G" stood for glider. However, the glider pilots, disdained by many power pilots, being an independent and resolute group of trained pilots, determined that "The 'G' is for Guts!"*[158] *Glider pilots were not part of the airborne organizations. On graduation, USAAF glider pilots were assigned to Troop Carrier Command along with C-47 pilots who would tow the gliders into battle.*

Glider pilot wings and glider infantry wings. *Author's collection.*

WWII CG-4A GLIDER SOARING OVER A FRANCE LANDSCAPE

Consoweld paper laminate "Dura Beauty" mosaic by Gib Endrezzi, artist, for the 2010 Second National World War II Glider Symposium, 2010. *Designer Ed Statskewicz, U.S. Marine, Vietnam veteran.*

Aircraft production increased. The *Marshfield Herald* reported that Roddis Plywood Corporation was[159] "manufacturing 1,400,000 square feet of aircraft plywood per month…wing skins for the British Mosquito Bomber, as well as skins and other plywood units for gliders and other aircraft."[160]

"Gliders and other aircraft" plywood were a major contribution to the war effort.[161] The English wrote about their airborne troops as a "New Phase of Warfare":

> *A great stride has been made in modern methods of warfare by the creation of a separate airborne Army…Welded into one great fighting unit—troops, aircraft, gliders, everything—their task is to conduct operations…to put troops down on the land. We may recognize this pattern of future warfare in which extremely mobile air armies will develop their own strategies. All ranks are trained to a degree of skill unsurpassed in any form of any service in history. Volunteers all.*[162]

Airborne was and is a proud service branch of the Armed Forces.

"On a basis of 500 cargo planes per month, for example, we will have to log 600 Million board feet more than we are taking out each month in logs...5 Billion board feet will substitute Wood for metal with the annual consumption of the estimated 38 Billion board feet."[163]

FORD MOTOR COMPANY, KINGSFORD, MICHIGAN

The Ford Motor Company's manufacturing plant in Kingsford, Michigan, was the largest manufacturer of gliders during World War II. Of the total 13,903 CG-4A gliders built, Ford Motor Company would build 4,190. This did not include 87 Ford-built CG-13A gliders.[164] The contracts for glider delivery and the exigencies for war required new techniques. In 1941, the

Ford Motor Company, Iron Mountain, Michigan. *Courtesy of Charles Day, author* Silent Ones: WWII Glider Invasion: Test and Experiment.

Troops unloading a trailer. *Courtesy of Charles Day, author of* Silent Ones: World War II Glider Invasion: Test and Experiment.

United States Army Air Corps had already decided that aluminum would be reserved for power plant aircraft. In addition, any facility involved in manufacturing airplanes with engines could not produce gliders. Ford Motor Company was eventually contracted to make the B-24 Bomber at Willow Run in lower Michigan, but it could not share any of the manufacturing materials with Kingsford's plant in the Upper Peninsula of Michigan. The B-24 featured laminated phenol resin "gun turrets, seats, shields, and ammunition boxes on the bomber."[165]

The first CG-4A glider that Ford Motor Company "delivered in September, 1942 was built entirely at the Ford Airport hangar in Dearborn… across the field from the now Henry Ford Museum. All the jigs…were built first and run through production tests. If they passed, they were shipped to Kingsford, Michigan to be set up for production."[166]

With over seventy thousand parts involved in glider construction,[167] the conditions and obstacles for the manufacturing of gliders were overwhelming. Contracts were changed regularly.

Even if the gliders themselves were constructed, difficulty obtaining wheels, tires or crates slowed delivery. Five shipping containers were required for one glider readied for the war theater. Sending the gliders on board a Liberty ship, each shipping crate measured "twenty-five feet five inches long

Over seven hundred mules were carried on CG-4A gliders in Burma. *Charles Day Collection.*

and eleven feet seven inches high. All five crates contained over 10,000 board feet of lumber. Depending on the manufacturer, the wood was No. 1 Pine or hardwood."[168] Wisconsin, the Upper Peninsula of Michigan and Michigan's lumber industry supplied the over 41 million board feet of lumber required for the Ford glider crates.

Skilled aircraft employees were not available. The Ford Motor Company Kingsford plant employed 7,500 people manufacturing car and truck bodies. Kingsford was also the home of what would later become Kingsford Charcoal. Prior to World War II, the automobile-manufacturing processes switched from wood to steel in construction. The 313,000-acre facility was limited to wood construction of the decorative panels for the Ford "Woody" station wagon. Eventually, over 5,000 skilled carpenters and employees at Ford Motor Company would assemble the "honeycomb plywood floor, plywood and fabric covered wings and cockpit, plywood bench seats, and stabilizers" at Kingsford.

Much of the plywood for the glider wings would come from Wisconsin's Roddis Lumber and Veneer Company, Marshfield, as a subcontractor for Steinway & Sons through General Aircraft. The length of the glider was

World War II glider pilot veteran Lawrence Kubale at the 2010 Second National World War II Glider Symposium, Madison. *Author's collection.*

48 feet, 3¾ inches. The tow speed was one hundred miles per hour. The wing span was 83 feet, 8 inches, with a maximum weight of nine thousand pounds.[169] The wings were made of mahogany plywood because of the surplus of mahogany in the lumber market.[170]

During World War II, Ford Motor Company's production of gliders averaged two hundred per month. Some of the gliders were towed out of the Kingsford airport in a regular parade of C-47 aircraft lifting these "Gentle Giants" into the sky.

Flight Officer Lawrence Kubale of Middleton, born in Reedsville, Wisconsin, flew CG-4A gliders in the Normandy, Southern France and Operation Market Garden missions. He said of the Operation Market Garden mission, "I was wounded in the back by flack that came through the back of my seat and I blacked out. The trooper in the co-pilot seat flew the glider until I came to…Our landing spot was a field full of burning airplanes and gliders, but I was able to land the glider troopers safely." Kubale received the Purple Heart, Air Medal, Bronze Star and Orange Lanyard for the Operation Market Garden mission.[171]

NORTHWESTERN AERONAUTICAL CORPORATION

At the height of the Great Depression and with no financial stability, the aircraft industry in the United States was floundering. The choices were bankruptcy, liquidation or mergers. The Great Depression had wreaked havoc on the worldwide economy. The aircraft industry was no exception.

John E. Parker, CEO of Northwestern Aeronautical Corporation. *Courtesy of the University of Minnesota, Charles Babbage Institute, Center for the History of Information Technology.*

In 1937, John E. Parker surveyed the wreckage. No one saw the economic impact more clearly than Parker, eventual president of Northwestern Aeronautical Corporation. He was an investment banker. With Parker's military background and his experience in Washington, D.C., he had knowledge of the precariousness and lack of aviation preparedness in the face of another world war. Parker would form Northwestern Aeronautical Corporation, which would become the second-largest glider producer behind Ford Motor Company.

John E. Parker was a young Naval Academy graduate who had joined his father-in-law's investment banking house of C. Murphy. The firm later became Horn Blower Weeks. After his father-in-law died, Parker was able to wrest control of the Baltimore, Washington and New York offices for his own.

In New York, he formed a partnership with Auchincloss and Redpath. Their firm of Auchincloss, Parker, and Redpath took an early interest in American aviation firms. The partnership would survey the aircraft industry in 1937. As investment bankers for Bell, Boeing, Beech and Cessna, Auchincloss, Parker, and Redpath also had a controlling interest in Northwest Airlines

Captain John E. Parker (back row). *Courtesy of the University of Minnesota, Charles Babbage Institute, Center for the History of Information Technology.*

and Board of Director representation. Parker's firm financed 70 percent of all the airlines. Auchincloss would invest by himself, initially $25,000 in 1938, and his partner, Parker, would purchase Porterfield Aviation in Kansas City. By year's end, the amount invested had risen to $140,000.[172]

Porterfield Aviation Company in Kansas City was in foreclosure. It was trying to get an army contract building an aircraft trainer for the United States Army Air Corps. However, the United States government "contracting source for the glider program was in Dayton." Colonel Nelson Talbot administered the program in Chicago.

Through John E. Parker's acquisition of Porterfield Aviation Company, he received a government contract to manufacture experimental gliders and CG-4A WACO cargo gliders with a letter of intent on February 28, 1942, followed by a formal contract on March 4, 1942.[173]

The initial investment was $1,000 plus $9,000 worth of equipment. It was estimated that to produce the initial thirty-seven gliders, it would cost $512,100.

The total contract value was $626,986.75.[174] That figure would grow to over $14 million as 1,507 gliders were eventually made by Northwestern Aeronautical Corporation.[175] As a co-founder of Northwest Airlines and member of the first Board of Directors, Parker drew heavily on Northwest Airlines for personnel, engineering expertise and a manufacturing facility.

Parker founded and transformed Northwestern Aeronautical Corporation into a glider manufacturer. He said, "I found out at Wright Field it [the bid on the trainer airplane] was going to go somewhere else, but they were going to put out a request for bids for a glider…They actually gave me a contract to build 13 airplanes on an experimental contract…by the end of the war, we were doing about a dozen or 15 a day."[176]

During the war, Parker's Northwestern Aeronautical Corporation had an enormous manufacturing facility on Minnehaha Avenue in St. Paul, as well

Two Villaume Corporation employees stand proudly in front of a CG-4A glider holding a glider tow rope. *Courtesy of Nick Linsmayer, president of Villaume Corp., St. Paul, Minnesota.*

World War II glider construction at Villaume Corporation. *Courtesy of Nick Linsmayer, president of Villaume Corp., St. Paul, Minnesota.*

as a facility at Chamberlain Field. Northwestern Aeronautical Corporation had glider pilot training facilities at Aero Ways in Cleveland, Ohio, and Hood Aviation in Northampton, Massachusetts.[177]

In the postwar period, through his involvement as vice-president of Sperry Rand Corporation, John E. Parker saw the application of new computer

World War II glider construction at Villaume Corporation. *Courtesy of Nick Linsmayer, president of Villaume Corp., St. Paul, Minnesota.*

technology to Northwest Airlines' reservation system. He was involved in the development of National Security with General Douglas A. MacArthur.

Although the contract for three hundred gliders had begun in 1942, only one experimental glider and one prototype CG-4A were constructed during that year. Serious production did not begin until 1943.

A howitzer being unloaded from a CG-4A glider. *Author's collection.*

The CG-4A carried a small bulldozer. *Courtesy of Charles Day, author of* Silent Ones: WWII Invasion Glider: Test and Experiment.

A CG-4A Northwestern Aeronautical Corporation glider constructed by Villaume Corporation in flight. *Courtesy of Nick Linsmayer, president of Villaume Corp., St. Paul, Minnesota.*

Nationally, over six million women were in the workforce. Several hundred worked at Villaume Box and Lumber Company. Villaume Corporation, now headed by the grandson of the founder, Nick Linsmayer, was a major subcontractor for Northwestern Aeronautical Corporation, as was DuPonti Aviation Company.[178]

Northwestern Aeronautical Corporation produced 1,509 CG-4As. "CG" stood for cargo glider. By producing forty-seven CG-13As, these gliders, even bigger than the CG-4As, would carry more troops, more ammunition and more vehicles.[179]

Other gliders were powered with engines. Northwestern Aeronautical Corporation built ten PG-2As ("PG" stood for power glider).[180] Under contract with the United States Army Air Corps, the total number of gliders to be built by Northwestern Aeronautical Corporation would have been 1,710, but 140 were cancelled.

The CG-13A would hold "airborne troops and their equipment or the equivalent weight in military vehicles or ordnance."[181]

World War II glider pilot Ralph C. Lester received his dead stick training at Janesville. In the first glider pilot training class, he arrived on June 1, 1942. His recollection of Janesville is living in the YMCA and flying from the same field every day (there were three in use for training). Lester recalls the Atkinson name and an aircraft maintenance building; his assigned field was presumably the Atkinson farm field. Lester's Janesville flying training was thirty-six hours total, including 180 dead-stick landings, mostly from five hundred feet. His "landing to the mark" training required a coast-roll to a stop within fifteen feet of a white line on the field.

From Janesville, Lester went to Lockbourne and then Stuttgart, where he received his "G" wings and was kept on as an instructor. Flight Officer

Herb Huebschen of Beloit fought in Normandy, Operation Market Garden and the Bulge. *Courtesy of Herb Huebchen.*

Lester was promoted to first lieutenant and shipped to the Philippines, where he flew a CG-4A glider in the Appari combat mission.[182]

The average time of survivability of the glider pilot was seventeen seconds. They called the release time to the ground "available air time."

At the conclusion of the war, it was recorded: "The outstanding record attained by Northwestern Aeronautical Corporation in the production of gliders for the Army Air Forces is an excellent example of the ingenuity exhibited by American industry in converting from peace-time production to the supplying of the implements of war to the Armed Forces of the United States."[183] Northwestern Aeronautical Corporation worked hard to complete its war mission.

Lieutenant Colonel Edward Finch, later ambassador to Panama who served in World War II in Strategic Planning in the Pentagon and on General Arnold's staff, said, "The greatest contribution by General 'Hap' Arnold was the development of the computer in the Pentagon at the end of World War II."[184] Captain John E. Parker parlayed the computer into Sperry Rand Corporation after having had glider contracts at Northwestern Aeronautical Corporation in St. Paul/ Minneapolis. What a technological revolution!

Herb Huebschen of Beloit fought in Normandy, Operation Market Garden and the Bulge. He said:

My entire Army Service in WWII was with the 325ᵗʰ Glider Infantry Regiment, 82ⁿᵈ Airborne Division…I participated in the Allied Airborne invasion of Normandy…Upon landing in a small field bounded by thick hedge-rows, our pilot hit the brakes and tipped the glider up on its underbody skis for a quick jolting halt. Small arms fire could be heard all around... Glider [pilots and] troops wore no parachutes, gliders were unarmed, and having no engine, obviously had no second chances to land. (One might say "we were roped in.") Our Normandy mission was to prevent the Germans from attacking Allied sea-borne forces that were trying to establish a beach-head on the coast of Normandy. While my unit was attacking a village in Normandy, an artillery shell exploded in our midst, and killed my battalion commander, for whom I was carrying a radio. I was wounded by the same blast and evacuated to a hospital in England. I rejoined the 325th...I learned that two men of my radio section had been killed...They were carrying the same radios that I had handed off to them when I was wounded.[185]

Northwestern Aeronautical Corporation was not the only company with a glider contract from the War Production Board. There were sixteen prime glider contractors and about fifty subcontractors making pieces and parts for the gliders.[186] Skilled woodworking craftsmen were needed for glider manufacturing. No one debated the woodworking skills at Steinway & Sons in New York.

From May to August 1943, Steinway & Sons paid Roddis Lumber and Veneer Company in Marshfield, Wisconsin, $16,773.16.[187] One purchase order was dated May 6, 1943. At that time, Steinway & Sons was located at 36th and 19th Avenues in Long Island City. The purchase order was for eighty-one pieces and 9,625 square feet for a total amount of $3,118.50. On May 19, 1943, an additional sixty-four pieces of plywood were ordered in the amount of $1,758.48. The specifications were for "5 ply Gum, 45 degree."[188] This meant that the facing and the core of the plywood were from red gum.

Red gum and Tupelo gum were tested extensively for tensile strength. It is thought that it was red gum, as opposed to Tupelo gum, that was used for

Steinway & Sons logo. *Courtesy of Steinway & Sons.*

This photo of the "Susie Bell" shows a man attaching a tow rope to the glider for which Steinway & Sons made parts. *Courtesy of LaGuardia and Wagner Archives, LaGuardia Community College/City University of New York, New York.*

the gliders. Tupelo gum was harder to cut, and the sweet gum or red gum was distributed more widely and would be more readily available. The cross-banded plywood was shipped again to Long Island City. Orders for veneer and plywood would follow. "Ninety-one sheets of ⅟₁₆ x 49 x 120 gum-gum 45 degrees" in the amount of $1,426.88 were ordered on June 10, 1943.[189] Some of the orders were "mahogany-poplar, 90 degrees," and some were birch-birch 90 degrees."[190] William Roddis II stated that the mahogany-poplar specifications were a center core of poplar with a mahogany outside.[191] A July 23, 1943 order was extensive—$6,326.97. It included varying sizes and thicknesses from ⅟₁₆ to ⅝ inch, primarily of birch-birch and mahogany-poplar.[192] All the pianos, equipment and wood were moved to accommodate glider manufacturing.[193]

Accommodations were also made for the more than seven hundred women who were hired. Theodore Steinway commented about the hiring of women, "We had to reconfigure the factory to build toilets for them. Up until that time, Steinway & Sons had been all men."[194] By 1943, women made up one-third of the total national workforce.[195]

Women handling glider panels at Steinway & Sons. *Courtesy of Steinway & Sons and the La Guardia and Wagner Archives, La Guardia Community College/City University of New York.*

Research has shown that Steinway had its own patents for tools developed to assist with making gliders, as well as patents for plywood glue and glue applications. The "cage nut tool" patent was the work of Michael Schultz.[196] Patent Number 2,384,347 was filed on November 11, 1943, and granted on September 4, 1945: "This invention relates to tools for clinching cage nuts to plywood skins used in gliders and aeroplane construction."[197] Without the cage nut tool, screws used would split the plywood. The cage nut tool allowed an anchoring device on the back or secured within the plywood to prevent wood splitting.

Another patent was the work of George Beiter and called "securing means for adhesively held parts."[198] The patent was filed on July 3, 1943, and approved on March 28, 1944.[199]

The removal of nails in canvas and wood would not only be a problem in constructing Steinway's gliders. This tool would be a precursor for Howard Hughes's construction of the "Spruce Goose." Hughes Aircraft Company would submit a patent for a similar tool to remove the eight tons of nails after the gluing process.

While tools were invented to assist with the wooden construction of the gliders, Steinway & Sons was also working on a process to improve the glue

The Griswold nose. *Courtesy of the La Guardia and Wagner Archives, La Guardia Community College/City University of New York.*

line on the wood edges. It was making seats for gliders. Other applications for the gliders required precision and speed. Steinway & Sons was the first company with the "quick dry" glue system.

It was able to manufacture spars and noses more quickly than other manufacturers. "The First was the 'real' Griswold nose, which was a complete nose. The 'bolt-on' Ludington-Griswold nose and skid came out of the Griswold nose."[200] It was designed by Roger Griswold of the Ludington-Griswold Company.

There were glider door frames,[201] some from Roddis Lumber and Veneer Company. Steinway was a subcontractor for General Aircraft in Astoria, two miles from the Steinway factory.[202] Steinway supplied the plywood and veneer pieces and parts for the gliders to General Aircraft Company, as well as Pratt and Read & Company. Steinway & Sons gave General Aircraft its building at "43-02 Ditmars, and they [General Aircraft] subcontracted all the woodworking to us, which included wings, tail surfaces, floors, nose, and even seats for the troops."[203]

Steinway & Sons supplied Ford Motor Company in Kingsford, Michigan.[204] General Aircraft Company was supplying parts to Ford Motor Company,

Steinway wing construction. *Courtesy of the LaGuardia and Wagner Archives, La Guardia Community College/City University of New York.*

the largest manufacturer of gliders during World War II. Roddis Plywood and Veneer Company supplied plywood to Ford indirectly through Steinway & Sons and then through General Aircraft.[205] As Roddis Lumber and Veneer Company had potentially supplied Laister-Kauffmann indirectly from Northwestern Aeronautical Corporation, Roddis supplied plywood to Ford indirectly through Steinway & Sons and then through General Aircraft.

Piano production during World War II was not allowed because of the use of metals. However, entertainment of the troops was also needed. The U.S. government would relent to allow Steinway & Sons to build "Victory Verticals."[206] Its German Hamburg factory was bombed by U.S. aircraft.

Pratt Read & Co. logo. *Courtesy of the Pratt Read & Company, Deep River, Connecticut.*

Steinway & Sons also supplied spars to Pratt, Read & Company, a piano parts manufacturer located in Deep River, Connecticut, and founded in 1860. With an elephant head for a logo, the elephant's tusks represented the supply for ivory piano keyboards. The company also made keyboard actions. Out of ivory, it made combs. The company invented the comb lathe in the late 1700s. During World War II, Pratt, Read & Company had skilled woodworkers. They built 956 CG-4A gliders.[207]

Some of the English Hadrian gliders were made by Pratt, Read & Company, including the famous "Voo-Doo." In 1943, the Royal Air Force flew a trans-Atlantic flight to test the feasibility of transatlantic cargo glider transport. Gliders were sent to England in huge wooden crates. Many of the crates were made by Phillips Flooring and Veneer Company in Phillips, Wisconsin. The gliders were "unassembled in wooden crates. Just one CG-4A glider, for example, required five huge wooden crates to be shipped overseas."[208] At the end of the war, people utilized the crates as houses or hunting shacks.

The United States Lend-Lease–built glider by Pratt, Read & Company was the only one towed by a C-47 that flew from Montreal, Canada, to Scotland. The pilot of the glider was Wing Commander Richard G. Seys, DFCAFC. The glider was called the "Voo-Doo" after some tricky maneuvering in the Atlantic crossing resembled the Indian rope trick. In discussing his flight, Wing Commander Seys said:

> *About the end of June, I got permission from my boss to have a shot at the Atlantic crossing. We started off at about noon on a lovely day and flew about three hours—we could see weather ahead. We tried to climb over it, but we didn't have the engine power to do so, so we went underneath. We were forced down at one time to below one thousand feet and went through*

three belts of thunderstorms, sleet, and snow—generally very unpleasant…
At one particular time it was not snowing outside, but snowing inside. It's
difficult to make allowances for that when planning a flight.

We carried about 1¼ ton of freight which consisted of vaccines and
blood plasma for Russia, equipment for the Free French and parts for B-24
bombers, Ford trucks and a lot of radio parts. The radio parts were very
delicate. We had to treat them carefully.

I also carried a bunch of bananas. Bananas do not exist in England and
won't for the duration of the war. I thought it would be nice to take some
back to the family in England, but they were frostbitten.

We flew north for 28 hours, three minutes, for a total of 3,500 miles.
We arrived safely and very tired at the other end.[209]

The flight took eight days. It was decided, at the conclusion of this harrowing trip, that transatlantic glider transport flight was unfeasible.[210]

In 2003, one hundred Roddis mahogany glider wing panels were found "in a garage loft" and were given to the Stone House Historical Society in Deep River, Connecticut.[211] When William H. Roddis II was asked why this was not yellow birch but mahogany, he said, "The mahogany was in plentiful supply during the war." The mahogany veneer was purchased in Indiana from Oscar Witt Veneer Buyers and Hoosier Veneer Company, as well as Louisville Veneer Company in Louisville, Kentucky. "They had machines which could slice the veneer lengthwise in longer lengths than the Roddis Lumber and Veneer Company could cut on their rotary lathes."

Pratt Read & Co. CG-4A 26th Production #42-52802. This glider was also fitted with the "real" Griswold nose. *Courtesy of Charles Day Collection.*

Loading the wing truck on its way to Deep River. *Courtesy of the Stone House Museum, Deep River, Connecticut.*

The longer lengths would fit into the Roddis sixteen-foot presses.[212] One glider wing panel in an exhibit was approximately four by five feet and ³⁄₃₂ of an inch.[213] During World War II, Pratt, Read & Company employed its former customers as subcontracters and suppliers, allowing all companies to survive wartime product restrictions.

After the war, Pratt, Read & Company returned to the music business and later became a toolwork company.

Cessna logo. *Courtesy of Cessna Aircraft Company.*

Cessna Aircraft Company had been building gliders since the 1930s. While the Great Depression had almost bankrupted the company, it received a contract from Canada's Royal Canadian Air Force (RCAF) to manufacture

Cessna Bobcat. *Courtesy of Cessna Aircraft Company.*

trainer aircraft, which saved it from financial ruin.[214] Over three thousand Bobcats were manufactured.

Roddis Lumber and Veneer Company supplied not only plywood for the Cessna glider wing panels but also the plywood for the AT-17 Bobcats. It is possible that Roddis supplied the plywood for the prototype C-106 and C-106A transport planes developed near the end of the war, as well. This government contract was cancelled. The planes were purposely destroyed in Wichita.

Cessna, Beech and Boeing worked in concert to produce the gliders. Cessna built the outer wing panels.[215] Cessna's manufacture of glider wing panels was not unfamiliar to the company. "During 1930, Cessna produced 84 single-seat gliders, each with a wing span of 35' 2"."[216] Beech was "assigned to build the inner wing panels, tail surfaces, all forgings and castings. The company subcontracted most of the work to outside firms, who delivered the part on time and to specifications." Boeing did the final glider assembly. Boeing had an aircraft division in Wichita, as did Beech. Like Roddis Plywood Corporation conducting shear stress tests in cooperation with the U.S. Forest Products Laboratory, Boeing conducted its own shear test on plywood.[217]

Remarkably, during World War II, Cessna built an entirely new "108,000 square foot factory in just over 30 days" to complete the glider contract. On a site of "110 acres of land, east of Hutchinson, Kansas…Three shifts labored hard hours to meet the deadline. Karl Boyd was supervisor… overseeing 315 workers initially and then more than twice that number as the job got rolling."[218] The cooperative effort of Cessna, Beech and Boeing resulted in 750 gliders.

The Bobcat was the twin-engine airplane in which pilots were trained to transition to bomber aircraft. Over three thousand Bobcats were manufactured. The Bobcat was thirty-two feet, nine inches long, with a wingspan of forty-one feet, eleven inches, and a maximum takeoff weight of 5,700 pounds, max speed of 195 miles per hour and range of 750 miles.[219]

After Pearl Harbor, aircraft manufacturing facilities like Cessna, Beechcraft and Boeing increased from forty-one to eighty-one. President Franklin D. Roosevelt had requested 60,000 aircraft for 1942 and 125,000 aircraft for 1943.

AIRCRAFT PRODUCTION TABLE

Date	Aircraft Plants	Plant space in sq. ft.	Employment	Production
1940	41	14 million	100,000	23,000
1943	81	170 million	85,898	
1944			2,000,000	96,318

The American strategy for aircraft use changed the tide of World War II. Aircraft was critical to America's success. President Roosevelt's projections were never realized, even at the war's peak. The United States aircraft production fell short by over twenty thousand. Still, within weeks of Pearl Harbor, the United States Congress had appropriated over $6 billion for aircraft construction and equipment. Gliders and new aircraft designs were an integral part of America's wartime successes in Europe and Asia.

CHAPTER 5

"WISCONSIN'S FLYING TREES"

THE BRITISH CONNECTION

Sir Geoffrey de Havilland had started building airplanes as a young man, and his first aircraft flew in 1909. It was a primitive biplane, but sophisticated designs would follow. The British aircraft design genius was knighted in 1944 for the design of the DH 98-Mosquito. The De Havilland Mosquito provided the British and their Allies with a superior aircraft during World War II.

In 1934, Sir de Havilland designed the record-setting DH 88-Comet.[220] Sir de Havilland's DH 88-Comet would be redesigned to become the Mosquito, affectionately known as the "Mossie." It would be the fastest airplane of World War II at 450 miles per hour. Pilots were known to polish their "Wooden Wonders" to coax even a few more knots from them. The "Timber Terror" would carry enormous bomb loads of up to ten thousand pounds. The Mosquito's first mission began on September 17, 1941.

The "Wooden Wonders" provided tactical support as Pathfinders. At first, the Pathfinders would lead the bombing runs and mark the "path" with fire bombs. The subsequent Mosquitoes would follow for bombing runs on enemy targets. A system called Gee, based on radio signals, was invented, but at the end of 1942, two newly developed radar systems known as Oboe and H2S would guide and assist the Pathfinders.[221]

As "Nightfighters," the Mosquitoes would shoot down German junker bombers over the English Channel and North Sea. The Germans flew to

Sir Geoffrey de Havilland (1882–1965). *Author's collection.*

England at night, and the "Nightfighter" Mosquitoes shot down many of their aircraft.

Most significantly in Operation Jericho, Mosquito raids on Amien released 258 French underground prisoners scheduled for execution by the Germans.[222] A raid on a Gestapo headquarters reduced to ashes the lists of German Jews scheduled for transport to concentration camps.

Gestapo headquarters were a favorite target. "On January 30, 1943, the commander of the Luftwaffe and World War I hero, Herman Goring, was scheduled to make a radio speech on the 10th anniversary of Adolph Hitler's ascent to power in Nazi broadcast. The explosions were caused by bombs dropped from three 'super-fast' twin-engine Mosquito bombers on the occasion of the first allied daylight raid on World War II…on the German capitol."[223]

At one point, the Dutch Resistance wanted the Gestapo headquarters bombed to prevent the revelation of the Resistance's identification papers.[224]

Different variants of the Mosquito identified the aircraft's use. Even though one was painted with red and white stripes, "not everyone managed to get that straight."[225] The Mosquito could fly low and avoid most flak by antiaircraft guns. The Mosquito "aimed at a particular building in the middle of the city, or even at a particular part of a building, and destroyed it without causing heavy casualties to the nearby friendly occupied population, and without being decimated by the enemy's anti-aircraft defenses."[226]

A Mosquito flight line. *Courtesy of Bill Groah, retired technical director of the Hardwood Plywood and Veneer Association, Reston, Virginia.*

The "Wooden Wonder," the Mosquito in flight. *Courtesy of Camp 5 Museum Foundation/Wisconsin Forestry Museum, Laona, Wisconsin.*

"Mosquito Got Nazi H.Q.; Oslo Wants More Raids" was the headline of the *Daily Mail.* "Details of the damage done by squadron Leader D.A.G. Parry's four Mosquitos new twin-engine British made light bombers in Friday's daylight raid on Oslo…The Mosquitos scored five direct hits on military objectives with seven bombs they released over the center of the Norwegian capitol."[227]

The Mosquito was also used as a "Dambuster" prototype. Whether the Mosquito was waiting over German airfields to shoot down German Junkers, thinking that they were home safely, or disrupting German lines of communication, it wreaked havoc wherever it was assigned.

The "Timber Terror" in flight. *Courtesy of Bill Groah, retired technical director of the Hardwood Plywood and Veneer Association, Reston, Virginia.*

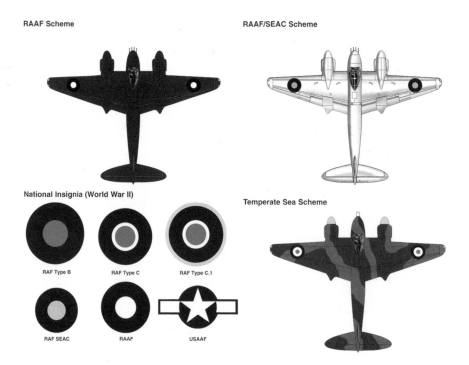

Courtesy of Squadron Signal Publications.

A Mosquito with single engine idling. *Courtesy of the National Museum of the United States Air Force, Dayton, Ohio, Wright Patterson Air Force Base.*

Sir Geoffrey de Havilland's "Wooden Wonder" Mosquito had taken form at Salisbury Hall, a famous English manor house that was disguised as a farm with a large barn. The barn was actually a working design center. The bureaucracy insisted that a wooden airplane could not fly; it could not have the flight characteristics needed for a sustainable war effort.

Group commander Donald Bennett, who later commanded the Pathfinder Force of Mosquito bombers, said:

> *I test flew the Mosquito by day and by night. At a meeting at the Air Ministry on the subject, Bomber Command and the Air Ministry both very strongly opposed the adoption of the Mosquito. They argued that it was a frail wood machine totally unsuited for Service conditions, that it would be shot down because of its absence of gun turrets, and that in any case it was far too small to carry equipment and an adequate Pathfinder crew. I dealt with each one of these points in turn, but finally they played their ace. They declared that the Mosquito had been tested thoroughly by the appropriate establishments and found quite unsuitable, and indeed impossible to fly at night. At this I raised an eyebrow, and said that I was very sorry to hear that it was quite impossible to fly at night, as I had been doing so regularly during the past week and had found nothing wrong. There was a deathly silence. I got my Mosquitoes.*[228]

RAF (DFC) Eric Loveland and his navigator, Jack Duffy, in the cockpit of their Mosquito. *Courtesy of Camp 5 Museum Foundation/Wisconsin Forestry Museum, Laona, Wisconsin.*

The British Air Ministry was convinced that metal airplanes were the only viable option. It dubbed the British air minister's support of Sir de Havilland's project "Freeman's Folly." That "folly" was to prove their folly and undoing at the beginning of World War II. Aluminum for aircraft was in short supply. The Germans dominated the skies.

Cecil Beaton said:

> *Life in London was bleak. Let me be un-British for a moment and refuse to minimize the sufferings of the civilians at home, for I don't think nearly enough people realize just what Londoners have been through. No one is starving, but a half-pound per week for meat is not very much, especially when there is no question of a chicken or game substitute. A shell egg, that is to say a real egg, is a marvel in London. There are queues for fish which is of the vilest quality. The Londoner has not seen any spoils of victory—a few oranges have been allotted to nursing infants but no sign of olive oil—no wine to speak of. Nerves are frayed, people are on edge, tempers are lost easily, rudeness, quarrels, and tragic little misunderstandings arise to the surface with surprising rapidity. People do not complain of their lot except when their patience is tried to snapping point.* [229]

The British Air Ministry would reconsider and turn to Sir de Havilland for support. Sir de Havilland's staunch ally Sir Wilfred Freeman would be vindicated. De Havilland by then had designed and built a Mosquito

Single-engine flying was the Mosquito's design coup. *Courtesy of Camp 5 Museum Foundation/ Wisconsin Forestry Museum, Laona, Wisconsin.*

The "Timber Terror" Mosquito. *Courtesy of the National Museum of the United States Air Force, Dayton, Ohio, Wright Patterson Air Force Base.*

prototype ready for demonstration at Hatfield. On November 25, 1940, it wowed the viewers with its capabilities.

No airplane had been as fast or could fly single-engine. No airplane had the quick turning radius or could outrun the enemy. Britain did not have the metal for airplanes, but it did have cabinet and woodworkers. Sir Geoffrey de Havilland received the first contract for 150 Mosquitoes on December 30, 1940.

The Mosquito had the highest return rate from bombing missions of any other airplane in the war. Describing several missions:

> *For the last three months of the war in Europe, I was stationed at a base about fifteen miles west of Norwich, attached to Elliot Roosevelt's reconnaissance group. This particular one had a squadron of Mosquitos,*

which flew combination radar "chaff" missions and photo reconnaissance mission. The Mosquito's flew ahead of the bombers and dumped chaff to disrupt German radar, flew off-target until the bombers released their bombs and then photographed the damage inflicted. In three of those four cases, the airplane had lost power in one engine...one of the German jet-fighters made a pass at the Mosquito, which was diving for cloud cover. It weakened the end of the wing and when it pulled out of the dive several feet of the wing broke off. It got back to base, but barely!

It happened that four of these planes crash-landed on returning to the base, fortunately with no casualties. When they crashed, plywood pieces from the fuselage flew in all directions. On that account, we had an opportunity to view it.[230]

De Havilland's design was "British invention in the face of adversity."

The Mosquito was versatile, quick and efficient. Roddis Lumber and Veneer Company would provide a large percentage of the yellow birch plywood for the "Timber Terror." British Intelligence, BRINY, No. 1232, cypher 30, dated October 30, 1940, as well as AVIA 38/669, said that the Roddis Lumber and Veneer Company plywood in crates had been "distributed to Roe, Gloster, De Havilland, Phillips & Powis, Venesta and others."[231] The BRINY cypher was from Sir Henry Self, who was in charge of Mosquito production, and addressed to the Ministry of Aircraft Production.

Regarding the BRINY 1232 cypher, on November 6, 1940, the Ministry of Aircraft Production sent a message to Sir Henry Self, MAP No. 1551 cypher:

> *Roddis Lumber and Veneer Co. plywood inspected by A.I.D. here from crates 267 and 3241 Lots Numbers 77712, 77414 and 77616...test report signed off by W.C. Nelson states shear test figures varying from 350 pounds to 551 pounds per square inch and that adhesion and bending are in accordance with 5 V 3. Plywood in question was shipped.*[232]

Further cables were sent between the Roddis Lumber and Veneer Company and the British Air Commission in 1941. On March 28, 1941, came BRINY 4083: "Cable 30, Have inspected Roddis...Assured satisfactory supplies can be shipped in the future. Recommend they proceed with contract. A.I.D. Inspector will be placed in works for 1 month. Roddis agrees to pay cost... Will meet any changes in sizes required." [233]

This cypher was sent to the "Director General (Air), Secretary of the Supply Council, A/C Pirie for Ambassador" and others. William H. Roddis II said:

> *Then in about 1939 or '40, the British came to us. They had learned somehow, that we had a 16 foot press and they needed long lengths of plywood for a plane they were developing and the result was that they placed orders early on...They had the Mosquito flying...and from then on we began getting orders. The initial orders were either solid core, rejected by the British. Our personnel didn't really understand the high perfection that the British expected and the product that we were making was aircraft plywood. As a result, my father appointed me and made me chief inspector...He was actually the main force to improve the quality and set up methods so that we could produce acceptable plywood for the Mosquito. To do so, we added a humidity room so that we could bring up the moisture content of the veneer...about 112 to 114 per cent and the hot plate presses for the type of glue...was a phenolic resin glue. Had to be pressed at 300 degrees...They* [De Havilland] *had inspectors on the presses.*

In Vilas County, Roddis Lumber and Veneer Company had purchased land from Claire Uihlein Trostel on March 2, 1943, after negotiations with Albert Trostel and Sons Company, Milwaukee, Wisconsin.[234] It had a vast growth of yellow birch. The yellow birch came from Wisconsin forests, particularly Vilas and Price Counties. William H. Roddis II said:

> *In World War II with the demand for birch veneer for the aircraft plywood we were using all the birch we could lay our hands on here in Wisconsin and as the war went on, my father realized that there wasn't enough birch available from the usual sources and one thing he did at the time was to purchase the Trostel estate...in the town of Winchester. It was all virgin timber...it was a big element in being able to product plywood for the Mosquito.*[235]

De Havilland sent representatives to Wisconsin and had inspectors at Roddis Lumber and Veneer Company. The veneer and plywood would be sent to England in crates built by the Phillips Flooring and Veneer Company in Phillips. Orville Peterson would write to his daughter:

> *Can you visualize how it was at our house in 1942 when I was 32? The war effort was getting in full swing...The mill ran six 8-hour days and*

Orville Peterson in Phillips, Wisconsin.
Courtesy of Karen Baumgartner, Phillips, Wisconsin.

often 10 hours a day producing lumber for the war...We made mostly crating to ship veneer from Butternut and Mellen to build airplane parts, so radar couldn't pick them up. Most everything that went overseas had to have a wooden crate to stand salt and rough handling.[236]

The pay was "$.30–$.35 per hour" at Phillips Flooring and Veneer Company.

The Royal Australian Air Force received 212 planes from Australia. Eventually, 7,781 "Wooden Wonders" were built.[237]

Franz Boschwitz, owner of Lullaby Furniture Company in Stevens Point, Wisconsin, provided the "plywood for one of three Mosquitoes."[238]

During the Second World War, Northern Hardwood Veneers, Incorporated. of Butternut manufactured plywood (or veneer) that was used to build the famous deHavilland "Mosquito" Bomber. Thirty-five percent of the wood going into this plane was from the plant at Butternut. It is recorded that one thousand carloads of Butternut veneer "winged its way over Europe"—the "Mosquito" Bomber.[239]

According to the Lullaby Furniture Company's own records, it was Northern Hardwood Veneers, Incorporated that manufactured the veneer and plywood, and Oshkosh Pluswood was the log supplier as the logs came through the Great Lakes from Canada.

Penokee Veneer Company in Mellen had veneer slicers. The *Manitowoc Herald Tribune* reported in 1946 that Eggers Plywood and Veneer Company in Two Rivers had provided aircraft plywood and veneer for the Mosquito and gliders. There were other minor producers manufacturing veneer and components for master contractors.[240]

THE DE HAVILLAND CANADIAN MOSQUITO: "O, CANADA"

As Canada had been heavily invested in World War I, it would again come to the assistance of Britain in World War II, this time with not only troops but also aircraft and Royal Canadian Air Force pilots.

The Canadian production of the Mosquitoes initially encountered problems with the subcontractors. De Havilland sent his chief engineer, W.D. Hunter, and production manager, H. Povey, to Canada for the manufacturing of the Mosquitoes.[241]

William H. Roddis II of Roddis Plywood Corporation in Marshfield, Wisconsin, worked with S.H. Morrow, inspector in charge of the British Air Commission—Materials Group at 5-231 General Motors Building in Detroit. The British Air Ministry had approached Canada for an initial contract of four hundred De Havilland Mosquitoes on September 11, 1941.

On a visit to Toronto arranged by Corr Harris, British Air Ministry, in 1942, William H. Roddis II said in a letter to Hamilton Roddis:

> *We were shown around by a fellow from one of the wood shops. Two types of planes are made here, an elementary trainer...At the DeHavilland plant we were taken to the experimental building where now one of the things they were working on was molded plywood. They have a pressure cylinder and have done much work along these lines. The building was definitely not for strangers, and I was very fortunate to see it. They make wooden wings for their elementary planes and tomorrow I can see the difference between making wings for elementary trainers, and wings for a two-motored bomber trainer.*[242]

William H. Roddis toured the De Havilland facility at 888 Dupont Street in 1942.

In his letter to his father, Roddis made reference to De Havilland's second manufacturing center at Downsview-Main. Later in life, he was proud that Roddis Plywood Corporation met the "British Standard Specification of 5V3 for stressed parts and V-34 for unstressed parts"[243] for the British Mosquito. The waterproof glue was also an important factor for Roddis.

The De Havilland plant in Canada eventually produced 1,076 Mosquitoes.[244] The 888 Dupont Street manufacturing plant was under the direction of W.J. Houston. The Dupont Street plant produced the Mosquito fuselage. It was two half shells put together with V-joints, which were concealed with long, thin strips of plywood.

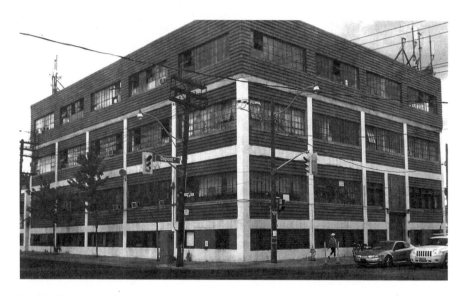

De Havilland manufacturing plant in Toronto, Canada. *Courtesy of Barbara McDonald, Toronto, whose brother, Richard Ellis, was RCAF.*

By June 1942, the British had formed the "Combined Raw Materials Board in Washington, D.C. with Deputies of the Minister of Production and the Chairman of the War Production Board...apprais[ing] Britain's raw material needs." The Canadian "project was definitely to be financed by the U.S. through the Lend-Lease Agreement."[245] It also resulted in the implementation of the British Ministry of Production.

By November of the same year, the Raw Materials Committee of the Commonwealth Supply Council dealing with Canadian production was established.[246] The assembly of the Mosquitoes was an amalgamation of Canadian manufacturers. Massey-Harris, which made farm machinery, "was to make the wings...Boeing Aircraft, Vancouver," made the tail empennage. Canadian Power Boat in Montreal built the flaps, and later it, too, would make the fuselage.

The wing production had begun to flourish. Soon, wing production outpaced fuselage production. Eventually, Central Aircraft stepped in and took over Mosquito production. The Royal Air Force (RAF) received 1,134 Mosquitoes from Canada.[247]

The British Air Ministry sent the Canadian Mosquitoes to the United States in a Royal Air Force exchange. Known as F-8s, they were sent to the 375th Service Squadron in Watton, Norfolk, and were later used in the war.[248]

In the postwar era, an official royal visit to Sault Ste. Marie on July 8, 1959, formally recognized the Roddis Lumber and Veneer Company's contribution to the Canadian war effort.[249] Mr. Gordon P. Connor was in Sault Ste. Marie in the summer of 1959 and recalled his grandfather's Beechcraft B-18 arriving. His grandparents both arrived to participate in the official luncheon.

MOSQUITO PILOT TRAINING

England sent 1,800 Royal Air Force cadets to the United States during the war to be trained as pilots. The skies over England were too crowded with German aircraft trying to bomb the United Kingdom and English aircraft trying to defend their homeland. Eric Loveland was one of those cadets sent to No. 5 BFTS in Clewiston, Florida.

In 2006, Loveland, a Royal Air Force Mosquito pilot and instructor, said, "It was a pilot's dream to fly the Mosquito, really. I did the demonstrations to the new recruits to show them that even if they lost an engine, the Mosquito would still be able to carry on. It was easy really, but they thought it was amazing. No other airplane had the quick turning radius or could outrun the enemy."[250]

Eric Loveland, RAF, DFC, retired (1922–2010). *Courtesy of Eric Loveland.*

Loveland also shared his thoughts with the author about the D-Day invasion. As a member of 68th Squadron, he said, "Our job was to provide aircraft cover during the invasion. Fortunately, we did not run into any opposition. However,

Eric Loveland, RAF, DFC, retired and his navigator, Jack Duffy. *Courtesy of Eric Loveland.*

the memory of seeing the waves of gliders coming over the beaches was unforgettable. We knew it was a one-way trip for them."[251]

The "Mossie" was equipped with four 20mm cannons and four machine guns.[252] In a dogfight, its ammunition could do the job. The added effectiveness of the Mosquito also was due to the airborne radar, a new invention.

During the war, the Mosquito pilots were credited with superior eyesight, "Cats-eye" Cunningham being the heralded example:[253]

On the night of March 3–4 [1945], one-hundred forty German intruders bombed fourteen airfields and shot down nineteen British bombers. Two weeks later, 68th Squadron was scrambled on the night of March 17 after intruders shot up Carnaby, Coltshall, and other English airfields.

Mosquito pilot Flying Officer Eric Loveland and Navigator Sgt. Jack Duffy of 68 Squadron were among those…Their brand new Mosquito

Moonlight Serenade, by Troy White. *Courtesy of Troy White.*

NF-30 was equipped with a pair of two-stage 1,690 hp Merlin engines and four 20mm cannons...After being vectored to the intruder by ground control, Loveland and Duffy were able to close in on the enemy and easily identify him as a German JU-88 as the aircraft was silhouetted against the clouds in the moonlit sky...

Eric sent the JU-88 diving to obtain cloud cover with a short gun burst. A second burst into the JU-88 produced flames and smoke from the port engine, and the intruder disappeared into the clouds.[254]

Loveland said:

We had top-secret airborne radar. If the ground radar suspected enemy aircraft in the area, they would try to direct us and put us on the same course behind them. The navigator would finally hear them. We would come in below the enemy aircraft so the radar would not get a ground return and we would not be seen...Unfortunately, if we were flying over the English Channel and had the Germans in our sight, we could not pursue them into Europe. We did not want the radar technology to fall into enemy hands, and we had to turn around.[255]

The Mosquito "fighters distinguished themselves in...night fighter roles, and destroyed 600 V1 flying bombs in defense of Britain."[256] The airborne radar could paint the enemy airplanes.

The effectiveness of the "Timber Terror" was a surprise to the Germans. What they did not know was that the Pathfinder, as well as the Mosquito bombers that would bomb Berlin, had the H2S radar. Along the English coast, there were twenty-one radar stations that could "detect enemy bombers 140 miles away and at altitudes up to 30,000 feet...[The radar] kept track of the enemy and RAF positions...'The British fighter was guided all the way from takeoff to his attack on German formations. For us, this was a surprise and a very bitter one,' Luftwaffe General Adolf Galland wrote later."[257]

Eric Loveland transferred to the 64th Squadron when the Hornet was developed.

De Havilland had developed an even faster airplane at the end of the war, the DH 103-Hornet. The goal was to create a Pacific Theater long-range fighter. A Mosquito derivative, it had counter-rotating propellers. Again the questions of whether the plywood could withstand tropical temperatures were studied in its development.[258] The Hornet was constructed with the two halves, or egg-carton construction, using the cold molding process

A De Havilland Hornet. *Courtesy of Camp 5 Museum Foundation/Wisconsin Forestry Museum Archives, Laona, Wisconsin.*

as well. Although the fuselage was shorter than the Mosquito, the use of composite wood and wood laminated to metal was a new process in 1943.[259] The Hornet squadron would be formed for training. The first flight of the Hornet was in 1944.

Eric Loveland would train pilots to fly a Hornet formation over Buckingham Palace on V-E Day, May 8, 1945. The *Daily Sketch* reported on Wednesday, May 9, 1945:

> *Over 100,000 people crowded Buckingham Palace...The crowd cheered the first time at the end of Winston Churchill's broadcast...While they were waving...A Mosquito came droning down Pall Mall at less than 1,000 feet and passed over the Royal Standard which flew so proudly from the Palace roof.*
>
> *At 4:15 PM, the balcony doors opened again. The scene was repeated.*[260]

Britain did not have enough plywood, so it built the Mosquitoes with imported Wisconsin plywood. The plywood had been originally sent over as "cabinet material." Under the Neutrality Act and soon-to-be Lend-Lease

Program, only so much could be sent as war material. No one would suspect that veneer and plywood would be used for aircraft. The Mosquito endeared itself to the pilots. They knew that more often than not, they would make it back to base after fearsome air battles.

AVRO ANSON

During World War II, returning after a grueling mission was the uppermost on all pilots' minds. They had great faith in the "Faithful Annie," the Avro Anson. Even poems were written about it:

> *Oh, the Crane may fly much faster*
> *Inside she may be neat,*
> *But to me the draughty Anson*
> *Is very hard to beat.*
> *Her plywood may be warping,*
> *Her window glass may be crack,*
> *But when you start out in an Anson,*
> *You know that you'll come back.*
> *—Andy, No. 7 SFTS (Fort Macleod) 1943*[261]

The "know that you'll come back" was a revealing line in the poem. The longevity (1968) of the Avro Anson into the postwar era illustrated its significant contribution to aviation history.

In England, the battle was over wood products for aircraft. Over eleven thousand Avro Ansons were constructed. Many were modified in Canada. "While initial agreements indicated that Canada's role in supplying aircraft was to be a small one, as it worked this decision actually instigated the largest Canadian wartime aircraft production program although the Anson was neither the largest nor the most numerous of the types produced."[262]

The "Faithful Annie" was a training aircraft to transition pilots to bombers, like the Lancaster. Being the first Royal Air Force aircraft to have retractable landing gear, it was an ideal trainer. However, what some pilots remember about it is the retractable landing gear requiring 160 turns to be raised after takeoff or lowered for landing.[263]

Training schools were located in Canada, England, South Africa and Australia. The British Commonwealth Air Training Plan to create

Avron Anson. *Courtesy of Nanton Lancaster Society Air Museum, Alberta, Canada.*

the Royal Canadian Air Force encompassed "schools operating 231 sites across Canada, 10,840 aircraft were involved, and the ground organization numbered 104,113 men and women, and three thousand trainees graduated each month. At a cost of more than $1.6 billion, 131,553 pilot, navigators, bomb aimers, wireless operators, air gunners, and flight engineers were graduated."[264]

The Anson was itself a light bomber, as well as being used for coastal reconnaissance. Powered by two Jacobs L-330 hsp engines, the length was forty-two feet, three inches. The cruising speed was 155 miles per hour.[265] The wingspan was fifty-six feet, six inches. While the initial contract called for the Anson to be made of metal, it was in short supply. The contract was changed to build the aircraft of plywood. Bristol Aircraft Products of Canada Limited in Belleville, Ontario, and Bristol, Virginia, was an early manufacturer. The cold molding process reached Canada through the National Research Council.

George Anson was a British Royal Navy admiral in the 1700s, and "Faithful Annie" was named after him. Prowling the coast, the Anson "made the first RAF attack on a German U-boat."[266] Also, it was estimated that had

111

transport planes like the Anson been used over the Burma Road, the "17,000 tons of material moved over it by 4,500 trucks could have been transported in less time by 21 transport planes."[267] The British were in desperate need of ships, materiel and support.

CHAPTER 6

THE "SPRUCE GOOSE," OR WAS IT WISCONSIN YELLOW BIRCH?

In the present conflict, wood and its derivatives are in great demand for an extraordinary variety of military and industrial uses. For the time being at least, the tables are turned. And wood in addition to the purposes for which it is normally utilized is being substituted extensively for other materials, notably metals, the supply of which are suddenly become inadequate for our needs. As a result, the production of logs for lumber, veneer, pulp, and other forest products is now at a higher level than for many years.[268]

Imagine the possibilities—and Henry Kaiser did with the HK-1 Flying Boat. Although the "Spruce Goose" did not fly until November 2, 1947, the HK-1 Flying Boat was conceived in 1942. It was under construction during World War II. Building techniques, aircraft design and the engines of the Flying Boat were revolutionary in the industry.

In 1942, when Kaiser conceived the Flying Boat, it was with the explicit instructions from the United States government that metals could not be used, nor could necessary engineers or laborers designated for the war effort be used in construction. Kaiser would not be hampered by these restrictions. He had already proved that men and women could be instructed with on-the-job training building Liberty ships. Sir Geoffrey de Havilland had already proven that wooden aircraft were valuable in the war effort with his "Wooden Wonder," the Mosquito.

In the United States, the discussion raged. What if war materials were sent by air to England in a large transport aircraft? The "Spruce Goose" was the idea of Henry Kaiser, a genius with a can-do attitude. The idea of a wooden transport plane excited the woodworking and aviation community. Dr. Wilson Compton, secretary of the National Lumber Manufacturers' Association, wrote:

> We aim to build cargo ships faster than they are sunk. At present, we are not doing it…For our overseas transportation should we keep our "eggs in one basket" and count on mastering the submarine? Or should we put the transportation in the air…
>
> For thousands of freight cargo planes, you might use lumber plastic laminated wood and molded plastic bonded plywood. These are strong enough, are no longer merely experimental, and cargo planes made of them certainly could be completely standardized. The production of plywood, except hardwood plywood is practically at the top of physical capacity… There is considerable capacity for laminated wood, not all of it is being used. The sawmills without more plant installations have capacity to produce considerably more lumber. They principally need logs and labor. There are enough trees. [269]

The new waterproof glue had made possible sturdy laminated wood products.[270] Planes designed specifically for cargo were now possible.

As Henry Kaiser suggested the largest transport plane in the world, Curtiss-Wright was building a smaller all "plastic-bonded plywood" plane in Kentucky. The C-76 cargo plane was even smaller than its C-46 aluminum plane but "offered the use of many workers skilled in wood-working so that builders of cargo planes would not find themselves 'stealing' workers from

Curtiss-Wright C-76 Transport. *Author's collection.*

present aircraft construction." In the end, twenty-five of the C-76 "Caravan" assault transport planes were manufactured.[271]

In fact, it was pointed out by Otto Timm,

> *president of Timm Aircraft Company, one of the pioneer developers of plywood planes now being built as trainers for Army use…there are 2100 wood-working plants in the country now in furniture, sash, door, and general millwork production, with 378,000 workers, who could be potential builders of plywood transports, trainers, and other such aircraft.*

The potential for the wooden aircraft being superior to the metal aircraft was described as:
1. The raw materials were readily available;
2. "fire resistance is superior to major aluminum alloys";
3. "corrosion resistance is higher near water";
4. "expansion of the plywood" from humidity has been reduced to a minimum;
5. "plywood eliminated riveting and is easily pressed"; and
6. "wood does not have to compete with aluminum."

In 1942, Henry Kaiser turned to the aviation genius Howard Hughes. Kaiser also would return to Wisconsin and the Roddis Plywood Corporation. The *News from Hughes* public relations newsletter summarized the project:

> *Design proposals were submitted to the government in late summer of 1942 and on November 16, a contract was let by the Defense Plant Corporation, as the governmental agency, to design and construct airplanes…*
>
> *The original proposal called for approximately 250,000 pounds. When the builders considered the airplane was to be designed around a 60 ton heavy tank, the present size gross weight of 400,000 pounds was established.*
>
> *…Regular aircraft birch, purchased in the northern part of the middle west—Wisconsin and Michigan, was selected because of past experiments with other planes and the strength ratio…Hughes Aircraft Company secured the franchise to use the Duramold process of wood lamination… Extreme precaution had to be taken and maintained to prevent parts and assemblies from being affected by moisture and temperature changes…*
>
> *All birch parts are made from veneer varying from ¹⁄₆₄ᵗʰ to ⅛" thick and laminated together with glue…Birch billets for wing spars were 6'x8'x90'…design and built scarfing and cutters and presses…*
>
> *The building for construction covered 8 acres and was built in two sections with a 3 story mezzanine equal to two large aircraft carriers.[272]*

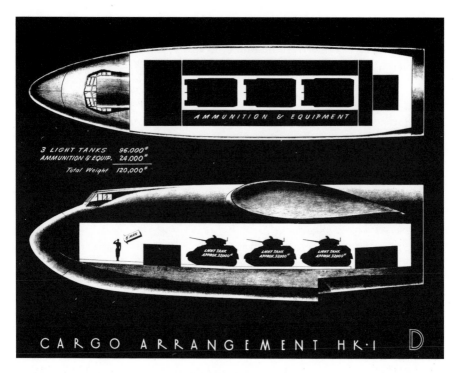

HK-1 cargo arrangement. *Courtesy of the U.S. Forest Products Laboratory Library, Madison, Wisconsin.*

Henry Kaiser was told by the War Production Board to build three prototypes.

Howard Hughes realized the importance of the revolutionary Duramold technique, which would reduce the plywood thickness, reduce the aircraft weight and increase the airspeed. The "sandwich construction" process was utilized by de Havilland in the Mosquito. Also, the Spruce Goose would have veneer cut to 1/90 and dried to 1/100.[273]

Although the Spruce Goose was constructed in Culver City, California, the veneer was cut by Herman Johnson at Roddis Lumber and Veneer Company in Marshfield, Wisconsin. Leroy Treutel of Stratford, who succeeded Johnson as lathe operator, said, "Johnson told me when he trained me to cut it that thin. You either cut it or you don't…It is so thin you can see your hand behind it."

Leroy Treutel cut the 1/90 veneer for U.S. Forest Products Laboratory samples. In cutting the yellow birch, Treutel said, "The only one that had greater tensile strength was Sitka spruce. The grain did not dare go one inch in eight feet. There was lots of lead on the knife…It would take all day

116

"Spruce Goose" fuselage construction at Culver City, California. *Courtesy of the Evergreen Aviation and Space Museum, McMinneville, Oregon.*

HK-1 Flying Boat wing. *Courtesy of the U.S. Forest Products Laboratory Library, Madison, Wisconsin.*

Opposite, top: HK-1 Flying Boat wing with engine nacelles. The wing is 225 feet long and 30 feet wide. *Courtesy of the U.S. Forest Products Laboratory Library, Madison, Wisconsin.*

Called the "Spruce Goose," the official name was the "Hughes H-4." *Courtesy of the U.S. Forest Products Laboratory Library, Madison, Wisconsin.*

to cut a thirty-inch log." He was the lathe operator at Roddis Plywood Corporation for fifteen years and the first lathe operator at the Canadian plant at Sault Ste. Marie. The lathe "could cut an eleven-foot-diameter log and a log ten feet long. Alex Lungren was the saw filer." Treutel later moved into sales.[274]

Although the Forest Products Laboratory had lathes of its own, they could not cut the birch veneer that thin. Whether it was a mechanical or

Roddis Lumber and Veneer Company circular lathe. *Author's collection.*

technique problem, the Forest Products Laboratory asked Roddis Lumber and Veneer Company to provide veneer samples. During World War II, most veneer was rotary cut in ⅟₆₄; the Roddis company veneer cut at 1/90 and dried at ⅟₁₀₀. Larry Wartner worked for Roddis for thirty-two years. He said that the Roddis Lumber and Veneer Company veneer was so thin that they "hung the veneer with clothespins on the third floor to dry."[275] It could not be kiln dried because it would shatter. Some veneer cut at ⅟₁₁₀ was considered "specialty veneer."[276] For Roddis, however, it was used in aircraft wing skins.[277] (The United States standard veneer today is cut ⅟₅₀ to ⅟₅₅.)

The "Spruce Goose" utilized plywood that was three-ply on either side with a basswood center core. The basswood core center to reduce plywood weight was engineered at the Roddis company by William H. Roddis II.

Developed by the United States Forest Products Laboratory was "electrostatic glue-setting, a process in which high frequency electrical energy was used to effect the cure of synthetic resin adhesive by raising the temperature of the glue."[278] Thousands (about eight tons) of small nails were used to provide pressure for attaching the hull and wing skins. After the adhesive had cured, they were removed with specially designed nail pullers. The result was an immense wooden airframe able to withstand the stresses of flight without being too heavy.

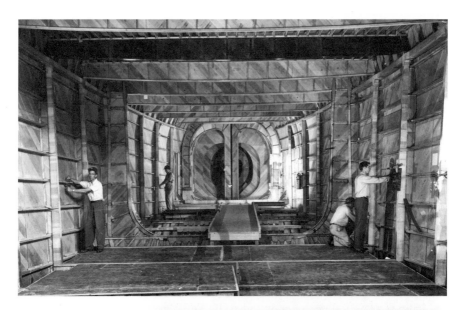

Above: Inside the "Spruce Goose" fuselage. *Courtesy of the U.S. Forest Products Laboratory Library, Madison, Wisconsin.*

Right: Bottom construction of the "Spruce Goose," H-4 Flying Boat. *Courtesy of the U.S. Forest Products Laboratory Library, Madison, Wisconsin.*

According to William H. Roddis II, chief inspector for the Roddis Lumber and Veneer Company in Marshfield, "shear tests" were conducted for the "Spruce Goose." He said, "The 'shear test' was the wood between two cuts. The cut was to test the glue box tension by trying to pull it apart." Glue was put on the wood and put in a press.

> *The shear test is a generally accepted method for evaluating the quality of glue joints in plywood, and the plywood shear testing machine... Considerable variation is commonly encountered in the shear-test values obtained on duplicate specimens of plywood.*
>
> *The causes of such variation are usually ascribed to variations of the wood, physical shape and arrangement, or in variation in the operation of the testing machine.*

Shear testing continued at the U.S. Forest Products Laboratory, testing the validity of wood versus metal as well. The debate of orthotropic versus isotropic raged on and would impinge on Howard Hughes's reputation.

Howard Hughes, while utilizing de Havilland's cold molding process, could have also learned from de Havilland about the vagaries of politics in creating new airplanes for military use. The completion of the H4-Hercules (also dubbed by the media the "Flying Lumberyard," although it was the "Spruce Goose" that stuck) was continually questioned in the governmental, press and aviation arenas.

The Roddis Plywood Corporation employees handling the HK-1 Flying Boat plywood had to wear gloves so that their skin oils would not penetrate the wood. William H. Roddis II said, "The thermo couples were

William H. Roddis II at the controls of the H-4 Flying Boat (Spruce Goose). *Courtesy of the Evergreen Aviation and Space Museum, McMinneville, Oregon.*

used to test the surface temperature of the press platens. We knew exactly if there was a problem." At the Roddis Plywood Corporation, in the press, "the average temperature varied with the thickness and the thermo coupler had to register 240 degrees for the platen temperature." Roddis said, "They were the largest

H-4 Flying Boat (Spruce Goose) airborne on November 2, 1947. *Courtesy of the Evergreen Aviation and Space Museum, McMinneville, Oregon.*

presses in the United States at that time." The presses were four by sixteen feet and five by sixteen feet.

Howard Hughes also required a tensile test. According to Roddis, "You cut a certain shape and test it. After making the shape, it is put in clamps and pulled with the grain. If it is a straight grain, it works well and it is the same on the outside." The Roddis Plywood Corporation did not have the measuring system for the tensile test. Tensile tests had been conducted on the birch ply with basswood cores as early as 1930. Samples were sent to the University of Wisconsin's Engineering Department. The plywood of yellow birch with a basswood core was used because it was strong and light.[279]

By 1944, it was clear that not only was the aircraft enormous (just longer than a football field in length) but so were the production schedule demands:

> *It seems that we were a little too hasty in calling our super-cargo flying boat the Hughes Hercules, so this name has been dropped for the designation, Hughes H-4, for the time being.*
>
> *The Kaiser-Hughes Corporation was dissolved in early spring of 1944. Mr. Kaiser became aware that mass production of these giant cargo planes was impractical so he retired from the project entirely at that time, since then a new corporation was formed and is known as the Hughes Aircraft Company.*[280]

It would be Howard Hughes who would fly his Hughes H-4 Flying Boat, dubbed by the media the "Spruce Goose," on November 2, 1947.

CHAPTER 7

"TEACHING WOOD TO FIGHT"

U.S. FOREST PRODUCTS LABORATORY, MADISON

Wood was crucial in aircraft production. The United States Forest Products Laboratory (FPL) had worked assiduously during World War I on aircraft and propeller design. During World War II, it again worked cooperatively with the forest products industry and aircraft manufacturers.

The Forest Products Laboratory led the way with diligent research. "In 1940, the U.S. Forest Products Laboratory had 175 employees and a budget of $600,000. By the end of 1944, U.S. Forest Products Laboratory had 700 employees and a budget of $2.5 M."[281] In 1940, it had begun changing direction "toward national defense problems":

> Research in plywood and laminated wood studies had turned more specifically toward aircraft requirements. A.J. Stamm and R.M. Seborg, the inventors of the resin-impregnated woods, had begun to concentrate upon the application of this material to aircraft manufacture and were busy preparing test samples for future tests. Don Brouse in Wood Preservation had turned his attention to the cutting of veneers and the gluing of test materials for aircraft studies. Research on waterproof coatings was being directed toward sealers and undercoatings suitable for aircraft plywood. Freas, March, and Luxford, and Erickson had begun making strength tests of plywood and similar tests on "compregnated" wood with a view...for aircraft manufacture. M. Dunlap in Timber

The USDA Forest Service Forest Products Laboratory, built in 1913 in the Art Deco period of architecture. *Courtesy of the U.S. Forest Products Laboratory Library, Madison, Wisconsin.*

Physics had begun a thorough study of electrostatic gluing and seasoning as related to aircraft manufacture. Loughbrough's chemical seasoning research was directed specifically to spruce aircraft stock problems, while others in the Division of Timber Physics initiated intensive tests on the kiln drying of aircraft woods.[282]

Director Winslow of the Forest Products Laboratory said, "We will be prepared in case of sudden call." The Forest Products Laboratory's motto during World War II was "Teaching Wood to Fight."[283]

The "fight" was an uphill battle with funding in 1941 until an increase in 1942. In addition, aircraft construction by the mid-1920s had resorted primarily to metal construction. The importance of aircraft plywood and glues was an outgrowth of World War I.[284]

Wooden aircraft construction had given way to metal because of the glue problems. The 1930s saw the development of the phenol resins, as well as "molded plywood":

The U.S. aircraft industry in 1941 lacked the fundamental design and engineering data necessary to undertake production. In late 1941, therefore, the aircraft industry called upon the Forest Products Laboratory to investigate and disseminate the latest technical information on plywood and plywood structures, modern glues and gluing practices, finishes, and finishing methods, laminated wood, and methods for testing aircraft woods…Demand for publications…resulted in "A Wood Aircraft Fabrication Manual and an ANC Handbook on the Design of Wood Aircraft Structures."[285]

The handbook is still used today for the building of experimental aircraft. The design and laminated studies for propellers are used today in drones.

In 1941, the aircraft industry representing twenty-three aircraft companies and government agencies had given the Forest Products Laboratory its support for future research and their marching orders. The result was that Wisconsin's forest product industry designation as a national defense priority meant that security was crucial for the industry. At FPL, research was conducted with great secrecy:

Guards stationed at the entrances to the laboratory checked the identification of each and every person who sought admittance. To facilitate identification, each employee was required to carry with him an "ID" card, with attached photograph, during working hours.[286]

With the looming war in Europe, L.J. Markwardt, a scientist and United States Forest Products Laboratory representative to the mission to Britain regarding aircraft manufacturing, would write prolifically about de Havilland's Mosquito Bomber.[287] In 1938, he published the "Resume of

A De Havilland Mosquito used on aircraft carriers with the folded wings. *Courtesy of Bill Groah, retired technical director of the Hardwood Plywood and Veneer Association, Reston, Virginia.*

Recent Developments in Wood, Plywood, and Conversion of Products of Interest in Aircraft Construction."[288] In discussing the importance of

> *adhesive in plywood and laminated construction, the phenolic resins…*
> *When formed in veneer, or in solid wood, they definitely 1) modify the*
> *mechanical properties, 2) greatly reduce the shrinking and swelling, 3) retard*
> *the absorption of moisture, 4) markedly improve weathering characteristics*
> *when exposed to the elements and 5) possibly increase the decay-resistance.*

The concern was the strength of the plywood and its durability for aircraft fuselages and wings, the impregnation effect of the resins and plasticization for molding and finally the laminations for propellers.

The Forest Products Laboratory was working in concert with corporations to test and develop waterproof glues. In 1937, it said:

> *When the Laboratory began its studies on wood adhesives, the gluing of*
> *wood was a traditional and secretive operation. By inventing new and*
> *improved glues and gluing methods, the Laboratory has eliminated many*
> *trade secrets from commercial gluing to the benefit of consumers and also*
> *greatly reduced the number of defective gluing practices.*

Since its inception in 1910, the Forest Products Laboratory had researched glue and gluing techniques. Through research, the Forest Products Laboratory developed testing techniques for glue and glue joints, as well as best practices to ensure glue product performance. By studying over forty American wood species and their receptivity to glue, the Forest Products Laboratory made great advances in wood properties. Its leading scientist in the late 1930s, regarding wood glues, was Don Brouse.

The Forest Products Laboratory had developed a "cheap strong, water-resistant casein glue…and…a blood glue" for a hot-press process.[289] However, it would be the phenol-formaldehyde resin technology that would enhance wood characteristics and develop the early plastics for aircraft and war production.[290]

The U.S. Forest Products Laboratory would continually assist the plywood industry in aircraft plywood development. The liaison between the forest products industry and the Forest Products Laboratory was Brouse. "Don Brouse in Wood Preservation had turned his attention to the cutting of veneers and the gluing of test materials for aircraft studies."[291] Later a veteran, Brouse said in 1949, "Phenol-formaldehyde and urea-formaldehyde are the most widely used synthetic glues. Melamine and resorcinol glues, were among the discoveries during WWII…a synthetic glue withstands continual wet exposure."[292]

The U.S. Forest Products Laboratory in 1939 was still researching humidity, fungi and mold in plywood. The "coal tar creosote" and an increase to a "25% solution of beta naphthol" improved the "durability of glue joints."[293] Irving Laucks would still try to defeat his rival, Dr. James A. Nevin, with U.S. patent #2,164,269 on June 27, 1939, with a fish-based recipe; the fish glue was insufficient.

George R. Meyercord, in a speech in 1940, concurred. Discussing phenolic resins, he said, "The use of resin in bonding plywood has greatly enlarged the field of usefulness of plywood, because the bonding material is so excellent."[294] To celebrate the victory of waterproof glue, Harbor Plywood constructed a small boat and floated it down the Colorado River. The glues from Germany were being used in aircraft development. In the United States, "Harbor's development provided the greatest single advancement in the plywood industry since…1905."[295]

Dr. Nevin's ceaseless work ethic caught up to him. Phenols caused skin irritation, and toxicity was being explored.[296] Dr. Nevin retired in 1940 and died of cancer in 1943. Dr. Nevin's phenol-aldehydes were now spreading throughout the industry.

During September and October 1943, at the height of World War II, a Forest Products Laboratory mission from the United States visited England. The title of the June 1944 resultant report was "The Use of Wood for Aircraft in the United Kingdom."[297] Under "Glues and Gluing Technique": "Nearly all the aircraft plywood is made with hot-pressed phenol-formaldehyde glues, mainly in the form of film; laminating and assembly gluing is done chiefly and the gluing of most propeller blocks and nearly all repair work is done with casein glues."[298] The report assayed that there was a similarity in the use of glues between the United States and the United Kingdom. Phenol-aldehydes were making their impact.

America was actually ahead in its research, and understandably so, as the British had been under attack since 1939. The report stated, "Melamine and resorcinol glues had not received much attention, it has been reported that a large user of wood in aircraft has adopted low-temperature setting phenolic glue."[299]

Since the Forest Product Laboratory rarely referred to manufacturers or companies by name, there is an inference and a little "reading between the lines." However, it is apparent that the "large user of wood in aircraft" was de Havilland. The "low-temperature setting phenolic glue" was a setting of

240 degrees Fahrenheit at the Roddis Plywood Corporation in Marshfield, Wisconsin, a supplier of plywood for the de Havilland Mosquito.[300]

England was testing glues throughout the war. Its focus was on the urea-formaldehydes. The lack of standardized assembly line manufacturing in favor of a more cottage industry approach at the beginning of the war meant less emphasis on the film glues. Small cabinet, piano and woodworking shops were involved in the manufacturing of aircraft pieces—stringers, spars, gussets, etc.

Glue testing in the United States was going on concurrently with the British studies. The Chemical Research Laboratory and National Physical Laboratory were exchanging information with Cambridge University and the Royal Aircraft Establishment. Studies of glues in relation to altitude, humidity and plywood stress factors were a determinant of aircraft manufacturing.

The supplier of the plywood with "melamine and resorcinol" was the Roddis Lumber and Veneer Company in Marshfield. It was during this time that two young chemists—Joe Schumann, who had worked at U.S. Plywood Corporation, and Ken Rapala, a graduate of the Institute of Paper Chemistry—utilized the Roddis glue, a Tego film phenolic glue for the aircraft plywood, and used the phenol-formaldehyde for the marine glue.[301] Gordie Schmoll was the "glue man" for Roddis. Recalling some of the formula for the glues, he said, "It was made of wheat flour, regular flour, alcohol, phenol-formaldehyde, ammonia…the smell was enough to knock you over. It had the consistency of maple syrup. You had to be careful because the glue gave you the itch."[302]

BELLANCA AIRCRAFT CORPORATION

The development of the phenol resin glue was implemented in the aircraft industry. As an example, Bellanca Aircraft Corporation submitted its "Process Specification for the Use and Application of Plastics Bonding Formulae 944-6 and 945-6" in January 1940. The use of plastics was the new innovation in aircraft construction. The report specified the mixing of the glue.

Consisting of "a viscous resin, powder, and a liquid catalyst," the mixture was "weighed by the laboratory…in three sized ice cream cartons in ½ lb, 1 lb, and 3lb weights respectively." The "mixing" read like a recipe:

Assume a one pound softwood mix is required. Proceed as follows:

Weigh out one pound of resin into mixing pot allowing for the weight of same.

Start the mixer and add one carton of powder labeled "Use with 1lb. resin" and mix three minutes or until mixture is smooth.

Add slowly, while the mixer is running, the contents of one bottle of catalyst mixture marked "Use with 1lb resin for softwood formula 944-6." Mix five minutes and the formula is ready for use.

In the same manner, multiple quantities may be made by weighing two (2) lbs. of resin using two (2) cartons of powder, and two bottles of catalyst mixture similarly marked.[303]

In using the glue formula, one was prepared for softwood to last seven hours. The other glue formula was prepared for hardwood with a four-hour application period. The glue was spread by hand or with a mechanical spreader and pressure applied in the assembly process. The report stated that "methods of computing and estimating pressures as recommended by the Forest Products Laboratory" should be followed.[304] Nailing strips to hold the glue until it was dry was industry standard.

HUGHES AIRCRAFT CORPORATION

Hughes Aircraft Company submitted its "Manual of Gluing Technique" stating that it had relied on its workers for input, but more importantly, the gluing technique was "mak[ing] the difference between a good job and a poor one."[305] The report was signed by Hughes Aircraft Company's chief chemist, G.O. Schull, and "approved by G.A. Allward, Chief of Research, and J.R. Jenman, Assistant Plant Manager."[306]

By 1941, phenol resins were sold under various labels. "Pregwood," a derivative, was a "product prepared by impregnating birch veneers with a phenolic resin and bonding them together with high pressure." Schull conducted "Curing-Time Tests" between phenolic resins using a Bakelite product and comparing it to urea hot and cold press products. He concluded that more tests were needed. However, the important result was the curing time reduction utilizing the phenolic resin, as well as the varied temperatures that could be incurred in the drying process.[307] Plastic plywood was the new terminology. Characteristics were determined by grain direction and bonding material:

- Plastic-plywood—built-up wood laminar having grain in various directions.
- Laminated—built-up wood laminar having grain in one direction.
- Molded—usually built-up wood laminar with no restriction in grain direction but formed to a given contour.

The distinction between types of "plastic-plywood" was the veneer composition. The use of phenolic resins, "hot setting" bond or the "impregnated bond" created aircraft "plastic plywoods" derivatives.

The Roddis Plywood Corporation had originally obtained the sixteen-foot presses in anticipation of a potential contract for the Carnegie Gallery (the National Gallery) in Washington, D.C., in 1936.[308] While it did not get the contract, ironically, the press initially was used for bar fronts at the end of Prohibition. The hot-platen press would be put to good use during World War II. The long presses allowed for extended wing panels. Again, Roddis Plywood Corporation led plywood manufacturers with imported German technology.

The Forest Products Laboratory would later report:

> *Plywood is generally quite as susceptible to decay as solid wood of the species from which it is made. Although some glues hinder passing of fungus from one layer of wood to another, wood or paper impregnated with a high content phenolic resin (as Impreg) strongly resists decay…decaying of wood used in aircraft is easily avoided.*[309]

As technologies advanced from the development of phenol-resin waterproof glues, more pressed-paper phenol-resin products started to appear in World War II glider floors, aircraft instrument consoles and packaging products. Also appearing were "plastic plywoods," especially for enhancing aircraft construction. The Canadian National Research Council developed the research for drop gas tanks on long-range bombers and fighters.[310]

> *We start with two-ply veneer, which is wound on a collapsible drum. Metal bands are loaded with a lever weight arrangement to apply pressure… Infrared lamps supply the heat necessary to set the cold-resin press as the two-ply ribbon is wound around the drum. The nose and tail are of the same shape and are composed of five layers of two-ply hot-press-molded wood…The tanks are flushed with a gasoline-resistant sealing compound.*

The "plastic plywood" drop tank would reduce the weight of the aircraft rather than using metal drop tanks. We have seen the British development of paper laminated phenol-resin "bee hive" tanks, and the plastic plywood was a new idea as well.

World War II progressed, and with it, people began to see the "light at the end of the tunnel." The plastic plywoods were for the future. Moving from aircraft uses to uses in the home:

> *The plywood planes that now roam the skies to clear them for the deafening dawn of victory are contributing, in more ways that may be apparent to the fulfillment of your dreams of a safe and happy future—a future that many of holds promise of a "dream house"...*
>
> *Appropriately enough, the gap between the building of today's bombers and tomorrow's homes is being closed by Canadian manufacturers whose experience and technique with plastic-bonded plywood of warplanes is already being tested in a practical way for peacetime civilian needs...The perfection of plastic-bonded plywood, made possible by chemistry's contribution of synthetic resin adhesives or bonding agents has lifted this material out of the "veneer" category... the plywood office building of Dominion Plywood Limited...has been designed and fabricated with all the cumulative skill and craftsmanship that goes into the manufacturer's output of plywood components for the Mosquito bomber...*
>
> *Here, then is our connecting link. Just as modern warfare is the "proving ground" for plywood planes, boats, and other weapons of war, this building is a proving ground for plywood as a material for tomorrow's homes.*[311]

Plastic plywood had come of age. In fact, it was reported that DuPont Company had created

> *a new chemical treatment which makes wood nearly as hard as steel, and will produce thousands of kinds of hardwood that never existed in nature...The chemical bath transmutes wood into virtually a new material, part wood and part plastic. It changes almost any softwood into hardwood...Some exceed the hardness of ebony, the hardest natural wood...An oxyacetylene torch takes almost twice as long to burn through a board of transmuted wood as through an equal thickness of steel.*[312]

De Havilland's genius was seen in the Mosquito construction. The two halves allowed easy access for wiring and control cables during the aircraft construction process. This process was also known as "Sandwich

Mosquito fuselage construction. *Courtesy of Bill Groah, retired executive director of the American Plywood Association/Hardwood Plywood Manufacturing Association Archives, Reston, Virginia.*

Construction." It was De Havilland's unique structure that set the stage for future aircraft construction.

The Duramold process was created in the United States by Sherman Fairchild under the auspices of Dr. Baekeland. Together with Bakelite Corporation, George Meyercord, president of Haskelite Corporation, ironically took credit for the phenolic resin. Haskelite was involved with laminates with metal, as well as the "molded plywood fuselage."[313] Some of the Bakelite product also was used in the Avro Anson.

The Mosquito was joined together at the center seam like an egg carton.

> *The Mosquito's wooden construction meant it could be very smooth. The fuselage was made in left and right halves, which were shaped in concrete rigs and then joined. They were made of balsa wood between two layers of birch plywood...The rest of the airframe was primarily Canadian spruce, with birch covering...The wing was built in one pieces and attached to the fuselage later. 550 brass screws held the aircraft together, along with the glue.*[314]

The thin plywood was molded around a form. The "face grain" of the plywood was "longitudinal to the axis of the plane." Cross-banded for extra strength, the thickness was ⅝ inch.[315] "Almost the entire plane was built of wood. The wings had two spars with double plywood skins on top and single

De Havilland Mosquito fuselage in production. *Courtesy of Bill Groah, retired technical director of the Hardwood Plywood and Veneer Association, Reston, Virginia.*

underneath. The fuselage was made of balsa between two ply skins built on spruce stringers…The hydraulic plain flaps were wood."[316]

Not only did de Havilland use the Duramold process, but the British, under the direction of Ralph Hare of De Havilland, as well as the Roddis Lumber and Veneer Company at the U.S. Forest Products Laboratory, conducted extensive "stress tests" and "sheer tests" on the plywood.[317] The tests utilized birch plywood with the Siempelkamp Tego glue.

> *The two test specimens were cut from two panels of yellow birch plywood each consisting of five 1/16 inch plies…The panels were received in a shipment of Tego-bonded aircraft plywood. Whether the tests were for the British or American aircraft, the reports issued stated that the reports were "prepared by the Forest Products Laboratory to further the nation's war effort."*

The war effort would be both American and British. The British Mosquito would be "superior to the metal equivalent."[318] While the fuselage would be 5/8 inch, the wing plies would be even thinner. The Mosquito, if it was damaged in battle, could be repaired with simple carpentry skills. The two thin plywood birch skins with balsa in between had cross-banding laid at forty-five-degree angles. The birch plies had extra strength. New waterproof glues meant that the plywood composition was strong and sturdy.

As the Mosquito was developed to have a service ceiling of 44,600 feet and bomb loads of over ten thousand pounds, a change in air tactical

The De Havilland "Mossie." *Courtesy of Camp 5 Museum Foundation/Wisconsin Forestry Museum, Laona, Wisconsin.*

warfare was imminent.[319] The Mosquito, with a crew of two, could carry the same bomb load as the larger bombers with crews of fifteen or more. The Mosquito had the same range. Seven hundred men could stand on each wing. With superior wing strength, each wing could support forty-one tons.

As if following the Roddis Plywood Corporation scenario, *Plywoods*, published in 1942, summarized the production of plywood aircraft:

> *During 1914–18 war, and for some years afterwards, plywood and solid spruce were largely used in the construction of aircraft, but, with the development of new and lightweight metals, wood gradually lost favor. The all-metal plane was evolved and for several years held the field both military and commercial work. Once resin adhesives had been proven to yield reliable waterproof plywood, this improved product of wood again became of interest to aircraft designers, who were alive to the fact that plywood possessed certain structural advantages over metal. By using plywood saving both in weight and power is affected. Plywood-covered wings have no rivets to offer resistance to the air, do not easily retain static charge of electricity, and are not liable to dent as*

are coverings of thin metal...Electrolytic action and excessive vibration do not cause the wood to "tire." It does not corrode.

Plywood made from...Birch is most generally used as it combines strength with light weight...The construction varies according to requirements, and thickness selected depends upon the degree of rigidity required: this may range from 0.6mm to 8mm. Plywood for use in aircraft must be manufactured in accordance with British Standard Specification 5V3 for stressed parts and V34 for unstressed parts. Resin-film adhesive is commonly used and continuous control under inspection is maintained during manufacture.

Plywood built with Birch veneers which are of even texture and straight grain is essential for all stressed parts...The inner core and gluing is finally tested by passing thin sheets of plywood over a specially constructed box housing lights of high intensity.[320]

At Roddis Lumber and Veneer Company, the phenolic resin Tego film glue was used for the Mosquito. The inspection of the plywood with new technology high-intensity lights detected unwanted defects in the wood. At Roddis Lumber and Veneer Company, uniform temperatures in the curing process were obtained with thermocouples inserted between the layers in the drying process. The temperatures were monitored by inspectors. One of those inspectors was Ellen Roddis, the sister of William H. Roddis II.[321] The *Plywoods* authors continued:

"Diagonal" plywood is used as a safeguard against torsion in positions liable [to be] subjected to heavy strains. The grain direction of the plies should be specified by the designer and, as a general rule, the grain of the two outer veneers runs at angles from 45 degrees to 60 degrees to the edges of the sheet. Both outer plies run in the same direction and are crossed by the grain of the core which is also cut at an angle 45 degrees to 60 degrees to the edge of the sheet. Diagonal plywood can be made to give the maximum resistance against diagonal strains.[322]

Studies were conducted by the Forest Products Laboratory for the most effective angles. Roddis Plywood Corporation used a forty-five-degree angle in its plywood, meeting the De Havilland Mosquito 5V3 and V34 specifications.[323]

Birch plywood 1½ mm thick is commonly used for covering the fuselage and wings being glued to the longerrons, struts, and stiffeners with...

synthetic resin adhesives...Birch plywood are glued and screwed to the solid spruce...By scarf-jointing several boards together, the entire upper surface of a wing running from the centre line of the frame spar to the trailing edge may be covered in one operation.[324]

In describing the Mosquito on its fiftieth anniversary at Hatfield British Aerospace, England, Mike Ramsden of de Havilland/British Aerospace said:

The Mosquito fuselage, made in halves by stretching two skins of birch plywood over concrete molds remain unique in aircraft construction. The plywood— three 1.5mm (.061 inches) to 2 mm (.08 inches) 45 degrees diagonal plies were stretched cold over the concrete mould...tests show the allowable stress of a birch plywood panel went approximately from 1,500 pounds per square inch to 5,000 pounds per square inch with a balsa sandwich core.

Birch plywood was found to give the best results. It was made of three-plies laid at 45 degrees to each other, so that when a shear load was applied, it was redistributed into a tension load along one ply grain and a compression load along the other two, the whole web taking a bigger load under compression. The lower wing skin was to a single plywood panel stiffened with spruce stringers.[325]

PAPER AND PACKAGING MATERIALS

New technologies also included the demand for pulpwood for paper and packaging materials. It was compounded by the demand for the new "plastic"—compressed paper with a phenolic resin. The "resinized paper [was pressed] together under heat and pressure."[326] With uses in the glider floors, "papreg" was also used to produce everything from ammunition boxes to aircraft instrument panels, as well as honeycombed gas tanks.

Like the advent of "plastic-bonded plywood," the phenolic impregnated pressed paper had many war uses. One of the most innovative uses of paper laminates was developed by George May.

[H]e was asked by DeHavilland Aircraft Company, Limited to concentrate on the possibility of constructing, from paper, an auxiliary aircraft fuel-tank of 50 gallon capacity...It had become highly important to extend the flying range of the Mosquito and the tanks, which normally would

The De Havilland Mosquito with drop tanks. *Courtesy of Camp 5 Museum Foundation/Wisconsin Forestry Museum, Laona, Wisconsin.*

have been of metal, could not be produced in sufficient quantity owing to shortage of material and skilled labor.[327]

With construction of the impregnated paper laminated tanks, they could be "sawn, planed, drilled, and screwed as readily as plywood." The construction time was four hours per tank.[328]

George May not only made fifty-gallon tanks, but by the end of World War II, tanks were also manufactured for one-hundred- and two-hundred-gallon fuel quantities. Fuel tank production included:[329]

FUEL TANK PRODUCTION TABLE[330]

Tank	Quantity
50-gallon capacity	25,000
100-gallon capacity	75,000
200-gallon capacity	2,000
Total	102,000

The design of the fuel tanks was of honeycomb construction. The lightweight honeycombed design would again be used in the design of the glider floor. The honeycombs were made with "paper, fabrics, and glass-fibre cloth. They were molded and stabilized by impregnation with suitable synthetic resins."[331] This was the beginning of fiberglass, but it had its origins in paper laminates. What is important to note is that the glues used were again the phenol-formaldehydes and "resorcinol-formaldehyde." Products from Bakelite Limited, British Resin Products Limited and Aero Research Limited were commercially available. George May continued paper laminate raydome for the Mosquito, too.[332]

The British would re-dominate the sky and conquer the enemy with the "made in Wisconsin" Mosquito. The British owed a huge debt of gratitude to Sir Geoffrey de Havilland.

The British tested the plywood of the gliders, with the United States Forest Products Laboratory searching for the strongest plywood and core combinations.[333] In addition, "papreg" was developed by the FPL and distributed to paper companies and other forest product businesses. Papreg would become a revolutionary new product used in everything from engine rooms in warships to construction materials Consolidated Water & Power Company made "paper floors" under its Consoweld subsidiary. The floors were phenolic resin pressed and heated. The heat acted as a catalyst and hardened the material to a plastic consistency.

Northwestern Aeronautical Corporation and Gibson Refrigerator Company made invasion gliders with paper laminates that were beginning to take on "plastic" characteristics. Paper laminate products were called

Consoweld, Wisconsin Rapids, manufacturing a CG-4A glider papreg floor for Northwestern Aeronautical Corporation, St. Paul/Minneapolis. Honeycombing lightens the floor load. *Courtesy of Gilbert Endrezzi, retired Consoweld engineer, Wisconsin Rapids, Wisconsin.*

Consoweld men with a glider floor in 1944. *Courtesy of Gilbert Endrezzi, retired Consoweld engineer, Wisconsin Rapids, Wisconsin.*

Dura Beauty, a trade name, by Consolidated Water & Power Company in Wisconsin Rapids, Wisconsin. Most people know the product by Consoweld's competitor's trade name, Formica. Formica was developed in 1912. Dura Beauty was developed by Jay Somers, a chemical engineer, who joined Consolidated in 1943.

Consoweld manufactured "decorative laminated plastic surfacing for the home, business, and various commercial uses."[334] As a "laminating and impregnating specialist," Somers said, "We were fortunate when we

Consoweld logo. *Courtesy of Gilbert Endrezzi, retired Consoweld engineer, Wisconsin Rapids, Wisconsin.*

started production because the demand for the war product paneling to was immediate."

> *It was to aid America's war effort that Consoweld's parent company began manufacturing laminated plastic in the first place. In a cooperative program with the government, it was found that laminated plastic…[has] strength characteristics similar to those found in most metals. And metals were at a premium. These factors combined made laminated plastic desirable.*

Consoweld manufactured "ammunition boxes and battery casings." Somers said, "We even made glider floors." He was "responsible for both the scientific and mechanical aspects of production. He assumed a significant role in the construction of laboratory and the establishment of a research staff." He continued, "We began experimenting with domestic uses for laminating early in 1943…We knew the war would eventually end and we would still be in business."[335] The reconversion and looking ahead was the thought process, despite full war production at Consoweld Corporation under Somers's leadership.

George Mead, president of Consolidated Papers, Incorporated, said later, "It was really the U.S. Forest Product Laboratory that developed the paper laminate and assisted us with developing the process." The "History of the Forest Products Laboratory" confirms Mead's comments:

Women handling papreg sheets. *Courtesy of Gilbert Endrezzi, retired Consoweld engineer, Wisconsin Rapids, Wisconsin.*

One of the most promising Forest Products Laboratory wartime developments in the general field of plastics was a paper-base laminated plastic known as "papreg."

This material, prepared by impregnating special paper with phenolic resins followed by the molding of the paper sheets into a laminated plastic, drew the interest of paper manufacturers and aircraft manufacturers because it was found to be half as heavy as aluminum and yet capable of developing a tensile strength of 35,000 to 50,000 pounds per square inch, which was comparable to that of certain aluminum alloys on a relative weight basis. Besides its high tensile strength, papreg proved to have exceptional dimensional stability, low abrasiveness, and high-impact resistance.

Late in 1942, FPL data on papreg were supplied to some 20 companies who had indicated an intention to develop the material commercially. By the end of 1943, a number of these companies were producing papreg materials in quantities worth $3 Million. [336]

Consolidated Water & Power Company in Wisconsin Rapids supplied 156 glider floors to Northwestern Aeronautical Corporation in Minneapolis/St. Paul. The first papreg floor was produced in 1943. [337]

Central Wisconsin would dominate the manufacturing process of the glider floors. The key to the paper floors for gliders was the high-impact resistance:

Papreg is a laminated paper plastic of high tensile strength and high modulus of Elasticity developed at the Forest Products Laboratory...The plastic can

Consolidated Water Power & Paper Co.
Plastics Div., Wisconsin Rapids, Wis.

Description: CG 4-A Glider Nose,

Snow Landing Model, showing sandwich

type Consoweld framework for Bottom

and Side Skin.

Group No.   21   Photo No.   4

Date 12/28/43   By   Fey For W.C.McL.

Description of the glider nose. *Courtesy of the U.S. Forest Products Laboratory, Madison, Wisconsin.*

be produced under low molding pressures and therefore has possibilities of use in large Application such as monocoque aircraft construction.[338]

The importance of Dr. James A. Nevin's work developing the phenol-formaldehyde glues was crucial to the development of papreg. Glider survivability was limited.

John Koning, a retired U.S. Forest Products Laboratory assistant director, found an actual piece of papreg and with it the description of the manufacturing process. The papreg was laminated together out of a 100 percent black spruce "mittsch sulfite" pulp. In the remarks section of the Forest Products Laboratory report, it said, "Beaten 5 minutes on Bed Plate;

This paper, dated November 30, 1942, was treated at the size press with compregnite and then un-dried."[339]

Koning said that it took 70 pieces to make the paper floor a quarter inch thick and 280 pieces to make it half an inch thick. In an e-mail to the author on February 8, 2010, he said:

Consoweld papreg nose. *Courtesy of Gilbert Endrezzi, retired Consoweld engineer, Wisconsin Rapids, Wisconsin.*

For experimental batches the laboratory would make the pulp, then make and treat the paper on the laboratory paper machine. The resin compounds used to treat the paper were developed by Consolidated Paper Company researchers, acquired from other companies, or modified formulations developed by Forest Products Laboratory staff. After multiple paper machine runs, varying the type of pulp used and chemical treatments, Consolidated would scale up the best combinations for production runs. By working with FPL, they were able to try numerous combinations to select the best chance of commercial success without interrupting their production. The laboratory's work helped speed the process and reduce the costs. Over the years, the laboratory has assisted many companies using this cooperative approach.[340]

Recent research revealed that Northwestern Aeronautical Corporation also utilized a "snow glider nose" made by Consoweld on the Northwestern Aeronautical Corporation glider #43-27314. The "43-27314 was the 61st Northwestern production article or their first 1943 contract…43-27314 had the Consoweld floor, as well as the Consoweld nose. The…photo ID sheet was dated December 28, 1943. John Harris inventoried the glider… He described it as…snow glider with an External type tow release. That is, of course, Consoweld Snow Glider w/ Griswold nose protection device." The "snow glider" had a papreg/plastic nose, ostensibly for sliding across the snow on landing. Consoweld had the contract for the "framework for Bottom and Side Skin," and photos were taken on December 28, 1943, in Wisconsin Rapids.[341]

The B-24 Liberator had started flying in the Pacific in 1942 and was most well-known for its operation in the Asian theater. Although considered an all-metal aircraft, it featured the Forest Products Laboratory–developed papreg in its "gun turrets, seats, shields, and ammunition boxes on the bomber."

In 1944, the United States had manufactured over ninety thousand aircraft, and in 1945, the manufacturing number would drop to forty-five thousand, still an impressive number.[342] The United States Forest Products Laboratory had indeed fulfilled its mission of "Teaching Wood to Fight."

CHAPTER 8

THE GERMAN CONNECTION

A STICKY SITUATION

With regard to plywood, I suppose there is not one man in the room who is not
familiar with the great contribution made by plywood. I have a notion that one of the
lessons that will be learned from this war will be the wide applications of gluing.
—*Dr. Wilson Compton, National Lumber Manufacturers' Association, before the*
Society of American Foresters, December 1942[343]

What made the development of phenolic resins so arresting was that Roddis Lumber and Veneer Company in Marshfield, during the 1930s had the only waterproof glue used for plywood and aircraft plywood in the United States. The Tego film glue had come from Germany, as had the hot-plate press from Siempelkamp in Krefeld, Germany. In the fall of 1938, Hamilton Roddis visited Siempelkamp, as well as plants with Siempelkamp equipment in England and other sawmill equipment manufacturers in Germany.

The United States Forest Products Laboratory had been working for years to develop a waterproof glue. In the United States, there had been an ongoing battle for over fifteen years between Irving Laucks of Haskelite and Dr. James Nevin at Harbor Plywood in developing waterproof glue. Dr. Nevin would finally prevail, filing a patent in 1937 and reaffirming the patent in 1939 for phenol-formaldehyde resin glue.[344]

Waterproof glue was a critical element in any wood construction but particularly in aircraft construction. Since it had the only waterproof glue

Bellanca "Cruiseair," aircraft plywood manufactured by Roddis Lumber and Veneer Company. *Author's collection.*

before World War II, Roddis Lumber and Veneer Company "was one of the largest manufacturers of airplane plywood in the United States." "It supplied airplane plywood to the government of France, Great Britain, as well as the United States."[345] Roddis Lumber and Veneer Company was very careful to explain that the Roddis glue was heat- and water-resistant. Heretofore, dairy-based glue and blood glue had been used. With the dairy-based glues, the wings would fall off the airplanes because of weakened glue joints. Airplanes were falling out of the sky. In tropical climates, mildew was an issue. The phenol-formaldehyde resin glues did not mildew, decay or change properties in heat or cold. This was an enormous technological revolution in aircraft and wood manufacturing.

THE GERMAN INFLUENCE ON WATERPROOF GLUE

After World War I, Roddis Lumber and Veneer Company had returned from making aircraft plywood to making doors for commercial and residential buildings. Despite the onset of the Great Depression, the plywood industry was undergoing monumental technological changes. The changes would begin with German innovation. Hamilton Roddis, like his father before him, admired German ingenuity. William H. Roddis II told the story of Baron von Maltitz's visit to Marshfield, Wisconsin. He said that the baron was impressive. He wore a black top hat, had a cape and carried a silver cane: "My father and I met him at the Hotel Charles in Marshfield for lunch. It was a hot summer day, and we sat outside at an umbrella table. What sold

Siempelkamp
Maschinen- und Anlagenbau

Courtesy of Siempelkamp, Krefeld, Germany.

All Roddis Lumber and Veneer departments were photographed in 1939. Note the Siempelkamp sign in the background. *Courtesy of Marshfield History Project, Marshfield, Wisconsin.*

the idea to my father was the waterproof glue. This had not been possible up to that point."[346]

The promise of waterproof plywood glue and a new manufacturing method with longer sixteen-foot plywood presses was the impetus for the meeting. That sale put Roddis Plywood and Veneer Company in the

Plywood
hot press.
Courtesy of
Siempelkamp,
Krefeld,
Germany.

forefront of plywood manufacturing for plywood quality and eventually aircraft plywood war production.

The author contacted Siempelkamp, the company that Baron von Maltitz had represented in Krefeld, Germany. It had developed the Tego film glue and hot presses for the plywood in the early 1930s. The German public relations and marketing director was very direct with its American counterpart: "Tell the woman that her grandfather's plywood sent to England for the Mosquito bombers bombed our archives, and we have no photos before 1945." They were intrigued that I had a photo of the "Men in the Glue Department—1939" with a large Siempelkamp sign in the background.

Graciously, Siempelkamp sent this information in German that was translated by Uta Patterson in its American office:

> *The development of glues for the plywood production basically took place in two stages. In about 1890, casein glues were introduced. This type of glue was the first glue that was reasonably water proofed glue. Up to the introduction of casein glue, blood albumin glues and glues made of bone were used.*
>
> *In the 1930's, so called Kaurit glues (urea-formaldehyde resins) and resole glues (alkaline hardening phenolic resins) were introduced.*
>
> *The latter two glues, in addition to Melamine based and isocyanates based glues, have been the foundation for the manufacturing of plywood and wood-based products into our days.*[347]

Siempelkamp's summary adds interest to its story of developing the hydraulic hot-platen press.[348]

In the early 1900s, Siempelkamp had produced the "cold presses for gluing of wood strips or veneers…the glues used needed a long curing time, sometimes up to three or four hours."[349] Siempelkamp credited I.G. Farben with the invention of casein glue. Its invention cut the curing time down to ten to fifteen minutes and also necessitated the application of "heat during the pressing cycle."[350] Later, with the development of urea-formaldehyde resins, Siempelkamp credited Bayer-Werke of Uerdingen, Germany, with the invention of the resin. E. von Maltitz was president of Plycor Company in Chicago. He was an intermediary supplier of sawmill and woodworking equipment for the German companies, including Siempelkamp, doing business in the United States.

In the summer of 1938, Hamilton Roddis planned to visit G. Siempelkamp and Company in Krefeld, Germany, as well as Adolf Fritz, GmbH (designating a private German company), in Stuttgart and F. Meyer and

Schwabedissen-Herford in Ramagen-on-Rhine. Von Maltitz wrote a long letter to Hamilton Roddis on August 2, 1938:

> *I will immediately inform Siempelkamp at Krefeld and Adolf Fritz at Stuttgart to communicate with you care of Hotel Royal Clarence, Exeter, England, sending a copy of all letters to the Regent Palace Hotel, London, England marked "please hold" on the envelope.*
>
> *However, we are still asking you to call at the American Express Company offices in London since we have already informed our friends over there to write you care of the Express Company.*
>
> *I have also asked Siempelkamp to instruct their London representative to get in touch with you since there are several very interesting plants in or near London which you should see. I enclose a list of concerns which have been furnished with our Hot-Plate Plywood Presses and other machinery during recent years. On this list I have marked with red companies near London, as well as those in Holland. Upon presentation of this list you may express your wishes as to which companies you would like to see.*
>
> *We certainly would advise you to call at the Siempelkamp factory at Krefeld which is just a very short distance from Dusseldorf. On your trip along the Rhine you will pass several plants where Siempelkamp ought to be able to obtain a permit for you to enter. On the way down to southern Germany, you should not miss going to Stuttgart—this city together with Munich belong among the most beautiful and interesting cities on the continent and it would be a pity if you missed them. In Stuttgart, of course, you would meet Adolf Fritz.*
>
> *You will find several interesting plants in France but Siempelkamp will be able to give you more detailed information than I am able to do.*
>
> *Again wishing you a very enjoyable and interesting trip to Europe and expressing the hope that you will be able to visit quite a number of European plywood plants equipped with modern machinery, I am with personal regards*[351]

The letter was signed by E. von Maltitz, president of Plycor Company.

G. Siempelkamp and Company followed with a letter to Hamilton Roddis on August 17, 1938:

> *We learn from our USA-representative, the Plycor Company, Chicago, that you are interested to see some plywood presses of our type in Germany and England. We have the pleasure in inviting you herewith to come to Krefeld*

where we are gladly prepared to show you our works. Moreover, there are some plywood plants in the neighborhood of Krefeld where you could see a number of machines supplied by us in operation.

In England our presses work at Flexo Plywood Industries, Ltd., London. We beg to hand you herewith a letter of introduction for these Gentlemen and hope that the inspection of these works will satisfy you.

Trusting to see you at Krefeld in short we are... [352]

This letter was addressed to Mr. Roddis, the author's grandfather, at the Hotel Royal Clarence in Exeter, England, August 17, 1938.

The trip had been planned for some time. A letter dated June 16, 1938, from F. Meyer and Schwabedillen was written to Hamilton Roddis in care of the London office of American Express:

By the "Plycor Company, Chicago" we have been informed that you can expect to pay a visit to Germany and to come to the continent early in July. The Plycor Company has written us that you are very interested to find out whether our core manufacturing process which does not use any glue, is applicable to your work, for which reason you would like to visit one plant in or near the Rhineland where you could inspect the work done with the core making machinery.

We beg to inform you that it will be possible to show you our core making machinery in a plant which is in Remagen-on-Rhine and we shall be glad to hear from you at what time you could be in Remagen so that we can make arrangements for you to visit the plant and to send one of our engineers to Remagen to meet you. [353]

Not only was the new core-making equipment of interest to Roddis, but a new "veneer edge-gluing machine" was of the type that Roddis was interested in and German made. From Adolf Fritz, GmbH, on August 16, 1938:

Our friends Messrs. Plycor Company Chicago inform us that you will come over to Germany during your stay in Europe and we shall be pleased to see you here.

From the enclosed folder, you will see that we make a wide range of machines, especially for dealing with veneers and we think that our new veneer edge-gluing machine will be of especial interest to you. We can show you this type in various factories near Stuttgart and you can inspect them under working conditions.

We therefore would kindly invite you to visit us here in Stuttgart and we shall be obliged to you if you will inform us in due course. [354]

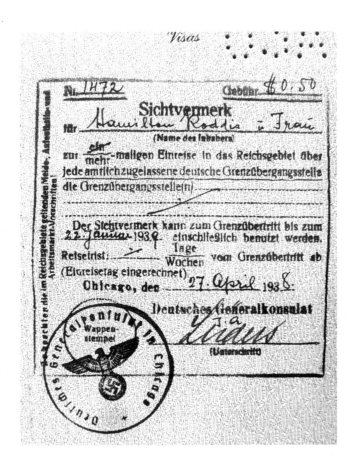

Visa "Sichtvemark" stamp, with the swastika Hitler entry dated April 27, 1938. *Author's collection.*

U.S. passport of Mr. and Mrs. Hamilton Roddis with their German trip stamp dated October 19, 1938. *Author's family collection.*

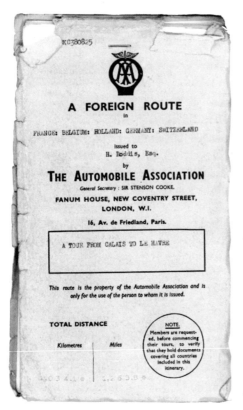

Automobile Triptic used by the Roddis family on their 1938 trip. *Author's family collection.*

Roddis did indeed tour the plants in England and Germany.

In addition, what had been perceived by his family as a "driving tour" was marked with Xs on a *National Geographic* map where visits took place, as well as listed in an itinerary driving guide. Krefeld, the home of Siempelkamp, was visited, as were Ramagen and Adolf Fritz in Stuttgart.[355]

His daughter, Augusta D. Roddis, would write of the trip fifty-four years later to her great-niece, Gillian Bostock:

One of my most vivid memories of the 1930s is the trip I took to Europe with my parents in 1938. Business conditions had finally improved, and although the business demanded the most careful attention, my father thought he could at last take another trip to Europe. He and my mother had had a wonderful trip in Europe in 1928 and he was anxious to see it again. He took a little Plymouth car we had with us and drove around England for about two weeks. I thought the English countryside was the most beautiful I had ever seen...I was, in fact, delighted with all I saw in London. We went to the continent next, and the Necker Valley in Germany, Heidelberg, Mannheim, the Swiss Alps...

There was a war scare crossing back from Europe in October, and many people were crowded onto the ship who were fleeing in fear of war. My mother's cousins who was traveling with us and I had to share our stateroom with a woman who had cut her trip to Europe short to avoid what she thought would be dangerous conditions in Europe. However, [Prime Minister Neville] Chamberlain signed the Munich Agreement, and the war was averted until the next year.[356]

Although war was averted, there was unease.

The rise of Germany in 1938 was focused on the youth. Hamilton Roddis was taken by his German host, Adolf Fritz, to a Nazi Youth Corps Camp in Wurttemberg, outside Stuttgart, to attend a September 18, 1938 performance of the *Merry Widow*.

"From the performance of elevating works, you will receive joy and strength for life."[357] This flowery translation of the director's letter followed the program title: "Hitler youth of the young workers."

In reexamination of the trip itinerary and directions, it is clear that it was a business trip to view and purchase the latest in plywood manufacturing

The program is entitled "The Talent Must Be With the Youth." *Author's family collection.*

Part of the leader's message says, "From the performance of elevating works, you will receive joy and strength for life."
The Nazi Youth Camp was composed of the "Hitler youth of the young workers."
Author's family collection.

equipment. Roddis purchased two Siempelkamp presses in Krefeld, the core machine in Ramagen and the new veneer edge-gluing machine in Stuttgart.[358] As we have seen, during World War II, the new presses for veneer and the edge-gluing machine used in splicing veneer were used in the aircraft plywood manufacturing process for British and American aircraft. The core machine was used for manufacturing fireproof doors for the Liberty ships and battleships.

By 1942, H.K. von Maltitz and Plycor Company was associated with Mereen-Johnson Machine Company in Minneapolis.[359] Adamson Machine Company in Louisville was also associated with Plycor in 1942.[360]

Reiterating the Roddis Plywood and Veneer Company's assertion that it had again turned to Germany for plywood manufacturing equipment, Dieter Siempelkamp later said, "My father introduced the first hot-platen presses in the U.S.A. However, the new resin was not yet known there. America did not have, as yet, the urea-formaldehyde resins or hot-platen presses."

One of the first presses delivered in the United States in 1936 was still operating in the 1980s.[361] That press was functioning at the Roddis Lumber and Veneer Company until its sale to Weyerhaeuser Company in 1961 and continued to operate at the Weyerhaeuser Company until 1986.

In Germany, glues had been patented by 1925, and waterproof glues were sold internationally by 1936. I.G. Farben would work with a U.S. vendor to bring the German patented products to the United States. Two men dominated the development of wood product glues in the United States from 1927 to 1946. Irving Laucks and Dr. James A. Nevin published their findings in the U.S. Chemical Society abstracts. Waterproof phenolic resin glue was a revolutionary product.

CHAPTER 9

TRADE ASSOCIATIONS

The American lumber industry has always been characterized by a certain degree of optimism, marked ingenuity and daring. It has faced difficulties, obstacles, and hardship before. It is ready to face them again…The indications are that neither the lumber industry nor the forests will fail America in an hour of need.[362]

Trade associations had initially been formed to facilitate international trade and to "establish a uniform system of grading rules for the measure and inspection of hardwood lumber…Since the original adoption of this grading system, no major changes in the standards have occurred that were not prompted by a change in the quality or availability of the timber supply."[363]

The National Hardwood Lumber Association (NHLA) was organized in 1898 and established the lumber grading system. Its "Rules for the Measurement and Inspection of Hardwood Lumber, Cypress, Veneers, and Thin Lumber, and the Sales Code of the NHLA" was put into effect in 1900.[364] Also a leader in "establishing grades was the White Pine Manufacturers Association in northern Wisconsin and Minnesota."[365] The American Forestry Association was also founded at the turn of the twentieth century.

The National Lumber Manufacturers' Association was organized in 1902. "George K. Smith was the first Secretary and was from the Yellow Pine Association. He was Secretary of both until 1908. Then Leonard Bronson until he became Editor of the *American Lumberman* in 1911."[366] Edward Hines of Hines Lumber Company in Chicago offered Royal S. Kellogg the position of secretary of the National Lumber Manufacturers' Association after Bronson, but it was given to J.E. Rhodes, who was the past secretary of the Northern Pine Manufacturers' Association and a private secretary for Frederick Weyerhaeuser.

Rhodes left the National Lumber Manufacturers' Association in 1915 for the Southern Pine Manufacturers' Association, and Kellogg became secretary from 1915 to 1918. Kellogg's main role during this period was "trade promotion, negotiating freight rates, and disputes between wooden and paper box manufacturers." Kellogg had come to the National Lumber Manufacturers' Association from a job as secretary of the Northern Hemlock and Hardwood Manufacturers' Association, formed in 1910 (later the Northern Hardwood and Pine Association).

Forest management techniques—plantation style for the paper companies and sustained-yield forestry for the lumber industry—are very different. Mill techniques (reducing the logs to chips and pulp) versus sawmills (sawing logs into lumber and grading systems) are also very different. Assuaging their differences—even the difference in the trade associations—has been a delicate balancing act. Kellogg, who had worked in the United States Forest Service and was an executive director of the National Lumber Manufacturers' Association, said, "Pulp and paper was as far removed from lumber as pulp and paper is from steel now."[367] Each industry has its own special characteristics. Before World War II, the forest products industry was "ranked at the top of the production scale nationally."[368]

During World War II, the National Lumber Manufacturers' Association, which worked to help men in combat, did its patriotic duty by contributing to the war effort and was composed of industry leaders—presidents of all the major lumber manufacturers and/or associations in the United States.[369] There were thousands of men and women who worked in the lumber industry throughout Wisconsin and the United States during World War II. Workers in Wisconsin's and Michigan's lumber industries were proud of their roles during the war.

The National Lumber Manufacturers' Association was composed of:

American Walnut Manufacturers' Association
Appalachian Hardwood Manufacturers, Incorporated
California Redwood Association
Mahogany Association
Maple Flooring Association
Northeastern Lumber Manufacturers' Association

Northern Hemlock and Hardwood Manufacturers' Association (of which the
  Wisconsin-Michigan Timber Producers' Association was an active member)
Northern Pine Manufacturers' Association
Southern Cypress Manufacturers' Association
Southern Hardwood Producers, Incorporated
Southern Pine Association
Veneer Association
West Coast Lumbermen's Association

The Board of Directors of the National Lumber Manufacturers'
Association was composed of representatives from each association
depending on their financial obligation. The Executive Committee
consisted of one representative from each organization. During World
War II, the National Lumber Manufacturers' Association had an executive
director.[370] Dr. Wilson Compton was well known, having served in the
Federal Trade Commission.

Under the auspices of the National Lumber Manufacturers' Association
was the American Forest Products Industries (AFPI), which was the
working end of the National Lumber Manufacturers' Association with
standing committees for Lumber Export Service; Taxation and Tariff;
Forest Conservation, Economics and Industry Planning; Standardization;
Transportation; Hardwood; Housing; Foreign Trade; Publicity;
Governmental Relations; Engineering; Research; Building Codes; and
Merchandising.[371] All were men dedicated to contributing to the war effort.
The regional organizations, as well as corporations, worked through the
National Lumber Manufacturers' Association.

The Northern Hemlock and Hardwood Manufacturers of Wisconsin
had just split off from the Northern Pine Manufacturers' Association and
became the Northern Hemlock and Hardwood Manufacturers' Association.
Headquartered in Wausau, Wisconsin, its first president was W.C. Landon,
president of a large lumber manufacturing firm in Wausau.[372] "At that time,
the primary role of Northern Hemlock and Hardwood Manufacturers'
Association was reporting statistics on actual sales of the quantity of lumber,
grades, and destinations…We were very thorough. We were even investigated
by the Federal Trade Commission, but to no avail."[373] E.A. Hamer of the
Upper Peninsula was the second president, and R.B. Goodman of Sawyer-
Goodman of Marinette was the third. Goodman was a lumberman with
great vision who led the industry. He was the advocate for sustained-yield
forestry management and Wisconsin's Forest Crop Act in 1929.

Board of directors of the Upper Michigan and Northern Wisconsin Timber Producers' Association, 1947. *Rear row, left to right*: Harry Theiler, Hancock, Michigan; Lawrence Welsh, Iron Mountain, Michigan; George Corrigan, Hurley, Wisconsin; Charles Noren, Amasa, Michigan; Arvey Ahonen, Ironwood, Michigan; Floyd Aldridge, Wakefield, Michigan; E.L. Kopke, Wild Rose, Wisconsin; L.J. Heinske; and H.L. Anderson. *Lower row, left to right*: W.S. Bromley; Tom Nordine; Gordon R. Connor, Wakefield, Michigan; Ray Aldrich, Mohawk, Michigan; Ivan Branham, Minocqua, Wisconsin; and Robert Ewing, Mellen, Wisconsin. *Courtesy of Tom Nordine, Bruce Crossing, Michigan.*

The Timber Producers' Association of Upper Michigan and Northern Wisconsin called a special meeting on May 13, 1941, to "organize a Mutual Insurance Company for loggers' compensation and also on cooperative buying of woods products."[374] The lumber industry was the most hazardous in the United States. For the first time, money was available to safely keep employees working—which also had been difficult for the previous ten years. Making a profit was made even more difficult with Canadian imports and over 85 percent of the pulp logs coming from other states. In the early 1940s, local pulping of timber was not being cut.[375]

On May 23, 1941, at a meeting of the Timber Producers' Association of Upper Michigan and Northern Wisconsin, it was reported that "Mr. White of the Forestry Department from Washington, D.C...gave a complete report on the possibility of cooperative marketing." This was followed several months later at the September 16 meeting as the complexities of the contracts and priorities were discussed: "Defense priority ratings were discussed by Gordon R. Connor," vice-president of Connor Lumber and Land Company and co-founder of the Timber Producers' Association of

Upper Michigan and Northern Wisconsin, "and suggestions were made that producers insist whenever possible on being given government order numbers on all government defense contracts for which forest products were supplied."[376]

"Priorities" were defined as "the means whereby precedence is established in the procurement programs after considering all urgent and essential needs of the Nation."[377] They took many forms, including "classification ratings," and were a powerful tool in resource allocation.

The Timber Producers' Association of Upper Michigan and Northern Wisconsin was a member of the Northern Hemlock and Hardwood Manufacturers' Association. The president was John Landon from Ironwood, Michigan; vice-president was A.L. McBean of Park Falls; and treasurer was W.W. Gamble Sr., Yawkey-Bissell Lumber Company, of White Lake, Wisconsin.[378] All were respected in the lumber industry. Payment problems and priorities were two of many issues that the Timber Producers' Association and the Northern Hemlock and Hardwood Manufacturers' Association—and thus O.T. Swan, secretary and manager at the National Lumber Manufacturers' Association—would deal with in the near future.

The War Production Board was established by Executive Order on December 11, 1941, under the auspices of the Office of Emergency Management. The War Production Board had the authority to:

> *a) Exercise general direction over the war procurement and production program*
> *b) Determine the policies, plans, procedures, and methods of the several Federal departments...*
> *c) Perform the functions and exercise the powers vested in the Supply Priorities and Allocations Board by Executive Order No. 8875 of August 28, 1941*
> *d) Supervise the Office of Production Management...*
> *e) Report...to the President*
> *Sweeping powers and authority were given to implement the war plans.*[379]

The "cost" of lumber production was reflected in a meeting of the Timber Producers' Association of Upper Michigan and Northern Wisconsin on May 11, 1945. The Timber Producers' Association had attended the Hardwood Advisory Committee meeting with the War Production Board in Washington in April. The Timber Producers' Association emphasized "that the WPB was vitally concerned over increased production, not only in war time needs but for civilian use. A.O. Anderson, President, stated that in the period of reconversion it appeared that all materials necessary for an extensive building program would be available with the exception of lumber."[380] In other words, lumber was still needed for the Pacific theater enough that even with the end of the war drawing near, civilian needs would not become the primary market.

The cost of production increased with added War Labor Board orders to the lumber industry. The timber industry was losing money with increased wages and price ceilings on logs and production.

The cost of doing business and production to meet the war effort was constant cooperation of the trade associations in meetings and reports with government agencies.

CHAPTER 10

WAR CONTRACTS
AND THE WISCONSIN
LUMBER INDUSTRY

There have been, I think, since the last war, three important developments in
lumber which have increased its ability to serve essential functions in war time.
Wider diversification of the uses of lumber and timber products and wood treatment.
Development of modern timber engineering, primarily through systems of
construction, which most ordinary contractors are able to handle great advances in
the gluing field, particularly in plywood and laminated wood.
—Dr. Wilson Compton, National Lumber Manufacturers Association[381]

The process of obtaining government war contracts at the beginning of World War II was confusing and tedious. Each corporation was required to contact the agency with which the contract was to be negotiated. It was a corporate and governmental bureaucratic nightmare.

On April 8, 1940, army procurement and purchasing was delineated in the "Plans of Industrial Mobilization":

In order that manufacturers capable of supplying the items required may
be able to place their facilities as the service of the Government, thereby
making available the maximum source of supply...Practically all Army
purchasing falls under the seven Supply, Arms and Services as follows,
arranged in order of volume of purchases.[382]
Corps of Engineers

Postcard. *Courtesy of Camp 5 Museum Foundation/Wisconsin Forestry Museum, Laona, Wisconsin.*

Air Corps
Quartermaster Corps
Ordnance Department
Signal Corps
Medical Department
Chemical Warfare Services

The U.S. Army Corps of Engineers' auction system was described by Lieutenant Colonel F.G. Sherrill in "Lumber Procurement for the War." He said:

> *We have a system whereby all of the services send their bills for materials to our office here in Washington or in Portland. We have representatives in most of the large cities, and throughout the country we hold auctions on lumber every week. We have tried to confine the orders to bill for a particular project in order to simplify the process. Our system is really to sell the building material rather than purchase lumber. The lumber is the medium of exchange for the building material. The auction is conducted in the open with our representatives acting in the capacity of the auctioneer. He offers the list for a certain camp or shipyard or navy shore station or the like. The process is seemingly very slow in that we break the list up into different items, that is into group 2, 3, or 4 in accordance with the desires of the representatives of the lumber industry, hoping that we will secure at least one bid for each group of items.*[383]

Was there any wonder that there was a chaotic search for contracts? These purchases were just for the army. In 1939, contracts had amounted to $457 million.[384]

Organizing the war effort in Washington, D.C., required cooperation between the bureaucracy and lumber industry. A Lumber and Lumber Products Division was established "as one of 40 divisions of the War Production Board." Its purpose was to coordinate with other national war agencies like the Office of Price Administration (OPA), War Labor Board, Selective Service System, War Labor Board, Tires Rationing Board, Office of Defense Transportation, Army-Navy, Munitions Board and others. The Lumber and Lumber Products Division was defined as an "industry branch, a materials branch, and in part a commodities branch because it is responsible for maintaining production of lumber for war purposes, for channeling that lumber to first uses first, and for the manufacture and flow of such commodities as plywood, millwork, certain other wood products, mobile housing, etc."

Employing 135 people, sections within the Lumber and Lumber Products Division included:

> *Domestic Lumber Production headed by H.E. Helman of the Society of American Foresters*
> *Foreign Woods*
> *Distribution*
> *Millwork*
> *Veneer and Plywood*
> *Mobile Housing*
> *Wood Fabrication*
> *Aircraft Lumber*
> *Across the sections were labor, machinery, equipment, planning and administration, statistics, requirements, research, administration of limit and conservation orders...the Industrial Advisory Committees are the industry group.*[385]

Coordination among the numerous government agencies with the lumber industry was constant throughout the war. Donald Nelson, a vice-president of Sears Roebuck, was appointed chairman of the War Production Board. The Lumber and Lumber Products Division dealt with the commodities, individual industries and raw materials.

> *There are many activities dealing with the production, specifications, purchases and use of lumber and timber products for defense. Because of the nature of the problems involved, it is generally difficult to coordinate our activities for maximum effectiveness...Some coordination of our activities and interchange of information appears to be desirable if we are to direct our efforts most intelligently.*
>
> *We want to do the best job we can with the facilities we have. If appropriate representatives of the government agencies dealing with the problem of lumber in defense will get together periodically with the representatives of the lumber and timber products industries to discuss frequently programs and activities, the interchange should develop a better understanding of our respective activities and facilities.*[386]

Patriotic fervor and potential profits after a disastrous market collapse during the Great Depression motivated the forest products industry. The members of the National Lumber Manufacturers' Association were trying to keep their businesses running, which had been difficult for the last ten years during the Great Depression. The regional forest products organizations, as well as lumbermen, through the National Lumber Manufacturers' Association in Washington, D.C., feverishly tried to learn how their members could obtain government contracts and assist in the war effort.

In one instance, the Hardwood Dimension Manufacturers' Association contacted the Conservation Section of the Office of Production Management. "Mr. John McClure of the National Hardwood Lumber Association reported to me on the conference he and other hardwood lumber and furniture interested parties met with you in Washington…McClure stated and I heartily concur in the thought, that the group which I represent—the Hardwood Dimension Industry would be intensely interested in your plans." The plan was to use dimensional hardwoods for substitute materials. The hardwood dimension business included parts for "wood furniture, automobiles, radio, refrigerator, and casket[s]."[387] The possibilities were endless.

The Hardwood Dimension Manufacturers' Association had been "working in close cooperation with as many government agencies as possible…There were many letters written requesting information about 'Procurement Procedures.'" One letter was written on February 14, 1941, to the National Lumber Manufacturers' Association. Wanting to participate in the auctions being held, Van Kreulen & Winchester Lumber Company in Grand Rapids, Michigan, inquired about the bidding procedures through the field offices of the U.S. quartermaster.[388]

It was difficult to be "greedy,"[389] as the changeover to war production was predicated on a price system. All aspects of the lumber industry were fixed by price, and the government contracts were negotiated on a "cost-plus-fixed-fee" (CPFF). Changes could only take place in the contract if there were significant changes in the contractor's circumstances or perhaps if the contract necessitated increases because of excessive, unreasonable demands of the contract. As a result of the Expediting Act of 1940, an incentive of up to 30 percent was given for corporations converting their manufacturing facilities. In addition, if the contract became cumbersome, the army and navy could give incentives along the way for completion. The CPFF contracts from 1940–41, in excess of $10,000, accounted for 46 percent of the value of all the Maritime Commission, army and navy contracts.

Those would not include contracts for construction, manufacturing facilities or foodstuffs. However, there was accelerated depreciation of purchases to reduce tax liability. "Capital loss after the war" was possible if the plant was too specialized, but mostly investment in facilities was to facilitate postwar production.[390] In the spring of 1940, Germany had marched into Denmark, Norway, Belgium, Holland and France.

By the fiscal year end of June 30, 1940, the United States War Department had awarded approximately 87 percent of its CPFF contracts. Some were awarded directly to the manufacturer and others through an invitational and bidding system. For those CPFF contracts, a fee of 7 percent was added to the contract cost.[391]

To pay for economic mobilization, in June 1940, the United States Congress again acted by passing the National Defense Tax Bill. Realizing the seriousness of a potential war, the national debt ceiling was raised to $49 billion. By July, recognizing the outcome of the China-Japanese War, Congress voted in favor of a $37 billion expenditure for a "two-ocean Navy," tanks for the army, aircraft for the United States Army Air Corps and aircraft for the navy.[392] Stockpiling for war had begun.

From June through December 1940, the United States military awarded over $11 billion in prime contracts. This was over and above the already appropriated $9.1 billion in federal spending. Of those contracts, the top one hundred corporations in the United States received over 86 percent of the business. The top twenty corporations received 60 percent of the contracts. Confusion led to action, and the contributions that the National Lumber Manufacturers' Association and the member industries made allowed the United States to rearm and prepare for war.

By the end of December 1942, 71 percent of all defense contracts were held by America's one hundred largest corporations.[393] During 1942, Yawkey-Bissell Lumber Company of White Lake provided lumber for larger lumber companies that had U.S. government war contracts. For example, orders for lumber went to Roddis Lumber and Veneer Company in Marshfield, the third-largest plywood manufacturer in the United States, on January 16 and continued throughout the war.[394] Lumber for glider parts was sold to Lloyd Manufacturing Company on January 28 for cargo glider assembly.

Problems still existed with the wartime bureaucracy for the forest products industry in Washington, D.C. Despite having a top priority rating under the War Production Board, the plywood industry struggled to meet production and distribution goals. Also, the Lumber and Timber Products Defense Committee, made up of thirty-one industry representatives, appealed to the Office of Price Management, Priorities Division, on "grades and dimensions."[395]

Throughout 1942, the National Lumber Manufacturers' Association and the Lumber and Timber Defense Committee asked that a chief of the Lumber and Lumber Production Branch be appointed:

> *Before appointing a Chairman for your Lumber Branch as announced in your press release today, I hope that you will consult with the Lumber and Timber Defense Committee of which I am Chairman. We are being asked to provide war and defense material in great quantities. We can provide substitutes for many critical materials. We need your cooperation with our effort to maintain needed production of lumber and timber products. This is our war, just as it is yours and whoever you appoint to head the lumber branch should command confidence and trust of this industry.*[396]

The point was to have someone in charge making decisions—someone who had knowledge of the forest products industry.[397] The National Lumber Manufacturers' Association, as well as the Lumber and Timber Defense Committee, worked tirelessly advocating for the lumber industry during the war.

Earlier in January, Dr. Wilson Compton, secretary of the National Lumber Manufacturers' Association, had sent a telegram to O.C. Lance of the Northwestern Lumbermen's Association in Minneapolis. It may have been shared with the Timber Producers' Association of Upper Michigan and Northern Wisconsin. Regarding an upcoming "building limitation order" and substitution of materials for steel, "the Lumber and Timber Products Defense Committee"

> *has been strongly urging with OPM* [Office of Price Management] *and other responsible defense officials that building which is otherwise permissible ought to be suspended because of lack of nails, screws, fasteners, and ordinary hardware…Believe your members should be prepared however for drastic restrictions at the end of this month of the use of existing stocks of metals involving virtual suspension of new housing except in defense areas…We are assured a ton of steel now for the defense program may be worth ten tons next year…we should insist…that critical materials be not hereafter used for purposes which may as well be served by other materials like lumber which are and we believe will continue in adequate supply.*

In other words, not only were metals in short supply, but wood could also be a substitute.

Owing to the scarcity of metals, increasing quantities of plywood are going into training and combat planes, gliders, and cargo planes. Plywood has been manufactured and used in airplanes in the United States for years. But before plywood goes into modern military craft in which the lives of American airmen are at stake, the Army and Navy must be assured that plywood can, as an engineering material, take the terrific punishment to which such planes are subjected. This calls for the immediate development and testing of mathematical formulas by which specific properties of plywood, such as resistance to fatigue, buckling, and torsion, can be more accurately calculated for design purposes. To obtain these formulas the laboratory's engineering staff has been greatly expanded and in order to expedite the testing required, a force of women is operating test equipment in two shifts from 6 o'clock in the morning until 11 p.m.[398]

The idea that wood could be a substitute for metal had already played out, encountering "terrific punishment," and the British Royal Air Force pilots were in harm's way. The Forest Products Laboratory in Madison, Wisconsin, had worked with de Havilland in testing wood for the Mosquito, which was already re-conquering the skies over Britain. Still, aerodynamics was in its infancy, and the Forest Products Laboratory was at the forefront of its field of study.

Dr. Compton would work tirelessly on contract issues. Contracts were also still a problem. Contract offices were in more populated areas, far from the forests of northern Wisconsin. The Contract Distribution Branch Field Offices were listed in Milwaukee, Appleton and Wausau. Dorance W. Walters was listed as head of the Eau Claire office, with John D. Howard being the head of the Madison office. In Michigan, Iron Mountain was the site of the Upper Peninsula office—also closest to forest operations. Herman K. Pleasant was in Grand Rapids and Warren Clarke in Detroit. One large issue, as we have seen, involved the differences in the auction versus a contract for lumber procurement. Dr. Compton wrote to Mr. D. MacKeachie of the War Production Board:

In conjunction with the announced policy of the War Production Board to rely on negotiated contracts rather than competitive bidding for war supplies, I ask appropriate consideration of the recommendations of the Lumber and Timber Products Defense Committee... These state the views of competent representatives of substantially all the timber products industries.

You well know the problems resulting from scattered and uncoordinated lumber buying a year and a half ago and of the vast improvement resulting

*from the program of centralized buying for the Army camps…under the
Corps of Engineers.*

*We are earnestly hopeful that the facilities thus developed for more
orderly lumber procurement will be maintained and strengthened…That
plan has worked well and is in fact the only plan which has worked well.
So far as we know it is entirely compatible with the policy of negotiated
contract buying* [399]

Often, contract issues revolved around the basic problem of meeting
production quotas, as well as procurement.

Underlying any problems, however, cooperation was paramount in all
the communications between Dr. Compton and Donald Nelson, director
of the War Productions Board. In fact, Dr. Compton would be offered a
job with the War Production Board but declined on December 29, 1942.[400]
In the meantime, in a letter dated May 21, 1942, Dr. Compton wrote to
Nelson about the "industry-wide cooperation for the maximum production
of lumber."[401]

The chairman of the War Production Board wrote to Dr. Compton on
May 22, 1942:

*Your ideas and suggestions were most helpful to the War Production Board
in deciding upon the character and scope of the provisions incorporated in
limitations Order L-121, which was issued and made affective May 13.
You, of course, have had a copy of that order…*

*I also appreciate your prompt action in disseminating my wire of May
5 throughout the lumber industry.*

*I am sure that if the expected favorable results of Order L-121 are to
materialize, we will need the continued cooperation of your organization,
and through it, all lumber manufacturers.* [402]

The telegram that Nelson referred to implored the lumber industry
to "inaugurate a full program of maximum production of all species."[403]
Realizing the lumber production shortages, Nelson in June announced a
new system liberalizing the policy of priority assistance to loggers and mill
operators regarding equipment repair parts and operating supplies. He was
well aware of the lumber shortages.[404]

The cordialities between the National Lumber Manufacturers Association
and the War Production Board were reiterated by Colonel W.S. Styer of
the U.S. Army Corps of Engineers: "The record of the lumber industry

in meeting its wartime obligations to date has been excellent...Because of efficient work of associations such as yours and their splendid cooperation with a sympathetic government."[405] Successful cooperation between government and the lumber industry was paramount.

All aspects of all industries were under production price ceilings and labor and equipment restrictions. It was as if the lumber industry was fighting a war on two fronts—one at home and one abroad. Still, the industries pressed on and accomplished the enormous contribution to the war effort.

It was thought that on July 9, 1943, some relief would be obtained by the "Reorganization of the Lumber and Lumber Products Division of the War Production Board." "Recognizing the importance of lumber and lumber products in the war program, the War Production Board has authorized the reorganization with increased staff to obtain maximum production and best distribution for war and essential civilian needs."[406]

However, the lumber industry still had to deal with the Program Branch, Operations Branch and Marketing and Control Branch. The good news was that the "technical advisory staff" was made up of lumbermen and wood product consultants who knew the business. The bad news was that there were still a plethora of other agencies with oversight power spread throughout the National Defense structure—the Office of Price Administration, Supply, Priorities and Allocation Board and Division of Priorities (one of nine offices under the Office of Production Management). Also, a "Manual of Policy and Procedures" set rules on meetings between industry and the War Production Board.[407]

In January 1944, the War Production Board was requesting that the timber industry's board footage for the year would be equal to or surpass that of 1943. In addition, the War Production Board had instituted "advisory committees and task groups." Restrictions on how the War Production Board representatives could meet with industry were implemented. New industrial committees had to be approved.

The War Production Board issued "General Administrative Order No. B-141" on January 14, 1944. Interestingly, the wording said that the War Production Board would have a better cross-section of industry representatives in making industry decisions by restricting how and with whom they could meet. However, the "Rules Applicable to Meeting with Groups of Industry Representatives" threatened industry with violation of "antitrust laws provided by agreements between the Attorney General and the General Counsel of the Board." The result was that the War Production Board could only solicit input from industry through an "Industry Advisory Committee or a Task Group."

The efficacy of the committee system was limited. The Industrial Advisory Committee had to be "approved by the Director of the Office of Industrial Advisory Committee, and have a government presiding officer." In addition, a committee would have to "submit to the Office of Industry Advisory Committees a memorandum" listing each member's name, address and relation to the industry, as well as the purpose and intention of the committee itself. The timber industry's Industrial Advisory Committee was composed of:

Hardwood Lumber Manufacturers' Association
Softwood Loggers and Lumber Manufacturers
Mahogany Importers-Manufacturers
Wholesale Distributors
Retail Distributors
Millwork Manufacturers
Softwood Plywood Manufacturers
Hardwood Plywood Manufacturers
House Trailer Manufacturers
Aircraft Lumber Manufacturers
Industry Transportation

The requirements for the Industrial Advisory Committee were to "fully represent segments of the industry involved. They must represent small, medium, and large operators in various geographic sections of the country, the various species of wood, the different methods of industry operations, and individuals and companies who are and who are not members of trade associations."[408]

The diversity of interest of the represented forest product groups made the work of the group laborious. Would not the patience of any industry be tied to the limit in the face of the war effort?

No wonder that by March 1944, according to J. Philip Boyd, director of the War Production Board—Lumber and Lumber Products Division, there were "weaknesses in the present distribution of lumber…Strict controls are in force in certain critical items…and the situation is becoming increasingly critical."

Still, the relations between the War Production Board and the National Lumber Manufacturers remained cordial and cooperative as the war effort increased. Arthur Upson of the Lumber and Lumber Products Division of the War Production Board said, "The following symposium evidences the helpful cooperation of the lumber industry with the federal government."[409] Multiple committees were formed to assist with the shortages.

The War Production Board reported a two-day meeting between the War Production Board, the Hardwood Lumber Manufacturers' Industrial Advisory Committee, the Softwood Loggers and Lumber Manufacturers' Industrial Advisory Committee. The result was that now not only aircraft plywood was in short supply, but

> *the heavy demand for lumber in 1944 has made all lumber critical instead of only certain species. The committee was informed that at least 17,000,000,000 board feet of lumber will be needed for boxing, crating, dunnage and industrial blocking this year. This is approximately half of total production...If necessary; this will be accomplished by allotting stated amounts of lumber to specific uses on a purchase authorization basis.*

Continuing, the War Production Board said, "Committee members concurred with WPB that some sort of over-all distribution controls are urgently needed. Stocks at mills and in the hands of distributors are so low that they can no longer be called upon to fill the gap between production and consumption. War and essential civilian needs for lumber must be met almost wholly by production."[410] With a total production of 34 billion board feet anticipated, the supply and demand chain needed to be rectified.

While 1943 saw lumber production of 34.65 billion board feet, consumption had, according to the War Production Board, exceeded production by 4.2 billion bdf. Still, the 1943 production was a reduction by 5 percent from 1942.

LUMBER PRODUCTION TABLE[411]

Year	Lumber Production (bdf)
1940	31.7 billion
1941	36.54 billion
1942	36.33 billion
1943	34.65 billion
1944	34 billion (anticipated)

The War Production Board—Lumber and Lumber Products Division eschewed that lumber production was "limited by manpower shortages and logging equipment shortages, chiefly tractors, trucks, heavy tires and repair parts."[412] The saga continued.

By the end of May 1944, the Forest Products Bureau of the War Production Board, again under the direction of Harold Boeschenstein, asked the National Lumber Manufacturers' Association to comment on the "Lumber Industry Report prepared by the Lumber Unit, Bureau of Foreign and Domestic Commerce, U.S. Department of Commerce, in cooperation with the Lumber Division, Forest Products Bureau, War Production Board and the U.S. Forest Service."[413] The draft of the report was also sent to forest products industry leaders asking "for input and suggestions so that future issues maybe of the fullest possible value to the industry."[414]

Dr. Compton said:

> *I have examined this* [the industry report on lumber] *with much interest and while I doubt the accuracy of some of the information…I recognize that it is official information of the War Production Board upon which are predicated findings and conclusions of its various lumber controls. Certainly nothing but benefit can result from as widespread as possible understanding of this underlying information.*
>
> *For about twelve years, I have participated in the preparation of a quarterly Lumber Survey Report to the Secretary of Commerce. This report has carried an unbroken series of comparable statistics on lumber consumption and lumber stocks.*
>
> *…The only affirmative suggestion that I care to make is that those who participate in the preparation of this information be cautioned to make use as reasonably as they can of industry information available from competent industry sources and thus avoid needless duplication of requests for current information.*

In short, the report was a duplication of efforts that had been going on for some time with cooperation from the lumber industry and government. The information in the U.S. Commerce reports better reflected the timber industry's actual figures. The National Lumber Manufacturers' Association had responded in light of the anticipation of even more stringent controls on distribution and lumber supply.[415]

In announcing L-335 and "over-all control of lumber," the War Production Board said:

> *This control affects all users of lumber, wholesale, retail distributors, and all but the very smallest of sawmills…Order L-335…sets up the procedure*

under which sawmills deliver lumber…Some fifty species are produced in scores of grades and sizes by approximately 37,000 sawmills. About 40 percent of all lumber is distributed by wholesale and retail distribution yards, numbering over 25,000. The demand for various species, sizes and grades varies as war requirements change…L-335 provides for the issuance of directions…and directives.[416]

The directions and directives for sawmills included Wisconsin's sawmills and members of the Timber Producers' Association of Upper Michigan and Northern Wisconsin. Every lumber order under L-335 had to be marked "Certified -L-335." At Yawkey-Bissell Lumber Company in White Lake, the orders also had to be certified and were signed by W.W. Gamble Jr., vice-president:

I certify that the above bill is correct and just, that payment therefore has not been received, that statutory requirements as to American production and labor standards, and all conditions of purchase applicable to the transactions have been complied with, and that State or Local Sales taxes are not included in the amount billed.[417]

Yawkey-Bissell Invoice #547 dated December 28, 1944, contained 20,878 board feet of 4/4 #2 Common Birch AD Rough costing $49.50 per board foot. The lumber was going to the Depot, Quartermaster, United States Marine Corps, Delaware and Oregon Avenues, Philadelphia, and also marked QMUSMC 1100 South Broad Street, Philadelphia.[418] Another invoice under L-335 was for the Foster-Lothman Mills in Oshkosh. Shipped in Car MP-48462 under Certified—L-335, the Yawkey-Bissell Lumber Company invoice was marked with three preference ratings: 15 percent AA-1, 15 percent AA-2X and the balance was AA-3. Included in the order was:

EXTRACT FROM
YAWKEY-BISSELL LUMBER COMPANY INVOICE[419]

109 2"x4"	6' 8$\frac{1}{16}$"	$\frac{10}{14}$"
2"x6"	6' $\frac{8}{16}$"	
1"x8"	$\frac{9}{16}$"	

Also included was over twenty thousand bdf of hemlock lumber.[420] Most of the December 1944 invoices at Yawkey-Bissell Lumber Company reflected the L-335 regulations. The military orders for thousands of bdf of hardwood lumber also had a top-priority preference, AA-1.

Sawmills producing over 100,000 bdf were included in L-335.[421] Of the thirty-seven thousand sawmills in the United States, the sawmill capacities ranged from 1 million bdf per day to 50,000 bdf per day. "Nearly half of all lumber produced comes from 28,000 mills, each of which has an output of less than 5,000,000 bdf per year."[422] "Sawmills covered by the order may sell lumber under the following conditions: (1) on certified and rated orders from a consumer or distributor; (2) on certified but unrated orders from Class 1 consumers or distributors; (3) to other sawmills, including concentration yards, without use of certifications."

The justification of L-335 by the War Production Board was that not all species were covered in other directives. The War Production Board stated that directives for hardwoods under MPR-364 covered seven species of hardwoods. The regulation for softwoods was partially covered under MPR-208 because other directives covered western softwoods.

In June, the War Production Board announced that the amount of lumber produced in the Great Lakes states during the spring of 1944 had increased by 5.2 percent. April 1944 production was 136,600,000 bdf, which was a 70.3 percent increase from the previous year. Overall, hardwoods had accounted for 5.5 million bdf produced in April. The Great Lakes states, therefore, had produced approximately 20 percent of the total national April hardwoods.[423] The Great Lakes states' lion share of production for April was attributed to weather conditions in other parts of the country.

The War Production Board announced at the end of November that September 1944 lumber production had been 2,731,863,000 bdf, with 93,500,000 bdf produced by the Great Lakes states.[424] Despite the efforts of the Great Lakes states, there were shortages of raw materials for the "military cargo truck body and the military cot program." To meet the shortages, the War Production Board tightened and amended L-335. "Species subject to this set-aside for military use are white oak (including 'WHND'—worm holes, not defect), red oak, birch, beech, pecan, rock elm, hard maple, and tough white ash. Grades and sizes affected are No. 1 common and better in ¾ and ⁵⁄₄ thicknesses (1¼ and 1½ inch)."[425]

With the amendment and addition of "Direction 6 and inclusion in Direction 7" of L-335, the large sawmills in the Timber Producers' Association of Upper Michigan and Northern Wisconsin were affected. "Sawmills subject to provisions of the direction are those producing 5,000 or more board feet of hardwood lumber of any kind per average eight hour day, or sawmills that produced this amount of hardwood per day while in operation from June 3, 1943 to December 3, 1943."[426]

This included the Connor Lumber and Land Company in Laona, with three sawmill carriages that could cut thirty thousand bdf per shift. Connor could cut fifty to sixty thousand bdf of hard maple with two sawmill carriages. Sawing 250 days per year, the output would be approximately fifteen million bdf.[427]

Roddis Lumber and Veneers Company in Park Falls reported cutting 100,000 bdf per day. C.M. Christiansen Company in Phelps, Yawkey-Bissell Lumber Company in White Lake, Goodman Lumber Company in Goodman and the Connor Lumber and Land Company in Laona run by R.M. Connor Sr. were running at full capacity.

All such sawmills are prohibited from selling, transferring, or delivering lumber of the grades, sizes, and species covered except to fill purchase orders (known as "Purchase Allocations") issued by the Central Procuring Agency of the U.S. Corps of Engineers, or as permitted as the result of appeals.

This prohibition stops the flow of the affected lumber from sawmills to all other consumers and to distributors. However, sale and delivery is permitted from one sawmill to another, and from producers of white ash to ash specialists, as provided by Direction 11 to L-335. An ash specialist is a person who operates a concentration yard dealing exclusively in ash.[428]

Even with L-335 directing all production, the October lumber production figures in the Great Lakes states had been 79,700,000 bdf. This was a 14-million-bdf decrease from September figures.

Despite lumber industry restrictions, the lumber industry was still trying to fill its military orders. Roddis reported being at full capacity in its aircraft plywood production. "The company was fortunate in landing a large gliders order recently which will take our full capacity in aircraft production. Our main difficulty now is help."[429] As we have seen, the British Horsa gliders and USAAC gliders played a significant role in 1944 in D-Day operations. Roddis Plywood Corporation's plywood "flew to war."

The Yawkey-Bissell Lumber Company in White Lake was also running at full capacity. While its initial foray into government contracts in 1944 was through other suppliers, it was not until June 9, 1944, that Yawkey-Bissell received its first direct government order. The order was for 20,754 board feet of #1 common birch, priced at $2,021.03, for the Terre Haute

Yawkey-Bissell Lumber Company, White Lake, Wisconsin. *Courtesy of Bill Gamble, White Lake, Wisconsin.*

Ordnance Depot by the Financial Division of Procurement.[430] There was a flurry of government activity from June 9 until August 10.

Orders poured in for over 200,000 more board feet of #1 common birch lumber and over $20,000 for the construction of the Terre Haute Ordnance Depot in Indiana.[431] The busiest months for government contracts for Yawkey-Bissell Lumber Company lumber sales were from October to December 1944, with more shipments to Terre Haute.[432] Interspersed with Terre Haute orders were other railroad carloads of lumber going to the U.S. Treasury Procurement, c/o Commanding Officer, Montgomery Railroad Station, Montgomery, Alabama. The load had a top-priority rating of AA-1 and contained over 18,000 board feet of lumber for $1,481.67.[433] Yawkey-Bissell Lumber Company also shipped to the 819th American Air Force in St. Louis; the Naval Supply Depot in Norfolk; the Navy Yard at Mare Island, California; and the Navy Yard at Port Huemene, California.[434] In Wisconsin, Yawkey-Bissell was also supplying lumber to Wisconsin Axle Division–Oshkosh and United States Motors in Oshkosh.[435] Today, both have been incorporated into a company that is known as Oshkosh Truck, a major military supplier.

Making production even more difficult was the implementation of a more stringent L-335. Additional steps were taken in December by the War Production Board. Although the supply of hardwoods had been adequate earlier in the year, it had been recently depleted by increased "demand for military and industrial programs and a drop in production of the better grades of hardwood." Not only was Direction 6 of L-335 in effect, but it had been expanded to apply to all hardwoods being produced. Also, the War Production Board expanded the exception of small sawmills cutting "less than 5,000 board feet of hardwood lumber per day. These mills are required to accept certified orders."[436] The result was that *all* hardwoods could only be sold on "certified orders."

The control of hardwood lumber production was additionally advanced by the Office of Price Administration. Every lumber order was still under the official price ceilings set by the Office of Price Administration, as well as L-335. For example, a Yawkey-Bissell Lumber Company Invoice #333 for the Wisconsin Axle Division, Oshkosh, United States Government Order #S132701, stated, "Yawkey-Bissell Lumber Company affirms that to the best of its knowledge, information, and belief the prices charges herein do not exceed the maximum prices established by any applicable price regulation issued by the Office of Price Administration."[437]

Hardwood prices were reduced further through the implementation of Maximum Price Regulation MPR-467, effective December 26, 1944. Merry Christmas! The shipping of hardwoods by railroad and their origination points were reconfigured, causing a decrease in prices. Also, the maximum price ceilings on hardwoods being sold at distributional yards—retail or wholesale—were reconfigured, causing a further decrease in prices.[438] Labor prices were about to increase, demand was decreasing and supply was in question. The War Production Board had just announced decreases in "new construction figures."[439]

Anticipation of improvement in lumber production was dashed immediately by the War Production Board in an industry-wide bulletin on New Year's Day 1945:

> *During the middle of 1944, everyone's hopes were high that the end of the European war was merely a matter of weeks or a few months at the most. This optimism was very understandable at the time, it is not understandable now. It is a great deal harder to pull ourselves back to a total war outlook after the let-down which we all experienced than it was to make the initial effort. However, we must pull ourselves back without the shock of another Pearl Harbor, although the recent German campaign should leave no doubts in anyone's mind of the seriousness of the situation. Lumber production for example, held up very well until September; since then it has been lagging…Instead of the 34 billion feet which we hoped for this year, we will not get over 32 billion.*[440]

J. Phillip Boyd continued in his summary to exhort the lumber industry to rededicate itself to production. How well received his words were, though, was doubtful. Even though aircraft and aircraft equipment accounted for 27.7 percent of the total United States exports by 1945, issues plaguing the timber industry were, according to Boyd, going to continue: "Manpower is not going to be better...lack of tires is going to continue and become more acute: equipment, while coming in about the same volume as last year, will not go as far because old equipment is closer to exhaustion."[441]

A stark contrast to the optimism of 1944, the real message in the proclamation was that the war was not over, as everyone had anticipated:

> *The time has passed when a sawmill or distributor should expect to receive help in the form of equipment, manpower or any other consideration... Tires, equipment, and other materials are too scarce and too precious... we have completely reversed...and have cancelled most of the relaxations of L-335 and are now back to the original order plus additionally stringent actions in the case of tight species such as...the higher grades of certain hardwoods.*[442]

An initial relaxation of L-335 controls over the lumber industry was reverted, and restrictions were tightened even more for the Great Lakes states hardwood producers. Boyd stated, "The situation on supply and demand of lumber is now tighter than at any time since the war began and your job of production or distribution is consequently more vital than it has ever been before. Every bit of the lumber now produced from any or all size mills must serve the war economy."

It was clearly a carrot and stick letter, as Boyd ended it by saying, "I want to impress upon each of you that your contribution from now on is not only twice as important as it has been before, but is your absolute duty as your part in the maintenance of this continued total war."[443]

To reiterate Boyd's communication to the lumber industry and to announce the specifics of L-335 restrictions, the War Production Board issued another press release on January 5 regarding the shortages of manpower, tires and production:

> *The lack of heavy duty tires, in particular, is expected to have an increasingly adverse effect on production through...the movement of logs and lumber.*
> *Order L-335 and eight directions to the order (Directions 1 through 8) were amended today to reduce the amount of lumber that may be sold*

without control—that is, on uncertified orders—and to establish additional controls over particular species and grades that are in critically short supply.

Direction 6 was specific to the Great Lakes states. It prevented sawmills and distributors from

receiving without specific WPB authorization any No. 1 common or better grades of eight species of hardwood produced by mills cutting 5,000 or more board feet per day of hardwood lumber. Species affected by Direction 6 are white oak, red oak, birch…hard maple, and white ash. The restriction also applies to special grades which are the equivalent of No. 1 common or better. Military requirements for these grades and species have increased and production of the better grades or hardwoods has fallen off, WPB officials said. Military requirements exceed anticipated supply for the first quarter of 1945.[444]

Four years and going into the fifth year of requesting "No. 1 common or better" for hardwood species was putting a strain on the Great Lake states' forests and timber producers.

Each sawmill covered by order L-335 is now permitted to ship lumber only on certified orders except when specifically authorized by WPB to fill uncertified orders. Authorization, for which request must be made by letter, will be granted to the individual sawmill only when certified orders cannot be obtained…

As a result of the tighter control established today, practically no lumber will be available for uncertified orders except the small amounts…Less than 3 per cent of all lumber produced comes from sawmills not covered by the order (those producing less than 100,000 board feet per year), they added.[445]

The L-335 lumber restrictions were over and above the "maximum prices established by the MPR-257, Maximum Price Regulation No. 257," applied to "pulpwood cut, peeled, and sold or contracted to be sold prior to November 7, 1942." The question was whether the pulpwood was subject to the pulpwood price ceiling. In the end, additional clarification was sought from Washington.

On April 27, Mr. Drucker of the Northern Hemlock and Hardwood Manufacturers' Association in Oshkosh wrote to Mr. Henry Bahr at the National Lumber Manufacturers' Association requesting fifty copies of

Minimum Pricing Regulations (MPRs) 222 and 223. MPR-222 covered softwood lumber prices. MPR-223 covered hardwoods in Amendment 8.[446] The Timber Producers' Association of Upper Michigan and Northern Wisconsin was concerned enough about the ceiling prices on logs to pass several resolutions at the April 27, 1944 meeting: "RESOLVED, That the Timber Producers' Association of Upper Michigan and Northern Wisconsin records that its members favor a continuance of maximum ceiling prices on logs; that its membership favors the present method of determining ceiling prices which is based upon the cost of stumpage, the cost of production, and inclusion of a reasonable margin of profit to the producers."

Addressing MPR-222 on softwood prices, the Timber Producers' Association of Upper Michigan and Northern Wisconsin passed a resolution: "BE IT FURTHER RESOLVED, that the chair appoint a committee to confer with Mr. Peter A. Stone, Chief of the Lumber Division of the Office of Price Administration, relative to the immediate establishment of a price differential for peeled hemlock logs over and above the present price of rough hemlock."

In answering the Office of Price Administration's MPR-223 on hardwood log pricing, the Timber Producers' Association further passed a resolution recommending that the Office of Price Administration not only increase the hemlock prices but also increase the prices of "white birch logs and white oak logs."

If, under MPR-223, the lumber was being bought by a War Procurement Agency, that could include the "War Department, Department of the Navy, the United States Maritime Commission, or the Lend Lease Section in the Procurement Division of the Treasury Department, or any agency of the foregoing." The prices were also established for hardwood lumber:

MILL PRICE TABLE—NORTHERN HARDWOOD LUMBER[447]
FOB MILL PRICE PER 1,000 FEET OF STANDARD OR NEAR STANDARD GRADES

BIRCH						
Thickness	*FAS*	*Selects*	*No. 1*	*No. 2*	*No. 3a*	*No. 3*
(FAS=First and Second)			*Common*	*Common*	*Common*	*Sound*
⅝"	$99	$53	$56.50	$37		
¾"	$111.50	$96.50	$62.50	$42.50		
1"	$131	$114	$75	$49.50	$41.50	$32

OAK						
Thickness	*FAS*	*Selects*	*No. 1*	*No. 2*	*No. 3a*	*No. 3*
(FAS=First and Second)			*Common*	*Common*	*Common*	*Sound*
1"	$91	$73.50	$61	$45	$34.50	$29
1¼"	$98	$80.50	$66.50	$48.50	$37	$30
1½"	$103.50	$86.50	$72.50	$49.50	$38	$31

These prices were per Appendix A but did not include the adjustment for kiln drying or air drying. The prices also did not include any adjustment for delivery or shipment. Per Appendix D, the shipping charges by truck were ruled to be at cost to the seller. The seller could add rail charges. However, if the lumber company hauled the lumber to the rail by truck and then loaded it by rail, the seller could not add, be reimbursed or bill for truck charges.[448]

Within the forest products industry, there were still the growing problems of price ceilings, shortages and supply to meet contracts. Attending the meeting were not only forest products industry representatives but also J.R. Neetzel of the United States Forest Service, Robert A. Parrington and George Wallner representing the War Production Board and E.J. Dunden of the Office of Price Administration. The minutes of the meeting stated that clarification was needed on Order No. 255 of the Office of Price Administration regarding "fixing ceiling prices within the states of Minnesota, Michigan, and Wisconsin and needed was an interpretation of the provision...Prices are f.o.b. common or contract carrier when a vehicle is available at the loading point at the time of delivery." The question was whether an extra charge would be made to load the railroad cars if no vehicle was available.

Issues of timber contracts and lumber supply continued. Illustrating the issue of logging contracts, the National Lumber Manufacturers' Association wrote to F. Drucker of the Northern Hemlock and Hardwood Manufacturers' Association, sending "fifty copies of the OPA's MPR-348, including Amendment 18 dated November 26, 1943."[449] Logging contract issues still lingered unresolved. The Office of Price Administration's price controls on logging contracts, MPR-348, was also onerous. The Timber Producers' Association sent a Western Union Telegram to the Lumber Branch of the office of Price Administration on April 22, 1943, petitioning the suspension of MPR-222, MPR-223 and MPR-348. The petition was signed by:[450]

Abbot M. Fox, Von Platen-Fox Company, Iron Mountain, MI
Vilas H. Ruhmore, C.M. Christiansen Company, Phelps, WI
Walter Gorman, Lake Superior Lumber Corporation, Ontonagon, MI
A.L. McBean, Edward Hines Lumber Company
W.W. Gamble Jr., Yawkey-Bissell Lumber Company, White Lake, WI
R.B. Goodman, Goodman Lumber Company, Goodman, WI
John Landon, Marathon Paper Mills Company, Ironwood, MI
H.H. Shopock, I. Stephenson Co. Wells, MI
Ray L. Prine, Michigan Dimension Company, Manistique, MI
J.D. Mylrea, Ahonen Lumber Co., Ironwood, MI
H.W. Johannos, Rib Lake Lumber Company, Rib Lake, WI
O.C. Lomko, Underwood Veneer Co., Wausau, WI
J.D. Mylrea, Thunder Lake Lumber Company, Rhinelander, WI
Munising Wood Products Company, Marquette, MI
S.D. Switzer, Oconto Company, Oconto, WI
Kurt Stoohr, Ray de Noguet Company, Nahma, MI

Tom Nordine, a logging contractor, represented the Timber Producers' Association of Upper Michigan and Northern Wisconsin in Chicago at a meeting with the Office of Price Administration. He said, "The price controls were imposed on the industry during WWII."[451] The Timber Producers' Association of Upper Michigan and Northern Wisconsin had passed a resolution, also at the April 27, 1944 meeting, regarding logging contract services:

> BE IT FURTHER RESOLVED, that the Association records its membership as being unanimously opposed to the establishment of a ceiling on contract services because of its belief that the widely varying conditions of contract logging services, which are rendered in the Lakes States area makes it impractical, if not entirely impossible, to establish a workable formula for the establishment of such ceiling price regulations on contract services.

Nordine, of Bruce Crossing, Michigan, worked with the pulp contractors, as well as the paper industry log buyers in Michigan and Wisconsin. He was later a board member of the Timber Producers' Association of Upper Michigan and Northern Wisconsin. The association was adamant in its opposition. Issues of ceiling prices on logs and production plus equipment problems would continue throughout the war years until the eventual Japanese surrender on September 2, 1945.

CHAPTER 11

TIRES, EQUIPMENT AND LUMBER SHORTAGES

Wisconsin children supported the war effort by canvassing their neighborhoods and having scavenger hunts for rubber bands, rubber balls and anything made of rubber that could be again used for tires. Scavenger hunters also sought scrap metal in early recycling for the war effort.

"War Machine Is Eating State's Timber Supply" was a blazing headline in the *Milwaukee Journal* on July 26, 1942.[452] To outfit each man in the military in 1942, it took five trees:

> *One makes possible his living quarters, mess halls, and chapels. Another provides the wooden crates necessary in shipping his food, clothing, tanks, and guns.*
>
> *Wood from the remaining three trees goes into the making of virtually every piece of equipment necessary in waging modern warfare—wood cellulose in high explosives, wood in training planes, wood in gun stocks, shipyards...*
>
> *By the end of the year 20,000,000 trees from our forests will be in the war backing up our fighting forces. Standing ten abreast and ten feet apart, this forest battalion would reach from New York to San Francisco.*[453]

The government had estimated a need of 38 billion bdf for 1942. That is enough lumber to "build a highway 30 feet wide and an inch thick 239,000 miles to the moon!"[454] As of July, lumber production was already 3 percent behind the 1941 total lumber consumption of 32.4 billion bdf.

Wisconsin's standing timber accounted for 16.6 billion bdf, and in 1941, Wisconsin had harvested 490 million bdf.[455] Much of Wisconsin's hardwood was being used for aircraft. In fact, Donald Nelson of the War Production Board had "asked lumber workers to give up vacations, draft boards to defer skilled forest and mill workers, operators to cut the best timber at once, and State governors to allow log hauling on Sundays."[456]

There were an estimated twenty-five thousand men working in the forest products industry. Sawmills were employing ten thousand men, with six thousand in veneer mills. It took a long time to train inexperienced men, and the result was reduced lumber production.

Wisconsin's wood uses were reported as the following:

Yellow birch…is now helping to drop bombs on Germany and Japanese outposts. Maple and basswood also go into planes. Maple and elm are used for sturdy trucks…maple, birch, white pine…for crates. Birch is second only to black walnut for gunstocks. Hemlock builds army cantonments.[457]

These uses did not include the paper and packaging industry. In fact, the War Production Board had perceived the shortages as important enough for packaging earlier in the year to conduct a survey to determine future policy regarding containers. The War Production Board had said:

We are now engaged in an all-out war effort. The war was not of our choosing. It was forced upon us by the Axis powers bent on world domination and enslavement. Some of our chief sources of supply of vital materials have been cut off for an indefinite period by the spread of war in the Southwest pacific and other sources are threatened. This, plus the tremendous demands of the Army and Navy, has resulted in shortages of materials used in the manufacture of containers.[458]

The Timber Producers' Association of Upper Michigan and Northern Wisconsin met on November 18, 1942, in Iron River, Michigan, to discuss the shortages of tires, equipment, raw materials and men.

THE TRUMAN COMMISSION ON FEDERAL REGULATION OF PRIVATE TIMBER LANDS

The Timber Producers' Association of Upper Michigan and Northern Wisconsin's concerns were manifested in Senator Harry Truman's investigation of the lumber industry, which began in December 1942. The reason for the investigation centered on why, in 1942 and potentially 1943, lumber war requirements were not going to be met. Over thirty-eight million board feet of lumber were needed, and the lumber industry was only going to produce thirty-two million board feet.

Truman's senatorial committee concluded, after the lumber industry testified, that the production was dependent on labor, which was in short supply, and equipment, which was also in short supply. "The Clapp Plan of the Forest Service would retard rather than increase production by the pirating of labor from manufacturers." C.M. Christiansen, president of C.M. Christiansen Company in Phelps, had written to the Truman Commission articulating those very points.[459] Other forest products industry representatives also testified that the army and navy specifications were too rigid. Dr. Wilson Compton, executive secretary/director of the National Lumber Manufacturers' Association in Washington, D.C., suggested consolidating the numerous agencies that were regulating the forest products industry because the bureaucracy was hindering lumber production.

The National Lumber Manufacturers' Association had been investigated in 1942 regarding the lumber standards. This was why lumber specifications were again addressed. Since the American Lumber Standards had been created in 1898 by the National Hardwood Lumber Manufacturers' Association and developed for the Weeks Act of 1911 for export, the standards were reaffirmed.

The Truman investigation was largely promulgated by the U.S. Forest Service's desire to co-opt not only all of the federal land but also state and private lands under the guise of ensuring the timber supply and management of timber for the war.[460] Hearings were held and reports were issued throughout the war; fortunately, the legislation was without success of implementation.[461] In a heavy-handed plan, all of the states were supposed to submit a plan for federal management of all timber lands within each state, to be approved by the secretary of agriculture. The Omnibus Forestry Bill would have withdrawn funding from the Clarke-McNary Act for any state in noncompliance.[462]

Truman's investigation subsequently came to an end, absolving the National Lumber Manufacturers' Association and thus the forest products industry nationally. Truman had a clearer understanding of the issue of why only thirty-two million bdf of lumber would be produced. Labor, equipment and restrictions were the problems resulting in low production outcomes.[463]

TIRE SHORTAGES

The Timber Producers' Association of Upper Michigan and Northern Wisconsin *Timber Producers' Association Bulletin* from January 1, 1942, said:

> *We have received a number of inquiries from members who want to know how they can get new tires for trucks and cars to replace those worn out. Since the recent order from Washington forbidding dealers to sell tires, many operators have been worried about getting replacements. Last week the Priorities Division of the O.P.A. announced the appointment of a State priority director...We have written Mr. Driscoll...informing him of the necessity of prompt action because of the limited hauling season during the period when iced and frozen roads are available as the only means of hauling timber over swamps, lakes, and streams.*[464]

This theme would be dealt with over and over again in the regional and national associations.

To try to alleviate the shortage problems, Donald Nelson, the War Production Board director, formed a Lumber Policy Committee. The Office of Price Administration hindered the process, contributing to the growing problem of equipment shortages. For example, tire shortages grew because the Office of Price Administration in July 1942 cut 364 trucks eligible for tires.[465]

The following table shows consumption of lumber in 1942 by the Armed Services:

LUMBER CONSUMPTION TABLE[466]

Army	1.75 billion bdf
Navy	250 million bdf
Shipyards	550 million bdf
American bases: Newfoundland, Greenland and Iceland	70 million bdf
Defense Housing	1.20 billion bdf
Total lumber in 1942	2.87 billion bdf

The 2.87 billion bdf was only a drop in the bucket for 1942 and far short of government estimates of total forest utilization.

O.T. Swan, secretary of the Northern Hemlock and Hardwood Manufacturers' Association in Oshkosh (and formerly of the U.S. Forest Service), reported shortages of tires, machinery and labor. The shortages were the reasons for lagging behind the 1941 figures. He estimated that 7,342 tires would need replacing. In the spring, Z.G. Driscoll, state director of commodity allotment, announced that "a supply of camelback material for re-treading tires has been allocated to this state…handled through the county tire boards. The matter of allocating new tires for passenger cars used by men engaged in supervising timber operations has been put up to Washington authorities for final decision."

Driscoll had already been to Washington, D.C., on behalf of the timber industry asking for an extra allotment of tires. The allotment "enable[d] operators to move their timber out of the swamps and to market before the spring break-up renders ice roads unfit for hauling." Synthetic rubber production plants were under construction.[467]

If timber operators needed new trucks, applications were sent to W.E. Hustleby, district director, Bureau of Motor Carriers in Minneapolis.[468] By June 1942, the Timber Producers' Association reported:

> We have sent out circular letters urging our members to use every precaution possible for tire conservation. We again call attention to the fact that the rubber supply is growing rapidly smaller and tires are going to be very hard to get in the near future.
>
> Mr. Eastman, who is Director of the nation's transportation facilities has *issued an order forbidding the hauling of any product by truck on highways* parallel to a railroad…In view of the scarcity of rubber and the difficulty in obtaining new tires or even retreads, it is up to everyone who has timber to haul…to save their tires and truck equipment in every way possible.
>
> …County Tire Boards have authority to refuse certificates to anyone who has let his tires wear too thin or who appears to have abused his tires, and the Tire Board may also refuse a certificate for the purchase of a new tire to any applicant who has failed to get his old tires retreaded in time.

The tire shortage was only at its beginning stages.

EQUIPMENT SHORTAGES

"Armed forces take 85% of the tractor production per month; leaving 15% for civilian and industrial use…79% of logs hauled from the woods to mill are on rubber tires. You know how necessary tires are to keep up lumber production."[469]

Again in 1943, meetings held by the Timber Producers' Association of Upper Michigan and Northern Wisconsin discussed "concerns about shortages of anti-freeze, repair parts for the equipment, tires, and chains for the trucks." The Timber Producers' Association meeting minutes record that

> *Mr. Eisele* [of the district office of the War Production Board] *stated that if there was a shortage of Prestone or other anti-freeze that the operators place his order with his dealer who, in turn, should immediately forward same fully itemized to his jobber or the producer of the material. The jobber then requests from the War Production Board an emergency rating and authorization to make delivery of the necessary quantity of Anti-Freeze for which definite orders have been placed.*
>
> *Charles Hutula suggested that the Equipment Committee, in cooperation with Mr. Eisele and the War Production Board Office, and the TPWP, endeavor to obtain a more adequate supply of repair parts for trucks and tractors. Several instances of delay from three weeks to four months have been experienced by operators in getting necessary repair parts for trucks during the past six month period.*[470]

The Timber Production War Project (TPWP) was under the auspices of the War Production Board. The United States Forest Service was the administrating agency, and it was under the Lumber and Lumber Products Division of the War Production Board. The idea of TPWP was to stimulate lumber production.[471]

In a resolution moved by Floyd Aldrige, seconded by Waino Komula and carried by a vote, the Timber Producers' Association of Upper Michigan and Northern Wisconsin:

> *RESOLVED, that the matter of increased allotment of tires to the logging industry of the district be referred to the equipment-tires-supplies committee of the Association, with instructions to take such steps as might be deemed advisable to assure the logging industry of a sufficient tire supply for the winter season, and that Mr. Culver* [district supply office of the

OPA] *be requested to take whatever steps he deemed advisable to assist in securing such increased allotment.*[472]

To assist with the multitude of shortages, the Timber Producers' Association Upper of Michigan and Northern Wisconsin had created committees:[473]

Membership Legislative Committee—Walter Henze

Log Bolts Committee—George Corrigan, successful logger in Wisconsin and Upper Peninsula of Michigan; later author of *Caulk Boots and Cant Hooks*

Pulpwood Ties and Mining Timbers Committee—Arvey Ahonen, Ahonen Lumber Company in Ironwood, Michigan

Sawmills Committee—Earl C. Poundstone, Penokee Veneer Company in Mellen Wisconsin; also in charge of Gogebic Lumber Company of Watersmeet, Michigan

Labor Manpower Committee—Charles Norem, Patton Lumber Company in Amasa, a subsidiary of Northern Paper Mills in Green Bay

Equipment/Supplies

Finance and Committee—Larry Peterson, logger east of Wakefield, Michigan, near Tula

When the Timber Producers' Association met, there were discussions of the "scaling and grading of veneer logs, price ceilings, less production prices for hemlock, labor supply problems caused by young men going off to war, log prices, travel time payments for loggers, meeting attendance in Washington, D.C. of the War Production Board, and meetings in Detroit and Lansing of the War Production Board."[474] In short, there were few aspects of the forest products industry in Wisconsin and Michigan that were not discussed.

The need for lumber was made even greater not only by a tire and truck shortage but also by the shortage of antifreeze, a critical component in Great Lakes states winter logging. In recognizing the shortage of antifreeze, the Timber Producers' Association of Upper Michigan and Northern Wisconsin said:[475]

The Lumber and Lumber Products Division of the WPB is making an effort to re-adjust the state quotas of Anti-Freeze for use in motor equipment by logging operators. They hope to provide larger quotas than were available in 1943.

Mr. McDonell of the Production Service Section requests that all operators of motor equipment in the timber producing industry put in their orders for

permanent type Anti-Freeze now. By doing so, you will be assured of an ample supply when you need it next winter. Also unresolved was the tire supply.

The annual meeting of the Timber Producers' Association of Upper Michigan and Northern Wisconsin had been held in mid-April, but it was reported in the May 1 *TPA Bulletin* that Office of Price Administration representatives from the Price Division (Mr. P.E. Zerby) and Tire Inspection and Distribution Services (Mr. V.A. Cooper)

warned truck operators that the quality of all new tires is poorer than formerly and that, therefore, it is more necessary than ever before that truck drivers give careful attention to the manufacturer's directions about air pressure and load weight or the consequences would be very expensive.[476]

The quality of the tires meant that logging trucks were in jeopardy if the tires on the trucks blew out.

The War Production Board reported that lumber production was "spotty… chiefly because of the shortage of tires for hauling." The lack of tires was nationwide.[477] The War Production Board revisited the tire rationing system and implemented a new certificate with a form to fill out with the idea to "simplify" the paperwork.

However, the Office of Price Administration chose to designate one War Price and Rationing Board as a "Truck Tire Board" to handle all applications for tires, tubes and recapping services by truck operators in the areas. An official "tire examiner" will be assigned to such areas…All inspections other than those recommending recapping, must be approved by the tire examiner, who will indicate his approval on the form.[478]

The Office of Price Administration order complicated the tire shortage. The OPA had already announced that the September quota of tires was 102,000. This was far short of the actual anticipated need of 150,000 heavy tires. The Lumber and Timber Products Committee composed of industry representatives had communicated with the National Lumber Manufacturers' Association, War Production Board, Office of Price Administration, the army and the assistant deputy rubber director regarding tire shortages.[479]

The Timber Producers' Association of Upper Michigan and Northern Wisconsin began again in September 1944 to warn its members about tires:

Heavy tires suitable for trucks engaged in hauling timber are scarce and are rapidly getting scarcer…It is up to each truck driver to make his tires last as long as he can. He must keep his speed down and not overload…The reasons cited for the scarcity were 1—A shortage of crude rubber and rayon cord stock, 2—A manpower shortage caused by the refusal of competent union tire builders to work more than 40 hours per week and also to the fact that many trained workers competent to build heavy truck tires have been drafted into military service.[480]

The implication of the lack of hours being worked by the union was in light of the many sawmill workers who were working over ninety hours per week. The lack of tires was also due to the "Army and Navy having first call on all tires produced and that means that civilian users must be satisfied with what is left." The Timber Producers' Association reported that the tire shortage was so acute that the "Army is considering the releasing of competent truck tire builders from selective service…where their services are most needed and are most important to the war effort."[481]

The Timber Producers' Association reminded the "timber trucker" to keep his equipment in good condition.

The Timber Producers' Association of Upper Michigan and Northern Wisconsin was justified in its tire concern. The War Production Board had sent to the National Lumber Manufacturers' Association "Emergency Recommendations for Use of Heavy Tires." These included a chart delineating the tire sizes, number of plies and the "load-carrying ability—pounds per tire." The War Production Board also warned of road maintenance issues regarding tire wear.[482] At the end of September, the War Production Board said:

Shortages of truck tires are now the chief factor curtailing lumber production. In the third quarter, 1944, there was a deficit of 124,000 tires for the lumber industry; in the fourth quarter, 1944, tires supplied to the industry will be about 150,000 less than known requirements. Total deficit of tires, as of January 1, 1945, is estimated to be 274,000 tires, of which 80 per cent are large tires (8.25 and larger).

WPB officials urged that in view of the serious tire shortage, trucks should be used only for hauling logs. Other means of transportation should be used for hauling lumber, whenever possible.[483]

The War Production Board painted a bleak picture for the continual tire shortage.

Although the lumber industry was a war priority industry and "tires for trucks moving logs from the woods to the mills are procured on No. 1

Tom Nordine, Bruce Crossing, Michigan. *Courtesy of Mike Monte, editor of* Pioneer Express, *Crandon, Wisconsin.*

priority, WPB officials said, but tires needed for moving lumber from the mills to the consumers are given only No. 3 priority."[484] No wonder there was a problem!

Tom Nordine explained the problem:

> *With a War Priority One, despite shortages of tires and men, we could cut and get the logs out of the woods. The problem came after the logs were out of the woods. The War Priority dropped from One to Three. Without trucks and equipment in good condition and gasoline shortages, we had to use the railroad, which added extra expense to the logging operation. We had to load the logs from the trucks in the woods to the railcars instead of taking the logs directly to the mill on the trucks.*
>
> *At the sawmill, the logs had to be offloaded from the railcars. The logs were then sawed into lumber. With a War Priority Three, there was no ability to rush the lumber to market. War Priority Three meant that transportation requirements for tires, gasoline and equipment were not as available. Therefore, the lumber would not get to market as quickly as it would have with a War Priority One.*[485]

The lumber shortage became acute.

Illustrating the reliance on trucks, the Roddis Plywood Corporation reported in the *Roddis Bulletin* on November 25, 1944: "The company has just purchased nine new semi-trucks for use at our seven camps, preparatory to a big logging season ahead…we will soon be in full swing at our logging camps with the cry of 'TIMBER' being heard thru the frosty air."[486] Logging in the north woods of Wisconsin was about to get underway.

The shortages of lumber, as well as labor, were illustrated by a list from the War Production Board. The materials listed were "insufficient for war and civilian demands (material substitution and supply)." They included Wisconsin species:

MATERIAL SUBSTITUTION TABLE[487]

Item	Authorized Substation
Hard Maple—First and Second (FAS) Selects	No. 1 in ¾" end thicker
Norway Pine—FAS	No. 2 and No. 3
White Ash	Selects, No. 1, No. 2
White Oak—FAS	Selects, No. 1
Yellow Birch—FAS	Selects, No. 1

These species were part of the list needed for war production. Other urgent orders were issued in July for "Navy Hardwood Requirements." The request for basswood would go to the navy yards in Boston and Charleston:

LUMBER REQUEST TABLE[488]

FOR BOSTON		
Size	Specie	Quantity in FBM
¾ x 6" and 8" R/L 12' to 16'	FAS Basswood	400,000'
¾ x 4" and 5" R/L 12' to 16'	FAS Basswood	200,000'
FOR CHARLESTON		
¾ x 4" & wider to avg. 8"	FAS Basswood	100,000'

FOB MILL, GOVERNMENT BILL OF LADING
National Hardwood Lumber Association rules apply, and certificate to accompany invoice. Cost of inspection, not to exceed $2.00 per thousand, may be added.

It was asked that the basswood be kiln dried or "thoroughly air dried."

Number one grades needed meant an even more difficult time meeting production requirements. Not only navy yards but also aircraft propeller manufacturers were short materials. In a War Production Board *Bulletin* entitled "WPB—Industry Cooperation Eases Propeller Problem," the story began:

> *In February of this year, there was considerable alarm among airplane propeller manufacturers as well as in the Aircraft Scheduling Unit...to obtain sufficient birch lumber to meet the requirements for the industry. The situation was brought on the attention of the Lumber and Lumber Products Division, WPB. Investigation showed that some of the lumber producers as well as secretaries of lumber associations were pessimistic. They declared it would be impossible to get the six million feet of lumber required for propellers.*[489]

Through strenuous work, cooperation and easement of import quotas and specifications, the lumber industry was finally able to provide the six million board feet for propellers.

Stumpage ceiling prices were an additional issue. This was promulgated by Maximum Price Regulation, or MPR-165, on June 16, 1943, by Office of Price Administration:

> *Ceilings on contract logging services—the top prices a contractor can charge for existing logs, half logs or cordwood from standing trees for the owner of the timber—have been transferred to Maximum Price Regulation No. 165 (Services). The Office of Price Administration announced today. The action will result in no increase in lumber prices, OPA said...*
>
> *Under Maximum Price Regulation No. 165, maximum prices for contract logging are to be based on the prices the contractor charged during the month of March, 1942, the same base date as was used to determine ceiling prices under the General Maximum Price Regulation.*[490]

The Office of Price Administration admitted that a profit was not possible under the March 1942 prices, even with adjustments:

> *Under the adjustment procedure, a contractor and an owner of standing trees jointly may adjust the final contract logging figure to an agreed amount reflecting any increased component costs. The upward adjustment must represent only the actual increase in cost of labor and materials, and the*

owner of the trees must agree to absorb the increase, and not pass it on in higher prices charged for the end products, such as lumber, which he may make out of the logs...

Within fifteen days prior to the use of the adjusted contract price, the contractor and the timber owner jointly must file with the OPA a simple statement of facts related to the adjustment on a form which may be obtained from OPA—form 687:116.

The absurdity of these restrictions was clear. The Office of Price Administration told the industry to pass the increased labor and material charges along to the consumer, i.e., the government, and penalized the business. The forest product associations were vexed by these Office of Price Administration restrictions.

Under MPR-460, when submitting a bid for a timber sale, the bidder had to justify the bid as contributing to the war effort. MPR-460 was adopted on August 31, 1943, but the "maximum selling price of all standing timber...is based upon the appraised values of publicly owned timber...the maximum price at which standing timber may be sold is the appraised price of the nearest comparable tract of publicly owned timber sold since September 1, 1942."[491] This limited competitive bidding because the bidder could only bid to the maximum bid of a previous sale. More importantly, the established prices to fulfill the contract were less than what it cost to actually recoup the cost of production.

The minutes of the November 12, 1943 Timber Producers' Association of Upper Michigan and Northern Wisconsin meeting record:

Waino Komula indicated that the present shortage of hemlock lumber was in no small way attributable to the $24.00 ceiling price of hemlock. Komula further indicated that the average stumpage price of hemlock in the district was $3.00, the loading coast, $2.50, and a logging cost from $21.00 to $25.00 per M' [per thousand]. Komula indicated that under present stumpage and loading cost, which totaled $5.50, that it was impossible to produce hemlock logs for $18.50; that as long as the present ceiling continued on hemlock that there would be a very restricted production on hemlock...[It was] suggested that the matter be referred to the Log-Bolt Committee with instructions to immediately file an application with the OPA to increase prices of hemlock logs to $27.00 per M' and Woods Run Maple to $35.00 per M' [from $32.00].[492]

As it turned out, dissatisfaction was expressed about the prices of white birch and white birch veneer. They were also added to the Office of Price Administration application. Logging operations were experiencing a loss because of stumpage ceiling prices and ceiling prices on lumber.

The Timber Producers' Association of Upper Michigan and Northern Wisconsin had a number of other price issues. MPR-348, regarding price restrictions on log bolts, caused a furor with corporations and other associations around the country. The Appalachian Hardwood Manufacturers' Association and National Lumber Manufacturers' Association were united in their objections.[493] MPR-348 established "log ceiling prices on logs delivered by truck." However, included was a surcharge based on distance of hauling that the supplier would have to pay to transport the logs. The Timber Producers' Association and the Northern Hemlock and Hardwood Manufacturers' Association filed objections with the War Production Board:

> *Persons holding small blocks of timber which have been under log contract, have begun to cancel these contracts (example, Pine Lumber Company, Park Falls, has lost two million feet), rather than absorb the delivery charge. They say that they can use a portable mill at the wood lot, and thus get maximum lumber and maximum log prices at the timber. This idea will spread with a resulting scattered manufacture of poorly made and graded lumber, more likely absorbed locally in some cases, the loss of some wood lot logs will be the margin which will cause one of the larger mills to give up. The Wisconsin Land and Lumber had that element in their difficulties when they closed September 1.[494]*

The Northern Hemlock and Hardwood Manufacturers' Association also filed a potential amendment: "The price for logs delivered to the mill by truck from within 35 miles of the plant shall be the same as f.o.b. cars prices. In the event the logs being delivered to the mill by truck from regions in excess of 35 miles from the buying plant the buyer may add not to exceed $1.00 per thousand feet log scale for every 10 miles or fraction thereof."[495] It was suggested that the specific miles could be adjusted depending on distance hauling logs to the railroad, road conditions and logging cost.

With shortages of logs, there was also a shortage of hemlock pulp. Amazingly, by the fall of 1943, some paper and pulp mills were down to one week's supply.[496] The shortage was considered so important that Sunday sermons stressed it. Women went into the woods to cut pulp.

The Pulpwood Parade. *Courtesy of Great Lakes Timber Professionals' Association, Rhinelander, Wisconsin.*

Tom Nordine was chairman of the Timber Producers' Association Pulpwood Committee. The price for pulpwood was eight to nine dollars a cord. He was cutting eight thousand cords per year. Dealing with all the paper companies, Nordine was logging by hand, without power saws. Although they had been invented and were encouraged for war use, the saw did not come to his operation until 1948. Men were in short supply.

Nordine was horse logging, hauling the logs to the side of the road, loading logs with an A-frame loader on the truck and finally loading the pulp in railroad cars at the siding. In getting timber contracts, Nordine also encouraged and worked with farmers to get pulp logs from their lands.[497]

To ease the pulp shortage, "county agents contacted farm woodlot owners and war bonds were offered as prizes for best-appearing and largest loads of wood at the Roundup. The climax was a grand parade down the street of Tomahawk, [Wisconsin,] on October 23, 1943…125 trucks and the biggest production since the war began."[498]

The parade was held in cooperation with the Timber Producers' Association of Upper Michigan and Northern Wisconsin. The Timber Producers' Association responded by working with the Northern Wisconsin Victory

Pulpwood Committee. It had begun the "Pulpwood Roundup" to encourage cutting and "publish[ed] a Pulpwood Tabloid." The Pulpwood Roundup was also sponsored by the War Production Board, United States Forest Service, Wisconsin State Conservation Board and the forest products industry.[499]

Lumber requirements at the same time were staggering. The 9.596 billion board feet that had been estimated for the third quarter of 1944 was reduced to a final quota of 9.152 billion bdf. Lumber required for the army, navy, Aircraft Resources Control Office, Maritime Commission, Foreign Economic Administration and Canadian Division, collectively, was first set at 1,669,051,000 bdf; this was reduced to 1,614,000,000 board feet in order to keep the overall total within the limits of supply. Included in some of the 1.6 billion bdf lumber used were:

LUMBER USAGE TABLE[500]

Application	Amount in Board Feet
Shipbuilding	135,546,000
Building Materials	37,014,000
Containers	1,871,337,000, which was already over the total allotment
Lumber and Lumber Products	1,128,419,000
Paper	24,615,000
Total	**1.6 billion bdf lumber**

Even though lumber production had increased nominally during the third quarter, the War Production Board reported continued shortages of Great Lakes state species with "grades of basswood, eastern hemlock, eastern white pine, hard maple, hickory, northern white pine, Norway pine, red oak, soft elm, soft maple, walnut, white ash, white oak, yellow birch."[501]

Despite the shortages, the May lumber production in the Great Lakes states (Michigan, Minnesota and Wisconsin) was reported in July by the War Production Board as 124,000,000 bdf, a 59 percent increase from 1943.[502] This was approximately 10 percent of the national total. J. Phillip Boyd, director of the Lumber Division of the War Production Board, sent a letter addressed to "The Lumber Industry" dated July 25, 1944, spelling out lumber's demand:

Now, when we are closer to the end of the war, although we all realize it is still a long way off...I want to assure the members of the industry that lumber demands are continuing in excess of supply and that every stick produced by the industry can find an essential use in the war program. Temporary mal-adjustments of supply and demand, however, cannot be avoided. Under WPB Order L-335 local and temporary surpluses may develop if local production or local availability of lumber is in excess of authorized purchase orders. On the other hand, the Lumber Division learns almost daily of demands for lumber of all types which are not being met. The Division, through its field Lumber Advisers, Timber Production War Project personnel, the Washington office, is prepared to assist producers and distributors in channeling their lumber to war uses if normal trade channels do not produce a ready market.[503]

This was an admission that L-335 was causing bottlenecks and that the overall goal to meet the war effort was inefficient. Shortages of tires, equipment, lumber and distribution were still issues.

CHAPTER 12

CONCLUSION

D uring World War II, the men and women who worked for the forest products industry in Wisconsin and the Upper Peninsula of Michigan provided millions of board feet of timber for national defense. Whether in the woods and logging camps, log yards, sawmills or manufacturing lumber, plywood and veneer war products, the civilian side on the homefront took pride in their contribution of winning the war. Many marched off to war and fought bravely "in the face of mortal combat."

The war began in Europe in late 1939, and the reaction in the United States in the manufacturing sector was almost instantaneous. The economic impact was reflected in the "Comparison of Sales—Laona" for the Connor Lumber and Land Company:

LUMBER SALES TABLE[504]

Year	Amount
1939	$695,082.78
1940	$805,240.75
1941	$1,259,444.40

The crescendo of the war was also demonstrated with the Adjusted Earnings Statement of the Yawkey-Bissell Lumber Company in White Lake, dated September 30, 1945:

YAWKEY-BISSELL LUMBER COMPANY
ADJUSTED EARNINGS TABLE[505]

Period	Amount
1938–1939	$53,452.97
1940–1941	$289,650.46
1941–1942	$361,753.93

As the United States was assisting England with the Lend-Lease program, wood was in demand. As World War II progressed, the timber industry and sawmills, like Yawkey-Bissell, were running three shifts to keep up with demand.

The exigencies of war continued into 1944, particularly manifested in demand for wooden aircraft and wood substitute materials. The forest products industry strained to meet not only aircraft production but lumber quotas in general. Issues related to the trials of wages and price ceilings, impositions of government regulations and equipment shortages were constant distractions to the job of providing lumber for the war effort. Manufacturing issues were hampered by price ceilings and production restrictions despite the exhortations of the War Production Board.

According to the War Production Board, in December 1943 alone, the Great Lakes states had produced 82.1 million board feet of lumber out of a December nationwide total of 2.6 billion bdf. During the same year, the plywood industry had been producing aircraft plywood "at the rate of approximately 8 Million feet per month." Other uses with anticipated increase in 1944 were described as:

ANTICIPATED PLYWOOD USAGE TABLE[506]
IN BILLION BDF

USE	1941	1942	1943
Boxing, Crating	5.50	9.546	
Dunnage			
Agriculture			2.530
General Industrial Commodities			4.000
Military			9.970
Factory	4.12	4.242	4.270

USE	1941	1942	1943
Civilian Construction	22.77	17.230	11.390
All Other			
Military Construction	5.00	12.135	6.625
Total	**37.39**	**43.153**	**38.785**

Of the 1943 total of 38,785 billion board feet of lumber used, "approximately 87 per cent of this total is for direct and indirect military use." Military use of lumber had been estimated as 7.284 billion board feet in the first quarter of 1944.

Wisconsin's industry, as well as the many men and women who were fighting so bravely, participated in D-Day on June 6, 1944, directly or indirectly. Wisconsin's timber industry was not the only industry experiencing shortages. Exemplifying the preparations feverishly leading up to D-Day and shortages of basic material for manufacturing, Auto Body Works, Inc. in Appleton had a "Priority" government contract to provide trailers for D-Day but was behind in the production schedule because of the lack of steel for four-inch tubing. An army captain arrived in Appleton as an "Expediter" to obtain steel for the trailer production and met with Eugene Pierce, president of Auto Body Works. Pierce explained that there was a steel shortage despite the priority and a delay. The captain expedited the steel. The trailers were manufactured and arrived at the seaport ready for shipment for D-Day. On D-Day, the trailers were towed by jeeps,[507] hauling tires and double tanks of gasoline to support the troops after landing.

On the homefront, by June 1944 the National Lumber Manufacturers' Association had established a Committee of Forest Conservation headed by G.F. Jewett of Potlatch Lumber Company; a Sub-Committee on Glue headed by T.D. Perry, chairman; and a Sub-Committee on Fabrication with A.S. Freidman and Verne Ketchum representing TECO industries. Among the Board of Directors were George Gerlinger, president; A.J. Glasscow, president of the American Forest Product Industries; Daniel K. Brown of Wisconsin's Neenah Paper Company and president of the American Paper and Pulp Association; John McClure, National Hardwood Lumber Association; and H.S. Crosby, Northern Hemlock and Hardwood Manufacturers' Association. Wisconsin was wisely represented.

The Timber Producers' Association of Upper Michigan and Northern Wisconsin reported that "the lumber situation continues to be critical; doubtless it will become increasingly so as the pace of the war accelerates."

The Timber Producers' Association communication was just before D-Day, June 6; the war would indeed accelerate. The regional trade associations were in constant contact with the National Lumber Manufacturers' Association, working cooperatively with the War Production Board and the Lumber and Lumber Products Division: "This week logging and lumbering were placed on the 'Production Urgency List' by the Production Executive Committee. This, lumber is included in the urgency list for first consideration in needs for labor. This action by representatives of the major war agencies re-affirms the War Production Board's previous statement that lumber is an extremely critical item."[508]

Another primary demand for lumber was for packaging, crating and boxing all the military materials needed in Europe and the Pacific. It was estimated, for example, that a 2,360-pound jeep needed "784 pounds of material about 85% of which is lumber and the rest moisture-proof paper and other corrosion preventative material."[509]

LUMBER REQUIREMENTS TABLE[510]
PACKING, CREATING AND BOXING

Year	Lumber in Board Feet
1941	5,500,000,000
1942	9,546,000,000
1943	16,500,000,000
1944 (estimated)	17,000,000,000

The United States Forest Products Laboratory stated without hesitation that its major contribution to World War II was the development of packaging materials.[511] Of the thirty-nine billion board feet of lumber of estimated use in 1942, it was estimated that eight billion board feet alone would be used for boxing and crating. This included not only military packaging but also civilian supplies abroad and requirements under the Lend-Lease program.

The Timber Producers' Association of Upper Michigan and Northern Wisconsin concurred with that assessment in 1944:

Experts have developed new plans and designs for crates and boxes...It has been estimated that this wartime research and study of crating, and packaging which has been going on for the past two or three years, has affected a saving which might not have been accomplished in a decade if the countries had not been faced by the great need for this material and the shortage of lumber to supply it.[512]

Research occurred with packaging materials made from paper, as well as lumber. However, the critical need for lumber meant that demand outstripped supply.

The gap between consumption and production in 1942 and 1943, necessitated heavy withdrawal from stocks. Stocks have declined from about 17,000,000,000 bdf at the beginning of 1941 to about 7,000,000,000 bdf. Hence, cuts in requirements, as reported, had to be made. The over-all amount allotted for the third quarter by the WPB Requirements Committee is 9,152,000,000 bdf, which equals the estimated supply for this quarter.[513]

The estimated use of 9.1 billion board feet for the third quarter of 1944 was over half of the amount estimated for the entire year.

The 1940's became a propitious time for change...retaining forest beauty. The advent of Caterpillar road building equipment developed in World War II could set up permanent forest paths for not only thinning and harvesting but for protection from the forest enemies of fire and insect blights. Building logging roads no longer needed wheeler-scrapers pulled by horsepower. Tractors and bulldozers took over...Then began the power saws, the end of railroad logging and the rail miles to maintain, the end of moving logging camps, the end of providing supplies or moving men for the camps.[514]

The 1945 New Year rang in with great expectations for war to end. Peace expectations meant that "Reconversion" to a peacetime economy would bring some uncertainty. Still, out of the war, new technologies advanced that meant a revolution in the lumber industry.

In patriotic fervor, lumberjacks were encouraged to use the new power saws rather than crosscut saws to increase log production in the woods. The first power saws were two-man models that weighed 150 pounds. Shortly after the war, through ingenuity and necessity, power saws had been reduced in weight to 70 pounds.

Gordon R. Connor, past president and chairman of the Board of Connor Forest Industries, said in 1981:

Power saws did not really come into full use until after World War II. Apparently, the first power saw was invented in Germany in 1926 by the Stihl's. Power saw development and usage was slower in the United States…

I think we had one of the first power saws in the Lake States. This was a German saw. At Connor Forest Industries, we had one early 150 pound two-man Titan power saws during World War II. Manpower was short and the pressure was on to use power saws and power machinery.

…We used these early power saws mainly for cutting wood at the logging camps. Camps required at least two men to constantly cut and provide fire wood for the Bunkhouses and Cook Shanty. These heavy, unhandy, hard to handle saws were not seriously considered for woods work until the single man power saws were developed in 1946–1948.[515]

The "modern" power saw now weighed approximately forty-eight pounds.

Still, lumberjacks were not too enthused about the power saw. Some, like the Miljevich brothers from Wakefield, Michigan, were "Gippos," or independent contractors, working for the Connor Lumber and Land Company. They could cut through a log faster than the power saw. They

World War II two-man power saw, Wakefield, Michigan. *Courtesy of Camp 5 Museum Foundation/Wisconsin Forestry Museum, Laona, Wisconsin.*

were guests on an early 1950s television game show, *I've Got a Secret*, to prove it.

The "modern" power saw also allowed "whole armies of 'Ma and Pa' and family pulpwood cutters [to enter] the woods. They still turn out a goodly pulpwood harvest for the state's hungry paper mills."[516] This new five-horsepower power saw could be yours for $500.

The largest sawmills throughout central and northern Wisconsin had been sawing over twenty-nine million board feet of lumber per year.[517] In Wakefield, Michigan, the Connor mill in 1943 had shipped lumber valued over $500,000.[518]

Supplying hardwoods for aircraft propellers at G.B. Lewis in Watertown and Sensenich, C.M. Christiansen Company had bought and sold timber lands throughout World War II as timber was cut for the war effort.

By September 1945, Roddis Plywood Corporation had purchased another sawmill in Ironwood, Michigan, from Marathon Corporation of Rothschild, Wisconsin. Included in the purchase was twenty-five thousand acres in Wisconsin and the Upper Peninsula of Michigan.[519]

Official Program

Second Annual Lake States Logging Congress

Houghton   Michigan

October 30-31 & November 1, 1947

Sponsored by

Timber Producers Association of Upper Michigan and Wisconsin

Timber Producers' Association Logging Congress program. *Courtesy of Tom Nordine, Bruce Crossing, Michigan.*

There was a supply of 3.1 million tons of wood pulp available for production. Of that, 2.6 million tons was from the United States, with the remainder from Canadian imports.[520] Lumber production nationally to date was reported in September as 32 billion bdf for 1944 and 29 billion bdf for 1945.[521]

In the timber industry, technology advanced with dramatic changes. "The first Logging Congress occurred on November 1 and 2nd, 1945 in Houghton, Michigan."

Under Gordon R. Connor's leadership, "Logging Congress" grew and traveled to venues throughout Wisconsin and Upper Michigan, "encouraging greater exposure and participation."[522] The focus was to demonstrate and experience new techniques in logging and heavy equipment. The now Timber Producers' Association of Upper Michigan and Northern Wisconsin Logging Congress exhibitors showed the latest developments in sawmill equipment, portable sawmills and logging equipment, including forwarders and tractors.[523]

In the timber industry, Gordon R. Connor said:

The development of large trucks was a major logging improvement. Single axle trucks, inadequate for the job were replaced by multiple drives and trucks were equipped with much larger tires. The increase in the hauling capacity of these machines was outstanding. Larger engines, heavier frames and springs along with diesel engines, improved hauling and handling of timber harvest. Two tier trucks have now become common, along with a loaded truck pulling an additional load on a pup trailer.[524]

Gordon R. Connor, Connor Lumber and Land Company. *Author's collection.*

Many of the logging roads were railroad beds reconstructed for trucks. In early truck logging, the trucks often were stuck as the roads were narrow, snow covered and icy. The original roads were plank roads but were improved as road-making equipment with big bulldozers developed.

Wisconsin's forest products industry had provided lumber

for aircraft, ships, army and navy bases and ordnance depots like Wisconsin's own Badger Ordnance Works in Baraboo. Wisconsin shipped billions of board feet of lumber to both the Pacific and Europe. America's Allies, especially the British, had relied on Wisconsin's forest products.

Connor said in 1981:

> *Railroad camps ended during and after World War II. We then had an entire new modern technology and what we call the "Gasoline Era." Remote railway logging camps gave way to permanent roads built by big bulldozers. Lumberjacks became settled family men, owning their own tools and driving to work in the family car. The industry finally had a more stable work force as well as many independent jobbers on which to rely.*[525]

Some loggers were independent "Gippos" and had contracts with the lumber companies. Many lumberjacks still worked for the lumber companies directly but went home each night. The logs were no longer hauled to the sawmills by railroad but by large trucks on a permanent road network.

Sawmill technology also changed. The large circular saws were supplanted with bandsaws, and the sawmill carriage was reinvented by Francis Cleereman of Newald, Wisconsin, revolutionizing the sawmill equipment industry.[526] Cleereman returned from Berlin in 1945.

New forest products, many invented during the war, became major industries. New

Francis Cleereman, later of Cleereman Industries, Newald, Wisconsin, with a Russian soldier in Berlin in 1945. *Courtesy of Mike Monte, editor of the* Pioneer Express, *Crandon, Wisconsin.*

Winter logging scene. *Courtesy of Tom Nordine, Bruce Crossing, Michigan.*

Bulldozer working on a Roddis Lumber and Veneer Company winter logging road, Park Falls, Wisconsin. *Courtesy of Camp 5 Museum Foundation/Wisconsin Forestry Museum, Laona, Wisconsin.*

technologies evolved. Leo Heikenen of Prentice founded his company in 1945 as a "chainsaw-repair and machine shop"[527] and developed the hydraulic loader. "Mechanical truck-mounted 'jammers,' like the one shown [above] came into use during World War II, when manpower shortages forced loggers and pulpwood-cutters to mechanize. Winches were made from the rear axles of old automobiles and trucks."[528]

Heikenen was a Wisconsinite from Brantwood. From 1941 to 1944, he worked in Milwaukee in a large machine shop "producing defense components."[529] At the urging of his brother, who operated Heikenen Brothers Construction and Logging, he moved to the Prentice area in 1945 to start his own machine-shop business. Working on mechanical jammers, Heikenen "patented a special tear drop log lifting winch for jammers." From the "cat jammer" to hydraulic loaders, the little machine shop would grow to the "Heikenen Machine Shop…a multi-million dollar worldwide leader, with 51% of the market share marketing the hydraulic loader worldwide."[530] Heikenen's success was lauded by *Timber Harvesting Magazine*: "Prentice Wisconsin's Leo Heikenen likely produced the first and perhaps only true forerunner to today's knuckleboom. Heikenen generally gets credit for first harnessing hydraulic power and using it to improve the design of his mechanically operated truck-mounted boom winch/cable hoist, or jammer."[531] A smaller crew of lumberjacks and one-man loading operation could load logs onto the back of the truck.

Along with the Prentice loader, woods crews worked with newly developed caterpillar tractors and bulldozers. The shortage of labor during World War II meant the creation of new equipment to move logs to the sawmills. Regarding bulldozers, Connor said, "Bulldozers of the 1940s and big caterpillar tractors made possible permanent road systems which in turn hastened the evolution of bigger trucks, bigger skidders, and bigger loaders. The transition was fortunate because the railroads were providing no innovations and were not providing sufficient log cars."[532]

Caterpillar tractors were advertised as "all around graders."[533] Connor continued, "Many loggers regarded the first big equipment dubiously. When my brother, Richard M. Connor, bought his first bulldozer with its 12 foot blade, the woods crew asked how they could ever be expected to get through the forest rock and trees with a twelve foot wide blade."[534]

The forest products industry was a priority industry mobilized during World War II.

An early Prentice loader. *Courtesy of Dale Heikenen, Heikenen Collection, Prentice, Wisconsin.*

The demand for forest products during World War II was truly insatiable. Wood in the form of lumber, plywood, paper, plastics, and other materials appeared in countless war uses. Some 25,000 trainer aircraft and gliders were made of wood and plywood. Wood was used in great quantities to build fighting ships, including minesweepers, submarine chasers, PT boats, and even battleships, not to mention the swarm of landing craft so important for amphibious invasion. Each minesweeper and subchaser contained enough timber to build ten average houses while the famous PT boat—constructed of spruce keels, mahogany planking, and plywood hulls—used 28,000 board feet of wood. The decking for the average battleship consumed 200,000 board feet of lumber and in the construction of the "Liberty" ship, nearly 700,000 board feet of lumber were used in shipway, staging, and scaffolding.

Three hundred thousand prefabricated dwelling units—together with vast numbers of conventional construction—were built largely of wood and plywood to house the multitude of workers that thronged to production centers of the Nation, while many thousands of other wood structures were erected at military encampments around the country and abroad. Government statistics reveal it required 1,400 board feet of lumber to house each fighting man, 300 feet to send him overseas, and 50 feet per month to keep him supplied...

...The tremendous quantities of lumber required for packaging materials of war. When it is realized that over 700,000 different military items had to be shipped overseas for the North African campaign... Lumber requirements for boxing and crating increased steadily from 1942 to 1944 nearly 17 Billion Board Feet of lumber. Nearly half the total lumber consumption was consumed in domestic and military packaging...For example, each 105mm Howitzer took 711 board feet, each 40 mm Bofors antiaircraft gun required 1,040 feet, while each giant bomber shipped overseas consumed 5,000 board feet of blocking and crating lumber.[535]

Charles Nelson's report of the contribution of the United States Forest Product's Laboratory's wood research on aircraft design and production is comprehensive.

The American forest products industries contributed much to the successful prosecution of the Second World War. In the process many of these industries assumed roles that were very strange to them. Furniture factories built gliders; lumber manufacturers produced truck bodies; plywood plants fabricated boats; as they undertook a variety of, for them, unusual functions,

Allis Chalmers D-5 bulldozer. *Courtesy of Camp 5 Museum Foundation/ Wisconsin Forestry Museum, Laona, Wisconsin.*

they developed new and exciting technologies that were effective in war and in some instances promised to be equally useful when directed toward peacetime manufacturing objectives.[536]

By the end of World War II, it was estimated that the United States had built:[537]

ESTIMATED U.S. WORLD WAR II PRODUCTION QUANTITY TABLE[538]

Quantity	Item
86,338	Tanks
297,000	Airplanes
17,400,000	Rifles and Side Arms
315,000	Field Artillery Pieces and Mortars
4,200,000	Artillery Shells
41,400,000,000	Rounds of Ammunition
6,500	Navy Ships
5,400	Cargo Ships
64,500	Landing Vessels

Over 12 million Americans had served their country. There were over 19 million more women and men who were employed in industries in the United States than had been employed in 1939;[539] 35 percent of the employees were women. Over 200,000 women were in the military by 1945.[540] Women had worked on the civilian side of the war effort as well, providing war materials.

It was estimated at the conclusion of World War II that the United States had used 215 billion board feet of lumber, or ten million acres of forests. That is the equivalent of 7.5 million football fields. The 215 billion board feet equals 40,312,903,103 eight-foot two-by-fours. If you laid the two-by-fours end to end, it would circle the globe 2,450 times, for 61 million miles. More impressively, it would reach the moon and back 120 times, for 238,862 miles. In terms of plywood used to cover all the wings of the gliders built, it is the equivalent of 27 million square feet, or 3,218 football fields.[541]

"Lumber Goes to War." *Courtesy of Northwestern University Archives, Evanston, Illinois.*

Wisconsin's "flying trees" flew over Europe and Asia. Wisconsin's sawmills supplied wing material, propellers and aircraft pieces and parts. With the research of the United States Forest Products Laboratory in Madison and the University of Wisconsin, the timber industry advanced the victory in World War II. The sawmills and paper mills provided lumber and materials for crating, houses, camps, battleships, cargo ships, battlements, aircraft and materials for Wisconsin's ammunition suppliers in new designs.

The numbers are impressive and a credit to Wisconsin and the Upper Peninsula's timber industry's ingenuity. Most importantly, this story is a tribute to the civilian women and men who worked so hard with dedication and perseverance in the forest products industry. It is an honor to tell their story and the story of the Wisconsin men who made the ultimate sacrifice and were veterans who flew "Wisconsin's Flying Trees" into "the face of mortal combat."[542] They are truly America's "Greatest Generation."[543]

CONNOR LUMBER AND LAND COMPANY

WORLD WAR II SERVICEMEN, LAONA, WISCONSIN

"Proudly We Pay Tribute to Members of Our Organization Who Answered the Call to the Colors"
*Denotes in Memory

Kenneth Allen
Emil Altaus
Orlan Andrews
*Edward Aschenbrenner
John Aschenbrenner
Theo Barnes Jr.
Edward Barney
Ray Bartlein
John Batease
Peter Baumgartner
Homer Belland
Mike Belland
P. Harvey Belland
Carl Betker
Roy Betker
*Clarence Beyers
Donald Bineham

Henry Boggs
Robert Bohman
Joe Bouck
Delbert Bowling
Charles Bowman
Anton Bradle Jr.
Donald Bradle
Frances Bradle
Robert Bradle
Gilbert Bradley
Eugene Breaker
Royal Breaker
Donald Brunkalla
Chester Brushafer
Ervin Brushafer
Clarence Bull
Ivan Calhoun

Clinton Chapman
Joseph Chitko
Douglas Collins
Elaine Collins
Kenneth Collins
Norman Collins
Lyle Conley
W.D. Connor Jr.
W.D. Connor III
*Arnold Cook
Theodore Cronick
Walter Crowley
Kasmer Dauksavage
Russell Dault
Walter Dault
Darrell Davis
Robert Davis
Osbert Derickson
Albert Di Ulio
Henry Drzweicke
Edward Duda
Fred Elam
Reinhart Elbe
*Robert Elfors
Harold Ernest
Frank Feucht
Leo Feucht
Clifford Flannery
Robert Flynn
Joe Fredericks
Robert Gentz
Earl Gibson
Albert Gillen
Elton Glenn
Edwin Godin
Lloyd Godin
Roy Godin
Stewart Hagen
Howard Hammes

Walter Hanson
Alfred Harris
Alois Hartel
Clarence Hendricks
Manley Homan
Isaac Hoyt
Ed Huff
Oliver Jacobs
Anton Jacubic
Peter Jaros
Oliver Johnson
Milo Jones
James Kadsow
Alvin Kalkhafen
Frank Kanack
Paul Kevilus
Vincent Kextel
Dale Kimball
Donovan King
Elmer King
Frank Kopecky
Chester Krause
Edward Krause
William Krauter
Otto Kuester
Melvin Kuntz
*Wenzel Kust
James Lacey
David La Fontain
Donald Lambert
Donald Lane
Leafy Lane
Herman Lange
Dorothy Lawrence
Charles Lawson
*Oliver Leichter
Edward Lemerande
Ernest Lewis
Theo Lewis

Porter Lockard
Rondal Lykins
Harley Magee
Harold Majeski
Ludger Majeski
Justin Mallow
Walter Manlick
*Chester Masel
John Masel
Harley Mentz
Arthur Mihalko
Floyd Mihalko
John Milak
Dale Miller
Arthur Newman
Donald Oettinger
Edward Oettinger
Marcellus Oettinger
Sylvester Oettinger
Ervin Olson
Ernest Ovitz Jr.
R.K. Palmer
Robert Pankratz
Robert Pantzer
Stanley Paszek
*Melvin Pearson
Andy Peterson
Walter Pitzlow
Joe Pivonka
Lewis Plummer
Ray Plummer
Clarence Powell
John Power
Albert Puza
Adrew Quella
Max Randall
Philip Rasmussen
Max Ratty
Delore Raymond

Richard Raymond
Glynton Roberts
Fred Rouse
Don Rudolph
Kurt Schneeweis
Karl Schneider
*Michael Seeman
Floyd Seversen
Frank Sharnek Jr.
George Sharnek
Milton Shelly
Rudolph Shodie
Victor Siefert
Gerald Simonis
Dale Slimmer
Frank Slimmer
Floyd Sorenson
Andy Stadjahar
Curis Starks
Norbert Stauber
Francis Sturzl
Richard Sturzl
Ed Summer
Harry Suppanz
Joe Synon
Virgil Tackett
Fred Thomas
Roy Thomas
Sterling Tipton
Francis Van Opens
Marvin Wald
Roscoe Walters
Adrian Webb
Willard Webb
George Weidner
David White
Glen Whitt
Roderick Williams
Edgar Wilson

Herbert Wilson
Arthur Winkelman
Ralph Wooland
Arleigh Yeager
Roy Yeager

CONSOWELD CORPORATION EMPLOYEES

A hdawagam Company became Consoweld Corporation and a subsidiary of Consolidated Paper Company in Wisconsin Rapids.

Jerry Altman
Gail Gene Anderson
Arne Arnesen
Jim Bowen
Barnard Bronk
Don Brown
Gerald Buhmbre—Rudolph
Mamie Buhmbre—Rudolph
Jon Cook—Nekoosa
Sandy Cook—Nekoosa
Jerry Delaney—Port Edwards
Dick Dent
William Eggett
Duke Ellregson
Gilbert "Gib" Endrezzi
Don Farresh

Bernie Flannery
Walter Fredette
Roger Gunz
J. Hein
Bill Hiles
Leroy Honeyard
Jim Hoogesteger
Dennis Jacob—Nekoosa
Don Jacobs—Nekoosa
John Jacobs—Nekoosa
Tom Jeffrey
Jim Johnson
Phil Johnson
Jim Kawleski
Gary Kessimer
Max Kneiss—Port Edwards

Roanald Koep
Tom Krien
John Kuehn
Ron Langsdorf
Arnold Leemeister—Nekoosa
Gary Linig
Francis Liveseh
Jack Luedtke
Ron Markwarth
Merlin McHugh
June Neitzel
Chuck Neuman
Earl M. Olde
Tom Oligney
James Perry
Jim Pfeiffer
Tom Phillis
Ron Radtke
Al Rasmusen—Nekoosa
Jim Reas
Harry Richman
R. Ristow
Gerald M. Rogers
Ray B. Rogers
Tim Ruesch

Harold Saeger—Port Edwards
Lee Scanlon
Robert Schiedy
Albert Schill
Donna Schooly
Bob Schuz
Bob Smalauck
Don Smith
Hank Smith
Jay Somers (vice-president and general manager of Consoweld)
Joan Steele
Don Stein
Dan Stranz—Vesper
Mke Swanson
Don H. Tarrish
Howard Theleman
Gary Tomfonder—Vesper
Emery Trickle
David Webb
Clarence Wirtz—Nekoosa
Nick Wirtz—Nekoosa
Tiny Younger
Herb Zynda

A tribute and grateful thanks to the men and women of Ahdawagam/Consoweld—Consolidated Paper Company, especially for their civilian and military service contribution to World War II.[544]

Note: This is not a complete list of Consolidate Paper Company employees but encompasses a great many from Ahdawagam/Consoweld. It is not to diminish the deserved recognition of the civilian and military service of all the employees during World War II.

C.M. CHRISTIANSEN COMPANY EMPLOYEES AND THOSE WHO SERVED DURING WORLD WAR II

DEPARTMENT: FILING AND SHIPPING UNIT AS OF DECEMBER 22, 1945

NAME	DATE OF EMPLOYMENT
Albrecht, Richard	January 29, 1941
Anderson, William	June 17, 1943
Benson, John	January 1930
Crass, William *Army	February 4, 1941
Hill, Armie	November 27, 1939
Johnson, Menard *Army	December 27, 1939
Kinner, Clarence *Army	May 26, 1942
Klabunde, Otto	December 1935
Kosky, William *Army	September 21, 1942
Lambert, Fred	September 1928
Larson, George	December 1932
Larson, Harold	January 1936

Lunde, Delmer *Army	November 13, 1942
Maki, Andrew *Army	August 25, 1941
Mikulandic, Louis	January 1929
Moshagen, Nils	October 1936
Olson, Emil B.	September 1928
Paulman, Ervin *Army	December 10, 1939
Schuster, Martin *Army	June 1932
Simpson, Cecil F.	October 1928
Tienhaara, Edwin *Army	September 7, 1943
Wyant, William	September 1928
Zironas, Sam	September 1928

DEPARTMENT: MANUFACTURING UNIT AS OF DECEMBER 22, 1945

NAME	DATE OF EMPLOYMENT
Alinen, Reino	February 8, 1938
Boone, Willard	September 1928
Braun, Art	June 16, 1943
Cadieu, Sidney	August 23, 1943
Cummings, Clifford *Army	December 18, 1940
Esque, Darl	March 1932
Filppula, Charles *Army	December 14, 1938
Freeland, Jake	October 1935
Freeland, James *Army (discharged 9/30/45)	December 18, 1938
Hansen, Andrew	July 21, 1941
Heehn, Henry *Army	September 3, 1941
Jaaska, T.J.	October 1934
Johnson, __.B.	September 1928
McKee, Smith	September 1928
Miller, Joe	November 1933
Monty, Lloyd	October 1935
Monty, Saul	September 1928

Olson, Sylvan, Jr. *Army	February 19, 1943
Olson, Vern	October 1928
Palo, John	May 11, 1943
Pier, John	September 1928
Pray, Albert	March 4, 1945
Rosner, Charles	September 1928
Rutledge, Frank	June 1, 1942
Sann, Charles	April 1929
Somers, Harry	August 1933
Somers, Ora *Navy	January 6, 1939
Southerland, George	February 8, 1943
St. Louis, Mark	October 1929
Sulstrom, Frank	January 6, 1939
Tienhaara, James *Army (discharged 9/30/45)	December 19, 1938
Tienhaara, Matt *Army (discharged 9/30/45)	December 19, 1938
Vyrant, Frank	November 1930
Youngquist, Jim	April 24, 1945

Agreement. C.M. Christiansen Co., Phelps dated December 22, 1945. Courtesy of the C.M. Christiansen Family. Phelps, Wisconsin.

Note: The original list was compiled by year of employment in both the Filing and Shipping Unit and the Manufacturing Units. The author has compiled the list by unit but alphabetically for ease of the reader. In addition, four men were listed on the Labor Agreement with dates of employment after World War II ended. They are included below because it appears that they are family members of other Christiansen employees and returned to Phelps.

Name	Date of Employment
Walter Hill	November 5, 1945
Larcene Lunde	October 24, 1945
Alfred McKee	December 10, 1945
Norman Olson	August 20, 1945

NOTES

CHAPTER 1

1. Colleen Holloran Austin and Verna Fohrman, interview by Sara W. Connor, February 10, 2006, Mosinee, WI.
2. Larson, *Voices of History*, 8. For Packer fans, the year ended with their rivals, the Chicago Bears, coached by George Halas, winning the NFL Championship. www.chicagobears.com.
3. Drake, interview.
4. Frei, *Third Down*.
5. Ibid., "Epilogue."
6. The Professional Football Hall of Fame, www.profootballhof.com. *USA Today*, January 28, 2004.
7. The University of Wisconsin Badger Athletics, www.uwbadgers.com.
8. *Marshfield Story: 1872–1997*, 34; *Marshfield Story: Windows to Our Past*, 102–3.
9. Larson, *Voices of History*, 8.
10. Ibid., 12.
11. Ibid.
12. Fohrman, interview.
13. Bailey, *Home Front*, 23.
14. Higgs, *Depression, War, and Cold War*, 74–75.
15. Treutel, interview.
16. *Journal of Forestry*, "More than Enough," 283.
17. Darrell Davis, postcard to W.D. Connor Jr., April 21, 1941. Connor Lumber and Land Company Collection, folder 21, box 9, Wisconsin Historical Society Archives, Madison, WI.

18. Darrell Davis, letter to W.D. Connor Jr., April 26, 1941. Connor Lumber and Land Company Collection, folder 29, box 9, Wisconsin Historical Society Archives, Madison, WI.

19. Letter from W.D. Connor Jr. to Darrell Davis, May 22, 1941. Connor Lumber and Land Company Collection, folder 29, box 9, Wisconsin Historical Society Archives, Madison, WI.

20. Brendemihl, letter to Mr. and Mrs. Hamilton Roddis.

21. Holloway, letter to Catherine Prindle Roddis.

22. Connor, "Lt. Verland Drake," 16–17; Drake, interview.

23. Winslow, "Wood Goes to War," *Journal of Forestry*, 913.

24. Upson, "Lumber and the War Production Board," 913.

25. Cash Book of the Connor Lumber and Land Company.

26. Richardson, discussion.

27. Day, e-mail, December 1, 2011.

28. Treutel, interview.

29. Schubert, interview.

30. Ibid.

31. Wirsbinski, interview.

32. Don Kircher, interview.

33. "Lumber for War Purposes Depends on Trucks and Tires," War Production Board—Lumber and Timber Products Defense Committee, Box 150, Forest History Society Archives, Durham. Underlining is in the original.

34. *Roddis Bulletin*, December 16, 1944.

35. Ibid., December 30, 1944.

36. Ibid., December 16, 1944.

37. War Production Board, press release, WPB7056, December 27, 1944.

38. *Roddis Bulletin*, December 2, 1944.

CHAPTER 2

39. *Journal of Forestry*, "More than Enough," 283.

40. Demmon, "Rubber Production Opportunities," 208. The United States had surveyed rubber production from 1927 to 1936. In 1927 in Liberia by Firestone, Henry Ford bought 2.5 million acres on the Tapajos River and more in 1933 in Brazil. In 1935, Goodyear surveyed Panama near the Gatun Locks and, in 1936, Costa Rica.

41. Ibid., 209.

42. Ibid., 210. The Department of Agriculture in 1942 was also promoting rubber growth in South America. Rubber trees grown in plantations were planted as two hundred trees per acre, yielding 400 pounds of rubber per

year. However, the Hevea tree species could not be harvested until they were between five and seven years old. Through plant manipulation by crossbreeding, production could increase to 1,200 pounds per year.

43. Bailey, *Home Front*, 82, 99, 155.

44. Author's papers.

45. Bailey, *Home Front*.

46. "We're Cutting Meat," *Vogue*, January 15, 1943. Roddis Dress Collection.

47. Don Kircher, interview.

48. Young, *Into the Valley*, 41.

49. Roddis Dress Collection Project.

50. Bata Shoe Museum, Toronto, Canada, May 16, 2012.

51. Don Kircher, interview.

52. $18.75 is worth $243.18 today. $1.00 in 1944 = $12.97 in 2012. William Blair & Co., Chicago.

53. Joyce and Don Kircher, interviews.

54. Roddis, speech to a civic group.

55. *Roddis Bulletin*, March 3, 1945.

56. Roddis employee photographs dated May 1939, Camp 5 Museum Archives, Laona, WI. (It has yet to be researched how many in the photos came home.)

57. *Roddis Bulletin*, November 18, 1944.

58. Ibid., December 9, 1944.

59. Ibid.

60. Ibid., January 6, 1944.

61. Ibid., January 6, 1945.

62. Ibid., November 25, 1944.

63. Ibid., December 9, 1944.

64. Ibid., December 18, 1944.

65. Ibid., January 20, 1945.

66. Schmoll, interview.

67. *Roddis Bulletin*, July 14, 1945.

68. Cady, interview. Cady was a B-24 pilot stationed in Italy flying over the Eastern Front.

69. *Roddis Bulletin*, February 3 and February 10, 1945.

70. Ibid., January 27, 1945.

71. Ibid., February 17 and February 24, 1945.

72. Ibid., March 31, 1945.

73. Ibid., December 30, 1944.

74. Ibid., December 9, 1944.

75. Ibid., January 15, 1945.

76. Don Kircher, interview.

77. *Roddis Bulletin*, January 15, 1945.

78. Ibid., April 24, 1945.

79. Ibid., May 5, May 12, May 19, 1945.

80. Ibid., April 7, April 14, April 21, April 28, 1945.

81. Ibid., April 7, 1945.

82. Maurer, "Airlines, Aviation, and Airports," October 25, 1944, in *History of Marshfield Aviation.*

83. Ibid.

84. *Roddis Bulletin*, December 9, 1944.

85. Ibid., December 2, 1944.

86. Ibid., December 5 and December 16, 1944.

87. Ibid., March 10, 1945.

88. Paragraphs and underlining not by the original Roddis "editor" but by the author.

89. *Roddis Bulletin*, January 6, 1945.

90. Austin, notes from Wartner, interview.

91. Treutel, interview.

92. Panshin, et al, *Forest Products*, 129.

93. Extra samples are on display with the "Wisconsin Flying Trees: Wisconsin Plywood Industry's Contribution to WWII" exhibit, Marshfield Airport, Marshfield, Wisconsin.

94. Domestically, too, it is generally ⅟₃₈ to ¼₅. In exports, it generally has been cut at ¹⁄₄₂ to ¹⁄₅₀. The agreement is between the buyer and the seller. Set in 1995, there was a "voluntary standard," and all the standards are voluntary. Overseas, they are cutting it thinner. Japan is apparently cutting it at ¹⁄₁₀₀ and even to ¹⁄₁₂₅.

95. *Roddis Bulletin*, January 15, 1945. Paragraphing and underlining by the author.

96. Austin, interview.

97. Wunrow, interview.

98. Polivka, interview.

99. Larson, *Voices of History*, 200.

100. Fohrman, interview.

101. Union Brotherhood, letter to Paupl.

102. Cour, *Plywood Age*, 133; Milward, *War, Economy, and Society*, 186.

103. Hunt and Garrett, *Wood Preservation*, 417.

104. *Roddis Bulletin*, January 20, 1945.

105. Lindberg and Todd, *Anglo-American Shipbuilding*, 171.

106. *Roddis Bulletin*, February 24, 1945.

107. Ibid., February 3, 1945.

108. Ibid.

109. Ibid., February 24, 1945.

110. War Production Board, Box-WPB.

111. Box 111, "E" Awards, Forest History Society Archives, Durham, NC.
112. Roddis, "Summary of Warehouse Profits."
113. Seymour, *Origin of the Wood Industry*, 40.
114. See chapter 10, "War Contracts."
115. *Roddis Bulletin*, March 3, 1945.
116. Ibid., March 24, 1945. The Office Building would become a showpiece for the wood species used by Roddis Plywood Corporation. Woods from around the world were installed in each office.
117. Ibid., March 24, 1945.
118. Ibid., March 17, 1945
119. Crowley, letter.
120. *Roddis Bulletin*, May 12, 1943.
121. Ibid., May 19, 1945.
122. "The People, Policies and Progress of the National Hardwood Lumber Association," 75th Annual Convention, St. Louis, MO, October 2–4, 1972, 16–17.
123. *Roddis Bulletin*, June 2, 1945.
124. Ibid., June 16 and June 30, 1945.
125. Ibid., July 28, 1945.

CHAPTER 3

126. Spencer, "Significance of Oil Progress Week."
127. *Roddis Bulletin*, December 9, 1944.
128. www.usmm.org/libertyships.html.
129. Ibid.
130. Cour, *Plywood Age*, 31.
131. Bailey, *Home Front*, 23.
132. Stokesbury, *Short History of World War II*, 118.
133. Bailey, *Home Front*, 26.
134. www.usmm.org/faq.html#faqs.
135. *Green Bay Press Gazette*, "Subchaser on Way to Coast," November 4, 2013, A5.
136. Lindberg and Todd, *Anglo-American Shipbuilding*, 155, 174.
137. *A Week of the War*, Box 148, folder 2, Forest History Society Archives.
138. Meyercord at a meeting on New Bakelite Rein Development, 4.
139. Koepke, interview. A partial monthly "Inventory Report" list in a Roddis "Inter-Office Communication" later revealed the extensive use of chemicals. The larger categories in "footage spread in square feet" and "glue spread per 1,000 square feet of single glue line" were:
Tego, Kimpreg

Roddisite—developed by Roddis chemists and patented

Roddisol #2— developed by Roddis chemists and patented

Casco 350

Catabond—The spread in footage was available for cold press and electronic

Uformite 553

Roddis Plywood Corporation, Inter-Office Communication, April 11, 1949.

140. Maurer, *History of Marshfield Aviation*.

141. Austin, interview.

142. Seymour, *Origin of the Wood Industry*, 26.

143. Ibid., 30.

144. Steven Ujifrussa, *America's National Flagship*; 1923–1938. Researcher for the Roddis Family Dress Collection Project. Frank O. Braynard Collection, Sea Cliff, NY.

145. *Golden Anniversary Catalogue*, 24.

146. Ibid., 21.

147. Seymour, *Origin of the Wood Industry*.

148. Ibid., 28.

149. *Marshfield News Herald*, November 6, 1942

CHAPTER 4

150. Megellas, *All the Way to Berlin*.

151. Connor and Day, "Primary Light Airplane Gliding School," 68.

152. Dedication of the 82nd Airborne Bridge Memorial, Stevens Point, June 2, 2013.

153. Connor and Day, "Primary Light Airplane Gliding School," 69.

154. Ibid., 62.

155. Megellas, Premiere of *Maggie's War*.

156. Tom Laney, ed., *WISCO Airborne Reporter*, Winter 2012–13, 2–8.

157. Lofaro, "Sword of St. Michael," 1–3. LTC Lofaro is an 82nd Ranger and Delta Force combat leader.

158. S.W. Maynes, *The "G" Is for Guts! An American Glider Pilot's Story*. N.p.: Booksurge, November 27, 2006.

159. *Marshfield News Herald*.

160. What the figures did not include was the small percentage available that was actually aircraft-grade material. If the 1.4 million square feet of plywood was supplied, the actual cut was far greater. Assuming the 1.4 million bdf, it would take 28 million bdf total. The 1.4 million board feet was 2 to 5 percent of the total to meet the aircraft specifications.

161. By 1942, species like Norway pine and yellow poplar were allowed for wood substitution. By 1943, the problems with inspections of aircraft, lumber and specifications had been the topic of discussion. Enormous volumes of lumber were being cut of one species, with small amounts being allowed for aircraft specifications of that species. Therefore, other species needed to be studied for substitution. Mahogany had filled the aircraft specification requirements, but birch for high stressed pieces and basswood were accepted as substitute materials.

162. *War Papers*, "Part 45."

163. Upson, "Lumber and the War Production Board," 911.

164. Day, "Ford Motor Company."

165. Koning, *Forest Products Laboratory*, 111.

166. Stevens, "Problems of Construction," 156–59.

167. Day, "Ford Motor Company."

168. Ibid. Day's article said, "After WWII ended, the buyers sought the wooden crates, not the gliders. Today, there still are cottages in the Pocono Mountains and parts of a warehouse in Lubbock, Texas built from glider crate wood. During WWII, a Bunkhouse for a Boy Scout camp was built from glider crate wood near the glider test base in Wilmington, Ohio. Glider assembly crews at Greenham Commons in England used the large crates for living space."

169. Taylor, *Jane's Encyclopedia of Aviation*, 888.

170. In the spring of 2006, airplane mechanic Al Hatz discovered Roddis plywood panels in the original NAC building on Chamberlain Field. They were given to Dan Maurer, a retired Northwest Airlines pilot and author of *The History of Marshfield Aviation*. The panels have the Roddis stamp on them and are included in the nationwide touring "Wisconsin's Flying Trees: Wisconsin Plywood Industry's Contribution to WWII" exhibit in Marshfield.

171. Connor and Day, "Primary Light Airplane Gliding School," 68

172. *History of the Glider Program*, 5.

173. Ibid., 7.

174. Ibid., 8.

175. Ibid., 15–18.

176. Parker, interview by J. Norberg, 4.

177. *Aircraft Yearbook*, 272.

178. *Minnesota Flyer*, January 2011, 4–5.

179. Roddis Lumber and Veneer Company supplied the aircraft glider wing panels and other components to Northwestern Aeronautical Corporation, with Villaume Corporation as the sub-contractor. Interestingly, as NAC also supplied ten wing sets to Laister Kauffmann

in St. Louis, Roddis Lumber and Veneer Company could have been the source for the aircraft plywood.

180. Gliders that were built as experimental aircraft included the 1-XPG (Experimental Power Glider), 1-XCG and 2-XCG-13as (also known as the YCG) for a grand total of 1,570. Day, *Silent Ones.*

181. Taylor, *Jane's Encyclopedia of Aviation*, 888.

182. Connor and Day, "Primary Light Airplane Gliding School," 67.

183. *History of the Glider Program.*

184. Finch, interview.

185. Connor and Day, "Primary Light Airplane Gliding School," 68.

186. Ibid.

187. In today's dollars, that is over $200,000. Bruce Radtke and Edward J. Dellin, William Blair and Company, Chicago.

188. Steinway & Sons Purchase Order No. 10908.

189. Ibid., June 10, 1043.

190. Ibid., July 21, 1943.

191. Roddis, interview, January 28, 2006.

192. Steinway & Sons Purchase Order No. 10908, July 23, 1943.

193. Steinway, *People and Pianos*, 127.

194. Ibid.

195. Bailey, *Home Front*, 90.

196. Ratcliffe, *Steinway*, 199.

197. United States Patent Office, no. 2,384,347.

198. Ratcliffe, *Steinway*, 199.

199. United States Patent Office, no. 2,345,025

200. Day, e-mail, October 30, 2006.

201. A Steinway glider door frame became part of the "Wisconsin Flying Trees: Wisconsin Plywood Industry's Contribution to WWII" nationwide traveling museum exhibit.

202. Day, e-mail, October 31, 2006.

203. Steinway, *People and Pianos*, 127.

204. www.exploringthenorth.com/gliders/history.html; Day, *Silent Ones*, 77.

205. In the summer of 2006, a Roddis Plywood Corporation veneer glider piece was found in the Ford Glider Restoration Project in Kingsford, Michigan, at the Cornish Pump Museum. On November 9, 2006, glider plywood door frames and wing panels with RLV stamps and Roddis Lumber and Veneer Company stamps were found in Wausau as part of the Ford Glider Restoration Project. In 2011, the restored Ford glider debuted at the new Menominee Range Historical Museum in Iron Mountain, Michigan.

206. Ratcliffe, *Steinway*, 49–56.

207. Day, *Voo-Doo Was My Name.*

208. www.exploringthenorth.com/gliders/history.html.

209. "Pratt-Read Workers Hear of Great Glider Flight," *The Leading Edge.*

210. Day, *Voo-Doo Was My Name.*

211. A mahogany panel is on loan from the Deep River Historical Society replete with the Roddis Lumber and Veneer Company and Roddiscraft manufacturing stamp, displayed as part of the "Wisconsin Flying Trees: Wisconsin Plywood Industry's Contribution to WWII" exhibit.

212. Roddis, interview, July 16, 2006.

213. Hoestetler, e-mail.

214. Cessna made 820 Crane-1 "Cranes" for the Canadian Commonwealth Air Training Plan. In the United States, these were called the A-8 or T-50. Similarly, the AT-17 or UC-78 "Bobcats" trained thousands of pilots for combat.

215. Phillips, *Cessna,* 119.

216. Taylor, *Jane's Encyclopedia of Aviation,* 243.

217. *Allowable Shear Stresses in Plywood.*

218. Phillips, *Cessna,* 119.

219. Taylor, *Jane's Encyclopedia of Aviation,* 243.

Chapter 5

220. *Wooden Wonder.* DH 88-Comet won the eleven-thousand-mile MacRobertson Air Race from London to Melbourne in a record seventy hours and fifty-four minutes.

221. Barker, *Epic of Flight,* 138–39.

222. *Wooden Wonder.*

223. Commonwealth Plywood Corporation, www.commonwealthplywood.com.

224. www.anu.edu.au/Forestry/wood/wfp/mosquito/Mosquito.html.

225. www.cbmp.com/profiles/quarter2/mosquitos.htm.

226. www.2worldwar2.com/mosquito.htm, 3–4.

227. *Daily Mail,* "War Papers."

228. www.2worldwar2.com/mosquito.htm, 3–4.

229. Beaton, "London Life in the Path of War," 62–63.

230. Smith, letter.

231. BRINY No. 1232, Cypher, October 30, 1940.

232. MAP No. 1551 CYPHER, November 6, 1940, To: Self, From: Ministry of Aircraft Production. British National Archives, London, Research for the author by T.R. Dellin.

233. BRINY No. 4083, March 28, 1941.

234. Minutes of a Special Meeting of the Board of Directors of the Roddis Lumber and Veneer Company, March 24, 1941, Warranty Deed on March 2, 1943, from Claire Uihlein Trostel to Roddis Lumber and Veneer Company.
235. Roddis, speech at the Upham Mansion, courtesy of Marcie Glaisner. Author's papers.
236. Peterson, letter to his daughter.
237. www.anu.edu.au/Forestry/wood/wfp/mosquito/Mosquito.html.
238. *Introduction to Pluswood.*
239. Ibid.
240. University of Wisconsin Digital Collection, Madison, WI.
241. DeHavilland DH-98 Mosquito.
242. Roddis, letter to Hamilton Roddis.
243. Ibid.
244. Bowman, *DeHavilland Mosquito,* 163.
245. Holliday, *Wooden Wonder Aircraft,* 61.
246. Ibid.
247. www.canadaatwar.ca.
248. Holliday, *Wooden Wonder Aircraft,* 62, 94, 124.
249. Meeting with Jane Bradbury, August 7, 2013; Connor, interview.
250. Loveland, interview.
251. Ibid.
252. channel12.org/ridddlefield/ew/bio.html.
253. *Mosquito Story.*
254. White, *Moonlight Serenade.*
255. Loveland, interview.
256. Taylor, *Jane's Encyclopedia of Aviation,* 315.
257. Barker, *Epic of Flight,* 53, 142.
258. Richards, "Some Structure Temperature Measurements."
259. www.flymodels.com/dehavill.htm.
260. *War Papers,* "Part 54."
261. *Avro Anson.*
262. DeHavilland DH-98 Mosquito.
263. Loveland, RAF personal papers, Avro Anson Flight Manual, 6.
264. www.lancastermuseum.ca/bcatp.html.
265. Ibid.
266. www.rafmuseum.org.uk/avro-anson-1.htm.
267. Herrick, "Wood Transport Planes," 10–12.

Chapter 6

268. *Journal of Forestry*, "Editorial: Forestry and the War," June 1942, 439.

269. Compton, letter to Don Nelson, July 23, 1942.

270. Connor, *Wisconsin's Flying Trees*, University of Wisconsin.

271. Taylor, *Jane's Encyclopedia of Aviation*, 277.

272. *News from Hughes*, Public Relations Department, Hughes Aircraft Company. Culver City, California. U.S. Forest Products Laboratory Library, #333 H87.

273. Roddis, interview, October 2006.

274. Treutel, interview, February 10, 2006.

275. Austin, notes from Larry Wartner, interview, February 10, 2006.

276. Panshin, et al, *Forest Products*, 129.

277. Extra samples are on display with the "Wisconsin Flying Trees: Wisconsin Plywood Industry's Contribution to WWII" exhibit.

278. Markwardt, *Mosquito*, 238.

279. Roddis, interview, November 13, 2006.

280. Press release dated August 15, 1944. Hughes Aircraft Company. Acquired by the U.S. Forest Products Laboratory, December 17, 1964. U.S. Forest Products Laboratory Library, Madison, WI.

Chapter 7

281. Nelson, *History of the U.S. Forest Products Laboratory*, 125.

282. Ibid.

283. Ibid.

284. U.S. Forest Products Laboratory, *Wood Aircraft Inspection*, 100–2.

285. Nelson, *History of the U.S. Forest Products Laboratory*, 128–29.

286. Ibid., 123

287. Markwardt, *Mosquito*.

288. Brouse, *Effects of Treating Plywood*.

289. *Some Accomplishments of the Forest Products Laboratory*, 16.

290. Markwardt, *Resume of Recent Developments*, 1, 2.

291. Brouse, "Methods of Increasing Durability," 30–31, 33.

292. Brouse, "Gluing of Wood," 637–39.

293. Markwardt, *Resume of Recent Developments*, 21.

294. Meyercord, at a meeting on New Bakelite Resin Developments.

295. Cour, *Plywood Age*, 92.

296. Royal Aircraft Establishment.

297. "Use of Wood for Aircraft."

298. Ibid., 4.

299. Ibid., 5.

300. Roddis, interview, July 16, 2006.

301. Koepke, interview.

302. Schmoll, interview.

303. Bellanca Aircraft Corporation, *Process Specifications.*

304. Ibid., 3

305. Schull, *Manual of Gluing Techniques*, 1.

306. Ibid.,

307. Schull, *Curing Time Tests*, 1–4.

308. *Golden Anniversary Catalogue*, 19.

309. Harley, "Fungi and Wood," 631–33.

310. Hiscocks, "Plastic Plywoods in Aircraft Construction," 169–75.

311. Welsh, "Plywood Preferred," 20.

312. *Timber Producers' Bulletin* 84, May 1, 1944, Forest History Society Archives, Durham, NC.

313. Meyercord, at a meeting on New Bakelite Rein Development.

314. www.anu.edu.au/Forestry/wood/wfp/mosquito/Mosquito.html.

315. Markwardt, *Mosquito*, 238.

316. www.diggerhistory.com.

317. BRINY No. 413, Cypher.

318. *Wooden Wonder.*

319. Sweetman, *Mosquito*, 20; www.2worldwar2.com/mosquito.htm.

320. Wood and Linn, *Plywoods*, 404–5.

321. William H. Roddis II, interview by Sara W. Connor, October 2006.

322. Wood and Linn, *Plywoods*, 404–5.

323. Roddis, letter to Dan Maurer.

324. Wood and Linn, *Plywoods*, 405.

325. Bowman, *DeHavilland Mosquito*, 16.

326. Reynolds, "Timber," 464–65.

327. May, *Paper, Plastics*, 2.

328. Ibid.

329. Ibid., photos.

330. Ibid.

331. Ibid., 11.

332. Ibid., 7.

333. Minute Sheet, June 14, 1942.

334. *Building Supplies*, 36.

335. Ibid.

336. Nelson, *History of the U.S. Forest Products Laboratory*, 125.

337. Jay Somers, when asked by the author a month before his death in 2009 about manufacturing of World War II glider floors, said, "Why are you asking me now and not twenty years ago when all the other men who

contributed to the war effort were still alive?" An appendix of some of the Consoweld employees is at the end of this book. We honor those men and women and all Consoweld employees for their civilian contribution to World War II.

338. U.S. Forest Products Laboratory, *Wood Aircraft Inspection*, 100–2.

339. Recently, the Yanks Aviation Museum in Chino, California, provided a 3½-inch by 5½-inch piece of its "paper/papreg" floor from its Northwestern Aeronautical Corporation restored glider. It is on loan to USFPL and "Wisconsin Flying Trees: Wisconsin Plywood Industry's Contribution to WWII." The botanists/wood anatomist at USFPL described the floor piece as "conifer fibers in a paper Matrix."

340. Koning, *Forest Products Laboratory*, 532.

341. Day, e-mail, October 31, 2006.

342. Dupuy, *Military History of World War II*, 22.

CHAPTER 8

343. Compton, "Lumber Industry," 914.

344. Connor, "Wisconsin's Flying Trees," *Wisconsin History Magazine*, 16–27.

345. Seymour, *Origin of the Wood Industry*.

346. Roddis, interview, October 2005.

347. Patterson, e-mail.

348. Siempelkamp, *Siempelkamp: 100 Years*, 9.

349. Ibid., 16.

350. Ibid.

351. Maltitz, letter.

352. Siempelkamp and Company, letter to Hamilton Roddis.

353. F. Meyer and Schwabedissen, letter.

354. Adolf Fritz, letter.

355. Map reviewed by Peter Bostock, 1938. Itinerary sent by e-mail.

356. Roddis, letter.

357. Translated by Ingrid McNeill, an Austrian, whose father was a pilot of a plane shot down by the Allies over Sicily. As a young girl of six to nine during the war, she remembers the deprivation of food and, as the oldest of three children, her mother's struggle as a twenty-six-year-old widow to find enough food during the war for her children. She said, "I swore that I would never eat lentils again!"

358. See chapter 2, "The Wisconsin Homefront," maintenance room section.

359. Mereen Today: Johnson is still a large supplier of sawmill equipment in the United States, and Mereen-Johnson, in the 1970s, supplied Connor Forest Industries with a router for SIFO's puzzle machines, a subsidiary

manufacturing toys. Merren-Johnson also supplied a double eenoner machine for the Connor kitchen cabinet doors and panels manufactured in Wausau. Interview with Gordon P. Connor, president of Nicolet Hardwoods Corporation, Laona, WI. Maltitz and Bolling, "Progress in Methods of Edge-Gluing Lumber," 387–92.

360. Maltitz and Bolling, "Progress in Methods of Edge-Gluing Lumber," 387–92.

361. Siempelkamp, *Siempelkamp: 100 Years.*

CHAPTER 9

362. *Journal of Forestry*, "More than Enough," 283–84.

363. Schaller Hardwood Company, www.schallerhardwood.com.

364. Ibid.

365. Kellogg, interview, 29.

366. Ibid.

367. Ibid., 8.

368. Bishop, "History of Trees for Tomorrow," 32.

369. In a review of all the correspondence between the National Lumber Manufacturers' Association and the War Production Board, the assertion of Paul Koistenen, a revisionist historian, of "untrustworthiness" by the National Lumber Manufacturers' Association cannot be substantiated.

Koistenen in his *Planning War, Pursuing Peace*, 163, stated, "Concerning the lumber association's offers to aid in planning, an OASW [Office of the Assistant Secretary of War] member expressed his doubts about 'anything coming from this association.' Officials are 'undoubtedly more interested in results right now than they are in war time preparedness' a ranking officer of the OASW characterized trade associations in general as untrustworthy."

370. The executive director position was known then as the secretary or secretary-manager.

371. National Lumber Manufacturers' Association, Organizational Chart.

372. Kellogg, interview, 19a, 23.

373. Ibid., 29.

374. Minutes of the Meeting of the Timber Producers' Association of Upper Michigan and Northern Wisconsin, May 13, 1941.

375. Bishop, "History of Trees for Tomorrow," 32.

376. Minutes of the Meeting of the Timber Producers' Assocation of Upper Michigan and Northern Wisconsin, September 16, 1941.

377. Northern Hemlock and Hardwood Manufacturers' Association, F-6, Box 38.

378. Ibid.

379. Executive Order Establishing the War Production Board in the Executive Office of the President, December 11, 1941.

380. Minutes of the meeting of the Timber Producers' Association of Upper Michigan and Northern Wisconsin, May 11, 1945.

Chapter 10

381. Compton, "Lumber Industry," 914.

382. National Defense and Industrial Mobilization, "How—Where–What."

383. Ibid.

384. Sherrill, "Lumber Procurement," 917.

385. Upson, "Lumber and the War Production Board," 910.

386. Bravo, Re: Timber Conference.

387. Bossee, letter.

388. Lumber and Timber Products—War Committee, Box 130.

389. Koistenen, *Planning War, Pursuing Peace*, 163.

390. Ibid.

391. Ibid., 39.

392. Stokesbury, *Short History of World War II*, 118.

393. Bailey, *Home Front*, 79.

394. Yawkey-Bissell Lumber Company, Invoice Book, 181.

395. Lumber and Timber Products—Defense Committee.

396. Fleishel, telegram to Phillip Reed.

397. Compton, letter to John Haynes.

398. Winslow, *Wood Goes to War.*

399. Compton, letter to D. MacKeache.

400. Compton, letter to Donald Nelson, December 29, 1942.

401. Ibid., May 21, 1942.

402. Nelson, letter to Dr. Wilson Compton.

403. Compton, telegram to Members of National Lumber Manufacturers' Association.

404. Lumber and Timber Products—War Committee, letter.

405. Styer, "Address to the West Coast Lumbermen's Association," 294.

406. War Production Board: Lumber and Lumber Products Division, *Administrative Bulletin* 2, July 1, 1943. Forest History Society Archives, Durham, NC.

407. GAO Order 2-141.

408. Upson, "Lumber and the War Production Board," 910.

409. Ibid., 909.

410. War Production Board, press release, March 4, 1944.

411. Ibid.

412. War Production Board, press release, March 8, 1944.

413. Boeschenstein, letter.

414. Boyd, letter.

415. Compton, letter to Harold Boeschenstein.

416. Ibid.

417. Yawkey-Bissell, Invoice #543.

418. Requisition Number: NM-36833-W.

419. Yawkey-Bissell, Invoice #543.

420. Ibid.

421. Ibid., 7.

422. War Production Board, press release WPB-5997, May 31, 1944.

423. War Production Board, press release, June, 29 1944.

424. War Production Board, advanced press release WPB-6890, November 27, 1944.

425. War Production Board, press release WPB-6840, November 18, 1944.

426. Ibid.

427. Connor, discussions.

428. Ibid.

429. *Roddis Bulletin*, November 18, 1944.

430. Yawkey-Bissell, Invoice Book, 1944, Order #280, Invoice 245. $1.00 in 1944 equaled $12.97 in 2012.

431. Yawkey-Bissell, Invoice Book, 1944, Order #285-371.

432. Yawkey-Bissell, Invoice Book, 1944, Orders #436–444.

433. Yawkey-Bissell, Invoice #508.

434. Yawkey-Bissell, Invoice #490; Yawkey-Bissell, Invoice, July 5, 1944, U.S. Order# NXsx 61997.

435. Yawkey-Bissell, Invoice Book, 1944.

436. War Production Board, press release WPB7008, December 18, 1944.

437. Yawkey-Bissell, Invoice #333.

438. Office of Price Administration, press release, December 20, 1944, OPA-5082.

439. War Production Board, press release WPB-6970, December 12, 1944.

440. War Production Board, WPB-2660, letter to the Lumber Industry, January 1, 1945.

441. Ibid.

442. Ibid.

443. Ibid.

444. War Production Board, press release WPB-7091, January 5, 1945.

445. Ibid.

446. Drucker, letter to Bahr.

447. Office of Price Administration, MPR-223.

448. Ibid.

449. Haumann, letter.

450. Western Union Telegram, April 22, 1943, Forest History Society Archives, Durham.

451. Monte, "Tom Nordine."

Chapter 11

452. *Milwaukee Journal*, "War Machine Is Eating State's Timber Supply."

453. Timber Producers' Association, *Bulletin* 62, July 1, 1942.

454. Connor, "Wisconsin's Flying Trees," exhibit.

455. Timber Producers' Association, *Bulletin* 61, June 1, 1942.

456. Nelson, telegram.

457. *Milwaukee Journal*, "War Machine Is Eating State's Timber Supply."

458. Department of Commerce, Washington, D.C., press release, February 22, 1942, War Production Board Folder, Forest History Society Archives, Durham, NC.

459. Christiansen, letter.

460. Compton, letter to Don Nelson; Christiansen, letter.

461. "Report of Hearing on Regulation and Control of Cutting and Timber on Privately Owned Lands," Iron Mountain, Michigan, September 19–21, 1945. State of Michigan, published by the *Norway Crescent*, Norway, MI. Author's papers.

462. "Public Regulation of Private Timber Cutting," 675–80.

463. Christiansen, letter.

464. Timber Producers' Association, *Bulletin* 56, January 1, 1942.

465. Office of Price Administration, news release, July 24, 1942.

466. Timber Producers' Association, *Bulletin* 60, May 1, 1942.

467. Timber Producers' Association, *Bulletin* 57, February 1, 1942.

468. Timber Producers' Association, *Bulletin* 59, April 1, 1942.

469. Upton, "Lumber and the War Production Board," 912.

470. Minutes of the Meeting of the Timber Producers' Association, November 12, 1943.

471. War Production Board, *Bulletin* 3.

472. Minutes of the Meeting of the Timber Producers' Association of Upper Michigan and Northern Wisconsin, November 12, 1943.

473. Nordine, interview. Nordine provided the information on committee members.

474. *History of the Wisconsin-Michigan Timber Producers' Association*, 6.

475. Timber Producers' Association, *Bulletin* 85, June 1, 1944.

476. Timber Producers' Association, *Bulletin* 84, May 1, 1944.

477. War Production Board, press release WPB 6262, August 9, 1944.

478. War Production Board, Activities and Orders.

479. Clark, letter.

480. Timber Producers' Association, *Bulletin* 88, September 1, 1944.

481. Ibid.

482. War Production Board, September 20, 1944.

483. War Production Board, press release WPB-6539, September 26, 1944.

484. War Production Board, press release WPB-7056.

485. Nordine, interview.

486. *Roddis Bulletin*, November 25, 1944.

487. War Production Board, list.

488. Ibid.

489. *WPB—Industry Cooperation.*

490. Office of Price Administration, Maximum Price Regulation, June 16, 1943.

491. Office of Price Administration, Maximum Price Regulation—460.

492. Minutes of the Meeting of the Timber Producers' Association of Upper Michigan and Northern Wisconsin, November 12, 1943.

493. Kenwood Corporation, letter.

494. Lumber and Timber Products—War Committee, MPR 348.

495. Swan, letter.

496. Bishop, "History of Trees for Tomorrow," 32.

497. Nordine, interview.

498. Ibid.

499. Bishop, "History of Trees for Tomorrow," 32.

500. War Production Board, press release, July 1, 1944.

501. War Production Board, Activities and Orders.

502. War Production Board, press release WPB-6128, July 20, 1944.

503. War Production Board, WPBI-2216, letter, July 25, 1944.

Chapter 12

504. Connor Lumber and Land Company, Comparison of Sales—Laona.

505. Yawkey-Bissell, Adjusted Earnings Statement.

506. War Production Board, press release, March 8, 1944, WPB-5139.

507. Pierce, interview.

508. *Timber Producers' Association Bulletin* 85, June 1, 1944.

509. War Production Board, advanced press release, WPB-5959, June 25, 1944.

510. Ibid.

511. Speech by the Director of the U.S. Forest Products Laboratory, September 22, 2010, Madison, WI. In Koning, *Forest Products Laboratory*, 109.

512. Timber Producers' Association, *Bulletin* 85, June 1, 1944.

513. War Production Board, advance press release, June 23, 1944.

514. Connor, *Century with Connor Timber*, 109–11. Mary R. Connor is the only woman inducted into the Wisconsin Forestry Hall of Fame.

515. Connor, *Logging Methods*, 17.

516. Ibid.

517. Guthrie, discussions. Conversion of "191,000 tons of logs," while dependent on the species, approximates 6.5 tons per 1,000 board feet. Therefore, 191,000 = 29,000,000 bdf. Discussions with Miles Benson, retired forester with Consolidated Paper Company, Wisconsin Rapids, WI; NLRB Board Decision, In Re: Connor Lumber and Land Co., 52 NLRB 641 (1943). Bloomberglaw.com, courtesy of Jack Schroder, Alston & Bird, Atlanta, GA. While the Connor Lumber and Land Company mill in Laona was the "largest hardwood mill in the United States" at the time, the smaller Connor mill in Laona today saws approximately 11 million board feet per year. Courtesy of Steve Guthrie, former forester for the Laona operations, February 12, 2013.

518. In 1942, $1.00 had the same buying power as $14.81 in 2013; annual inflation over this period was 3.87 percent. Bruce Radtke, William Blair & Company. E-mail on February 13, 2013. Therefore, $500,000 = over $7.4 million in 2013, The $500,000 figure is from NLRB Decision, In Re: Connor Lumber and Land Co., 47 NLRB 867 (1943), Bloomberglaw. com, courtesy of Jack Schroder, Alston & Bird, Atlanta.

519. *Roddis Bulletin*, June 30, 1945.

520. War Production Board, press release, September 11, 1945.

521. War Production Board, press release, September 12, 1945, WPB-9048; Schug, *United States History*, 190–94.

522. As an experienced and well-respected lumberman, Gordon R. Connor, then vice-president of the Connor Lumber and Land Company and co-founder of the Timber Producers' Association of Upper Michigan and Northern Wisconsin and the Timber Producers' Association's "Logging Congress," encouraged the lumber industry and saw the need to have everyone learn and implement the latest logging and sawmill equipment.

523. In 2011, the 66th Logging Congress was held in Escanaba, Michigan, with more than 875,000 square feet of exhibit space, 3,500 attendees daily and over three hundred booths.

524. Connor, *Logging Methods*, 18.

525. Ibid., 16.

526. Connor, "Loggers, Lumbermen, and Inventors"; Connor, *Cleereman Family*.

527. *Prentice People, Special Issue.*

528. Ibid.

529. *Business North,* "Town Leo Built," 14.

530. "Leo Heikenen Day," 3.

531. Ibid., 6.

532. Connor, *Logging Methods,* 16, 18. Both Mr. Connor and Mary Roddis Connor (Mrs. Gordon R. Connor), corporate secretary of the Connor Lumber and Land Company, had earlier been instrumental in changing railroad policy.

533. *Timberman,* 8, 10, 141.

534. Connor, *Logging Methods,* 18.

535. Nelson, *History of the U.S. Forest Products Laboratory,* 125–26.

536. Panshin, et al, *Forest Products.*

537. Higgs, *Depression, War, and Cold War,* 72, 73.

538. Ibid.

539. Brokaw, *Greatest Generation,* 11.

540. Bailey, *Home Front,* 50.

541. Ibid.

542. Megellas, "Leadership in the Face of Mortal Combat."

543. Brokaw, *Greatest Generation.*

Appendix II

544. The lists of employees are from the Consoweld employee meetings held on April 26, 2004, and April 25, 2005, as well as the lecture by the author at the Wisconsin Paper Making Museum on October 31, 2005. Unless otherwise noted, the Consoweld employees are from Wisconsin Rapids.

BIBLIOGRAPHY

Adolf Fritz, GmbH, Stuttgart, Germany. Letter to Hamilton Roddis, August 16, 1938. Wisconsin Historical Society Archives, Madison, WI.

The Aircraft Yearbook—1943, 272. Experimental Aircraft Association Library (Oshkosh). Susan A. Lurvey, EAA Librarian. E-mail message to Sara W. Connor, October 28, 2005.

Allowable Shear Stresses in Plywood. Report #6219. Wichita. U.S. Forest Products Laboratory Library, Madison, WI.

Austin, Colleen Holloran. Notes from Larry Wartner, interview by Sara W. Connor, September 10, 2006, Mosinee, WI.

Austin, Colleen Holloran, Verna Fohrman and Leroy Treutel. Interview by Sara Witter Connor, September 10, 2006, Mosinee, WI.

Avro Anson. Alberta, Canada: Nanton Lancaster Air Museum, n.d.

Bahr, Henry, National Lumber Manufacturers' Association. Letter to Warren Bailey, Division of Priorities, Office of Production Management, November 1, 1941. Production and Priorities. Forest History Society Archives, Durham, NC.

Bailey, Ronald H., ed. *The Home Front-USA.* Chicago: Time-Life Books, 1981.

Barker, Ralph. *The Epic of Flight: The RAF at War.* Alexandria, VA: Time Life Books, 1981.

Barton, Charles, Capt. Ret., USN. *Howard Hughes and His Flying Boat.* Revised ed. Vienna, VA, 1982.

The Bata Shoe Museum, Toronto, Canada.

Baumgartner, Karen. Family papers. Phillips, WI.

Beaton, Cecil. "London Life in the Path of War." *Vogue,* January 1, 1945. Wisconsin Historical Society Archives, Madison, WI.

Bellanca Aircraft Corporation. *Process Specifications for the Use and Application of Plastics Bonding Formulae 944-6 and 945-6.* Report #390. Bellanca Aircraft Corporation. New Castle, DE. January 4, 1940, 1–4. U.S. Forest Products Laboratory Library, Madison, WI.

Bishop, Maggie. "History of Trees for Tomorrow." *TPA* (January 2011).

Boeschenstein, Harold, Acting Director of the Forest Products Bureau, War Production Board. Letter to Wilson Compton, National Lumber Manufacturers' Association, May 26, 1944. Forest History Society Archives, Durham, NC.

Boettcher, John. Photo collection. Park Falls, WI.

Bossee, Louis. Letter to Mr. Dibrell, Office of Production Management, July 16, 1941. Forest History Society Archives, Durham, NC.

Bostock, Peter. Map review of the Roddis 1938 Itinerary. E-mail message to Sara Witter Connor. May 31, 2013. Author's papers.

Bowman, Martin W. *De Havilland Mosquito.* Ramsbury, Wiltshire, UK: Crowood Press, 2005.

Boyd, Phillip, Director of the Lumber and Lumber Products Division—War Production Board. Letter to M.L. Fleishel, President of Putnam Lumber Company, Shamrock, Florida, May 26, 1944. Box 148, folder 2. Forest History Society Archives, Durham, NC.

Bravo, E.L., Northern Hemlock and Hardwood Manufacturers' Association c/o Marshall Flooring Company. Washington, December 10, 1941. Re: Timber Conference. Forest History Society Archives, Durham, NC.

Brendemihl, Reverend. Letter to Mr. and Mrs. Hamilton Roddis and Family, December 30, 1941, Headquarters of the 2nd Cavalry. Fort Riley, Kansas. Wisconsin Historical Society Archives, Madison, WI.

BRINY No. 413. Cypher, August 26, 1940. British National Archives, London.

———. Cypher, October 30, 1940. British National Archives, London.

Brokaw, Tom. *The Greatest Generation.* New York: Random House, 2004.

Brouse, Don. *Effects of Treating Plywood with Tetrechlorphenol, Chlorothrphenylphenol, and Dinotrochlorbenzene on Durability of Glue Joints—Project L-157.* U.S. Forest Products Laboratory Library, Madison, WI.

———. "Gluing of Wood." *U.S. Dept. of Agriculture Yearbook: 1949, Trees.* Washington, D.C.: U.S. GPO, 1949.

———. "Methods of Increasing Durability of Plywood: 1932." *Wood Working Industries* 11, no. 2 (February 1932): 30–31, 33. U.S. Forest Products Laboratory Library, Madison, WI.

Building Supplies (May 1969): 36. Collection of Gilbert Endrezzi, retired mechanical engineer for Consoweld, Wisconsin Rapids, WI.

Business North. "The Town Leo Built." October 1996.

Cady, John. Interview by Sara W. Connor, January 9–11, 2011, Hillsboro, FL.

Cash Book of the Connor Lumber and Land Company (CL&L), January 29, 1942–September 21, 1944. Camp 5 Museum/Wisconsin Forestry Museum Archives. Laona, WI.

"The CG-4A Glider." www.exploringthenorth.com/gliders/history.html.

Chicago Bears. www.chicagobears.com.

Christiansen, C.M., President of C.M. Christiansen Company, Phelps, WI. Letter to Senator Truman with a copy to Dr. Wilson Compton, National Lumber Manufacturers' Association, December 2, 1942. Forest History Society Archives, Durham, NC.

Clark, J.F., Assistant Deputy Rubber Director. Letter to Mr. Fleishel, Chairman, Timber and Timber Products War Committee. National Lumber Manufacturers' Association. Forest History Society Archives, Durham, NC.

Commonwealth Plywood Corporation. www.commonwealthplywood.com.

Compton, Wilson, PhD. "The Lumber Industry: Our Forest Resources Are Contributing to Victory." *Journal of Forestry* 40, no. 12 (1942).

———, Lumber and Timber Products War Committee. Telegram to J.E. Kimberly, War Productions Board, December 17, 1942. Forest History Society Archives, Durham, NC.

———, National Lumber Manufacturers' Association. Letter to D. MacKeache, War Production Board. Forest History Society Archives, Durham, NC.

———, National Lumber Manufacturers' Association. Letter to Donald Nelson, War Production Board Chairman, December 29, 1942. Forest History Society Archives, Durham, NC.

———, National Lumber Manufacturers' Association. Letter to Don Nelson, War Production Board. Forest History Society Archives, Durham, NC.

———, National Lumber Manufacturers' Association. Letter to Ernest Kanzler, Director General of the Office of Price Supply: War Production Board, December 29, 1942. Lumber and Timber Committee. Forest History Society Archives, Durham, NC.

———, National Lumber Manufacturers' Association. Letter to Harold Boeschenstein, Acting Director of the Forest Products Bureau—War Production Board, June 5, 1944. Forest History Society Archives, Durham, NC.

———, National Lumber Manufacturers' Association. Letter to John Haynes, Building Materials Branch of the War Production Board, April 25, 1942. Forest History Society Archives, Durham, NC.

———, National Lumber Manufacturers' Association. Memorandum to Donald M. Nelson, War Production Board, July 23, 1942. Forest History Society Archives, Durham, NC.

————, National Lumber Manufacturers' Association. Postal Telegraph to O.C. Lance, Northwestern Lumbermen's Association, January 18, 1942. Forest History Society Archives, Durham, NC.

————, National Lumber Manufacturers' Association. Telegram to Members of National Lumber Manufacturers' Association, May 5, 1942. Forest History Society Archives, Durham, NC.

Connor, Gordon R., President, Connor Forest Industries. *Logging Methods in the River, the Railroad, and the Gasoline Era. 6th Annual Proceedings of the Forest History Association of Wisconsin.* Forest History Association of Wisconsin, Wisconsin Historical Society Archives, Madison, WI.

————, President, Nicolet Hardwoods Corporation. Discussions. February 16, 2012. Author's papers.

Connor Lumber and Land Company Collection. Comparison of Sales—Laona: 1939–1941. Wisconsin Historical Society Archives, Madison, WI.

————. Financial Records—Accounts Payable, Plant Operations, Production Records, and Supplies: 1925–1934, vols. 124–28. Wisconsin Historical Society Archives, Madison, WI.

————. Financial Statement—Lumber Costs for Fiscal Year Ending August 31, 1941, and Successive Months. Wisconsin Historical Society Archives, Madison, WI.

————. Lumber Sales Report, December 1941. Wisconsin Historical Society Archives, Madison, WI.

————. *Proudly We Pay Tribute to Members of Our Organization Who Answered the Call to the Colors.* List of Laona veterans who were employed and served during WWII. Plaque. Camp 5 Museum Foundation, Laona, WI.

————. *Shipping Journal*, vol. 12. Wisconsin Historical Society Archives, Madison, WI.

————. Wisconsin Historical Society Archives, Madison, WI. MSS 815, Box 3.

————. Wisconsin Historical Society Archives, Madison, WI. MSS 815, Box 8, Folders 7–14.

————. Wisconsin Historical Society Archives, Madison, WI. MSS 815, Box 9.

————. Wisconsin Historical Society Archives, Madison, WI. MSS 815, Box 10.

————. Wisconsin Historical Society Archives, Madison, WI. MSS 815, Box 14.

————. Wisconsin Historical Society Archives, Madison, WI. MSS 815, Box 21.

————. Wisconsin Historical Society Archives, Madison, WI. MSS 815, Box 22.

————. Wisconsin Historical Society Archives, Madison, WI. MSS 815, Box 35.

————. Wisconsin Historical Society Archives, Madison, WI. MSS 815, Box 40.

————. Wisconsin Historical Society Archives, Madison, WI. MSS 815, Box 45.

————. Wisconsin Historical Society Archives, Madison, WI. MSS 815, Box 46.

————. Wisconsin Historical Society Archives, Madison, WI. MSS 815, Box 51, Volume 11.

Connor, Mary Roddis. *A Century with Connor Timber.* Stevens Point, WI: Worzalla Publishing Co., 1972.

Connor, Sara Witter. *The Cleereman Family.* Newald, WI: Cleereman Industries, 2004.

————. "Loggers, Lumbermen, and Inventors: The Cleereman Family." *Chips and Sawdust.* Forest History Association of Wisconsin, 2004.

————. "Lt. Verland Drake." *WISCO Airborne Reporter* (Winter 2012–13): 16–17.

————. "Wisconsin's Flying Trees: Wisconsin Plywood Industry's Contribution to WWII." *Chips and Sawdust* 31, no. 3 (Summer 2006). Forest History Association of Wisconsin.

————. "Wisconsin's Flying Trees: Wisconsin Plywood Industry's Contribution to WWII." Exhibit, Marshfield Airport, Marshfield, WI.

————. "Wisconsin's Flying Trees: Wisconsin Plywood Industry's Contribution to WWII." Hamilton Roddis Lecture Series. No. 11. University of Wisconsin—Department of Forestry, Ecology and Wildlife. January 31, 2007. U.S. Forest Products Laboratory, Madison, WI.

————. "Wisconsin's Flying Trees: Wisconsin Plywood Industry's Contribution to WWII." Proceedings of the Forest History Association of Wisconsin. Camp 5 Museum/Wisconsin Forestry Museum. Laona: 2007. Wisconsin Historical Society Archives, Madison, WI.

————. "Wisconsin's Flying Trees: Wisconsin Plywood Industry's Contribution to WWII." *Wisconsin History Magazine* (Spring 2009). Wisconsin Historical Society.

Connor, Sara Witter, and Charles Day. "Primary Light Airplane Gliding School at Janesville, Wisconsin." American Aviation Historical Society. *AAHS Journal* 56, no. 1 (Spring 2011).

Connor, W.D., Jr. Letter to Darrell Davis, May 22, 1941. Connor Lumber and Land Company Collection, folder 29, box 9. Wisconsin Historical Society Archives, Madison, WI.

Cornish Pump Museum, Iron Mountain, Michigan.

Cour, Robert M. *The Plywood Age: A History of the Fir Plywood Industry's First Fifty Years.* Portland, OR: Binford and Mort, 2005.

Crowley, Leo T. Letter, May 10, 1945. War Production Board, Box 112-Lumber and Timber War Committee. Forest History Society Archives, Durham, NC.

Daily Mail. "The War Papers." Part 24. London. October 1, 1942. Camp 5 Museum/Wisconsin Forestry Museum Archives, Laona, WI.

Davis, Darrell. Postcard to W.D. Connor Jr., April 21, 1941. Connor Lumber and Land Company Collection, folder 21, box 9. Wisconsin Historical Society Archives, Madison, WI.

Day, Charles. E-mail to Sara Witter Connor, December 1, 2011.

———. E-mail to Sara Witter Connor, October 30, 2006.

———. E-mail to Sara Witter Connor, October 31, 2006.

———. Ford Motor Company, Kingsford, Michigan. Lambertville. December 6, 2007. Author's papers.

———. Photos of the Charles Day Collection.

———. *Silent Ones: WWII Glider Invasion: Test and Experiment, Clinton County Army Air Field.* Wilmington, OH, 2001.

———. *Voo-Doo Was My Name, Flying Was My Game.* Lambertville, OH. www.440thtroopcarriergroup.org/glidermen.shtml.

DeHavilland DH-98 Mosquito. British Columbia Aviation Museum Archives, Vancouver, BC.

Dellin, Edward J., William Blair and Company, Chicago. E-mail to Sara W. Connor, February 16, 2012. Monetary equivalents.

Demmon, E.L. "Rubber Production Opportunities in the American Tropics." *Journal of Forestry* 40, no. 3 (1942).

Drake, Verland. Interview by Sara Witter Connor, October 30, 2012. Whitefish, MT.

Drucker, Mr. Letter to Mr. Bahr, April 27, 1944, Box 148, Folder 1. Forest History Society Archives, Durham, NC.

Dupuy, Trevor Nevitt (ret.). *The Military History of World War II: Volume 7. The Air War in the West: June 1941–April 1945.* New York: Franklin Watts, Inc., 1963.

"E" Awards, Box 111. Forest History Society Archives, Durham, NC.

Executive Order Establishing the War Production Board in the Executive Office of the President, December 11, 1941. War Production Board. Forest History Society Archives, Durham, NC.

Finch, Ambassador Edward. Interview by Sara W. Connor, Hillsboro, FL, January 12, 2010.

Fleishel, M.L. Telegram to Phillip Reed, March 9, 1942, Lumber and Timber War Production. Forest History Society Archives, Durham, NC.

Fleishel, W.L., Chairman of the Lumber and Timber Products War Committee. Telegram to the Lumber Industry, Washington, D.C., May 5,

1942. Re: Request from Donald Nelson, Director of the War Production Board. Forest History Society Archives, Durham, NC.

Fleishel, W.L., National Lumber Manufacturers' Association. Telegram to Philip D. Reed, Bureau of Industry Branch—War Production Board, March 9, 1942. Forest History Society Archives, Durham, NC.

F. Meyer and Schwabedissen-Hereford. Remagen-on-Rhine. Letter to Hamilton Roddis, President of Lumber and Veneer Company, June 16, 1938. Wisconsin Historical Society Archives, Madison, WI.

Fohrman, Verna. Interview by Sara W. Connor, September 2006, Mosinee, WI.

Frei, Terry. *Third Down and a War to Go.* Madison: Wisconsin Historical Society Press, 2007.

GAO Order 2-141. War Production Board, Forest History Society Archives, Durham, NC.

Glaisner, Marcie. Correspondence, May 16, 2006. A Speech of William H. Roddis II to the Upham Mansion, Marshfield, WI.

The Golden Anniversary Catalogue—1890–1940: Fifty Years of Service. Marshfield, WI: Roddis Plywood Corporation. Roddis Collection. Wisconsin Historical Society Archives, Madison, WI.

Groah, Bill (ret.), Executive Director, Hardwood Plywood and Veneer Association, Reston Virginia. American Plywood Association.

Guthrie, Steve, Forester for Ottawa Forest Products, Amasa, MI. Discussions on February 12, 2013.

Harley, Carl. "Fungi and Wood." *United States Department of Agriculture Yearbook: Trees.* Washington, D.C.: United States GPO, 1949. U.S. Forest Products Laboratory Library, Madison, WI.

Haumann, K., Lumber and Timber Products—War Committee. Letter to Mr. Dunbar, Northern Hemlock and Hardwood Association, May 9, 1944. Forest History Society Archives, Durham, NC.

Herrick, George. "Wood Transport Planes...Now and to Come." *Veneers and Plywood.* 36, no. 9 (1942). United States Forest Products Laboratory Library, Madison, WI.

Higgs, Robert. *Depression, War, and Cold War: Studies in Political Economy.* Oxford: Oxford University Press, 2006.

Hiscocks, R.D. "Plastic Plywoods in Aircraft Construction." *Transactions of the American Society of Mechanical Engineers* 66, no. 3 (April 1944): 169–75. U.S. Forest Products Laboratory Library, Madison, WI.

The History of the Glider Program at Northwestern Aeronautical Corporation. Management Control Center: Central Division—ATSC. September 1945. University of Minnesota—Charles Babbage Institute. Minneapolis, MN.

History of the Wisconsin-Michigan Timber Producers Association. Rhinelander, WI: Great Lakes Timber Professionals, 1991.

Hoestetler Jeff, President of the Stone House Historical Society, Deep River, CT. E-mail message to Sara Witter Connor, March 15, 2006.

Holliday, Joe. *The Wooden Wonder Aircraft of World War II: Mosquito: The Exciting Story of the Unique Canadian Fighter.* Markham, Ontario: Paper Jacks, Limited, 1980.

Holloway, John. Childersburg, AL. Letter to Catherine Prindle Roddis, Marshfield, December 13, 1941. Wisconsin Historical Society Archives, Madison, WI.

Hunt, George M., and George A. Garrett. *Wood Preservation.* New York: McGraw-Hill Book Company, Incorporated, 1938.

An Introduction to Pluswood. University of Wisconsin–Stevens Point Archives. Stevens Point, WI.

Journal of Forestry. "Editorial: More than Enough Before It Is Needed." Society of American Foresters. 40, no 4 (1942).

Kellogg, Royal S., Former Executive Director of the National Lumber Manufacturers' Association in 1959. Interview by R. Maunder. Forest History Society Archives, Durham, NC.

———. Oral history interview conducted by Elwood R. Maunder on April 16, 1955, in Palmetto, FL. Forest History Society Archives, Durham, NC.

———. Oral history interview conducted by Elwood R. Maunder on February 9, 1959, in Palmetto, FL. Forest History Society Archives, Durham, NC.

———. Oral history interview conducted by Elwood R. Maunder on January 8, 1963, in Palmetto, FL. Forest History Society Archives, Durham, NC.

Kenwood Corporation. Letter to the Office of Price Administration, August 8, 1943, and letter from the Appalachian Hardwood Manufacturers' Association, Office of Price Administration. Forest History Society Archives, Durham, NC.

Kircher, Don. Interview by Sara Witter Connor, August 2011, Laona, WI.

Kircher, Joyce. Interview by Sara Witter Connor, August 2011, Laona, WI.

Koepke, Ron. Interview by Sara Witter Connor, May 2, 2006, Marshfield, WI.

Koistenen, Paul. *Planning War, Pursuing Peace: 1920–1939: The Political Economy of American Warfare.* Lawrence: University Press of Kansas, 1998.

Koning, John W., Jr. *Forest Products Laboratory: 1910–2010: Celebrating a Century of Accomplishment.* Madison: University of Wisconsin Press, 2011.

Larson, Bradley. *Voices of History: 1941–1945.* Oshkosh, WI: Oshkosh Public Museum, 2004.

"Leo Heikenen Day—August 31, 1996." *Prentice Progress Days—Prentice.* Prentice Weebr and Sons for the community of Prentice, 1996.

Lindberg, Michael, and Daniel Todd. *Anglo-American Shipbuilding in World War II: A Geographical Perspective.* Westport, CT: Praeger, 2004.

Linsmayer, Nick. CEO, Villaume Corporation, St. Paul, MN.

Lofaro, Guy. *The Sword of St. Michael.* Cambridge, MA: Da Capo Press, 2011.

———. "The Sword of St. Michael." *WISCO Airborne Reporter* (Winter 2012–13): 1–3.

Loveland, Eric. Interview by Sara Witter Connor, July 9, 2006, Laona, WI.

———. RAF personal papers. Avro Anson Flight Manual, 6.

Lumber and Timber Products Defense Committee. Letter to the Office of Price Administration, January 5, 1942, Box 148. Forest History Society Archives, Durham, NC.

Lumber and Timber Products—War Committee. Box 130. Forest History Society Archives, Durham, NC.

———. Box 148. Forest History Society Archives, Durham, NC.

———. Box 148, Folder 2. Forest History Society Archives, Durham, NC.

———. Letter to the National Lumber Manufacturers' Association. Forest History Society Archives, Durham, NC.

———. Logs and Bolts—Price Regulations—MPR-348. Box 113. Forest History Society Archives, Durham, NC.

———. Lumber Industry Capacity. Box 113. Forest History Society Archives, Durham, NC.

———. Truck Requirements. Box 150. Forest History Society Archives, Durham, NC.

———. Wage and Salary Stabilization. Box 149, Folder 2. Forest History Society Archives, Durham, NC.

———. *War Manpower Commission Regulation Under Executive Order 9328.* Forest History Society Archives, Durham, NC.

Lumber Limitations, L-335 and L-41. Box 103, Forest History Society Archives, Durham, NC.

"The Magnificent Mossie. Executive Brief." Hardwood Plywood Manufacturers' Association. Fourth Quarter, 1990. Reston, VA.

Maltitz, H. von, President of Plycor Company, Chicago. Letter to Hamilton Roddis, August 2, 1938. Wisconsin Historical Society Archives, Madison, WI.

Maltitz, H.K., and O. Bolling. "Progress in Methods of Edge-Gluing Lumber and Veneers." *Transactions of the A.S.M.E.* 64, no 4 (May 1942): 387–92. U.S. Forest Products Laboratory Library, Madison, WI.

Markwardt, L.J. *The Mosquito.* U.S. Forest Products Laboratory Library, Madison, WI.

———. *Resume of Recent Developments in Wood, Plywood and Conversion of Products of Interest in Aircraft Construction.* Manuscript. U.S. Forest Products

Laboratory in cooperation with the University of Wisconsin. June 17, 1938. U.S. Forest Products Laboratory Library, Madison, WI.

Marshfield News Herald, November 6, 1942.

The Marshfield Story: 1872–1997; Piecing Together Our Past. Marshfield History Project. Amherst, WI: Palmer Publications, Incorporated, 1997. First edition, vol. 1.

The Marshfield Story: Windows to Our Past. Marshfield History Project. Eagle River, WI: Hahn Printing, Incorporated, 2000. Vol. 2.

Marshfield, Wisconsin: Highlights of History: 1872–1972. Marshfield, WI: Marshfield Centennial Committee, 1972.

Maurer, Dan. *History of Marshfield Aviation.* Marshfield, WI, n.d.

May, George. *Paper, Plastics and Weight Saving Construction in Aircraft.* Boreham Wood, [England] Dufaylite Developments Limited. London. May 1957 [38], 2. Forest Products Laboratory Library, Madison, WI.

McNeill, Ingrid Sieder. German translation. July 2013.

Measurement and Inspection Rules. National Hardwood Lumber Association. Chicago, 1952.

Meeting of the Board of Directors Policy Committee. Timber Producers' Association of Michigan and Wisconsin. Wakefield, WI, November 28, 1944.

Megellas, LTC James. *All the Way to Berlin.* New York: Ballantine Books, 2003.

———. "Leadership in the Face of Mortal Combat." National World War II Glider Symposium. Madison, WI, 2010.

———. Premiere of *Maggie's War.* October 2012, Fond du Lac, WI.

Menominee Range Historical Museum, Iron Mountain, MI.

Menu. Thanksgiving at the Naval Air Technical Training. Corpus Christi, TX. November 1944. William H. Roddis II's personal papers. Marshfield, WI. Wisconsin Historical Society Archives, Madison, WI.

"Mexico's Timberland Awaits Development." *Timber of Canada* 4, no. 9 (May 1944). Roddis Plywood Corporation. Marshfield, WI. Wisconsin Historical Society Archives, Madison, WI.

Meyercord, George R., President of Haskelite Manufacturing Company, at a meeting on New Bakelite Rein Development in Laminated Plastics, Plywood and Veneers sponsored by Bakelite Corporation in the Lecture Hall of the Franklin Institute, Philadelphia. March 14, 1940. U.S. Forest Products Laboratory Library, Madison, WI.

Miller, Boswell K. *The First 50 Years of the Timber Producers Association of Michigan and Wisconsin, Incorporated.* Rhinelander, WI: 1991. Timber Producers Association of Michigan and Wisconsin, now Great Lakes Timber Professionals Association Archives.

Milquet, Steven R. "From Here to WWII." *Voyageur: Northeast Wisconsin's Historical Review* 8, no. 2 (Winter–Spring 1992).

Milward, Alan S. *War, Economy, and Society: 1939–1945*. Berkeley: University of California Press, 1979.

Milwaukee Journal. "War Machine Is Eating State's Timber Supply." July 26, 1942. Forest History Society Archives, Durham, NC.

Minute Sheet, June 14, 1942. Reference Number SB-37492. British National Archives, London.

Minutes of the Meeting of the Board of Directors. Timber Producers' Association of Upper Michigan and Northern Wisconsin. April 4, 1941. Great Lakes Timber Professionals' Association Archives, Rhinelander, WI.

———. Timber Producers' Association of Upper Michigan and Northern Wisconsin. Iron River, April 27, 1944. Great Lakes Timber Professionals, Association Archives, Rhinelander, WI.

———. Timber Producers' Association of Upper Michigan and Northern Wisconsin. Iron River, August 31, 1945. Great Lakes Timber Professionals, Association Archives, Rhinelander, WI.

———. Timber Producers' Association of Upper Michigan and Northern Wisconsin. Iron River, May 23, 1941. Great Lakes Timber Professionals' Association. Archives, Rhinelander, WI.

———. Timber Producers' Association of Upper Michigan and Northern Wisconsin. Iron River, November 14, 1942. *Timber Producers' Association of Michigan and Wisconsin Bulletin* 18 (November 18, 1942). Ontonagon. Great Lakes Timber Professionals' Association Archives, Rhinelander, WI.

———. Timber Producers' Association of Upper Michigan and Northern Wisconsin. Lakeview Inn, Wakefield, MI, November 28, 1944. Great Lakes Timber Professionals Association Archives, Rhinelander, WI.

———. Timber Producers' Association of Upper Michigan and Northern Wisconsin. May 11, 1945. Great Lakes Timber Professionals' Association Archives, Rhinelander, WI.

———. Timber Producers' Association of Upper Michigan and Northern Wisconsin. November 12, 1943. Great Lakes Timber Professionals' Association Archives, Rhinelander, WI.

———. Timber Producers' Association of Upper Michigan and Northern Wisconsin. Ontonagon, July 8, 1944. Great Lakes Timber Professionals, Association Archives, Rhinelander, WI.

———. Timber Producers' Association of Upper Michigan and Northern Wisconsin. September 16, 1941. Great Lakes Timber Professionals' Association Archives, Rhinelander, WI.

———. Timber Producers' Association of Upper Michigan and Northern Wisconsin. September 22, 1943. Great Lakes Timber Professionals' Association Archives, Rhinelander, WI.

————. Timber Producers' Association of Upper Michigan and Northern Wisconsin. Stambaugh, June 27, 1946. Great Lakes Timber Professionals' Association Archives, Rhinelander, WI.

————. Timber Producers' Association of Upper Michigan and Northern Wisconsin. Stambaugh, May 11, 1945. Great Lakes Timber Professionals' Association Archives, Rhinelander, WI.

Minutes of a Special Meeting of the Timber Producers' Association of Upper Michigan and Northern Wisconsin. August 31, 1945. Great Lakes Timber Professionals' Association Archives, Rhinelander, WI.

————. May 13, 1941. Great Lakes Timber Professionals' Association Archives, Rhinelander, WI.

Modern Plastics 41, no. 2. Tenth national exposition and conference. New York: Breskin Publications, October 1963.

Money, Time, and Work-saving Ideas. Roddiscraft Product Brochure. Roddiscraft Decorative Paneling, Roddis Plywood Corporation, Marshfield. Roddis Collection, Wisconsin Historical Society, Madison.

Monte, Mike. "Tom Nordine—A U.P. Treasure." *TPA* 11 (November 2010). Great Lakes Timber Professionals' Association. Rhinelander, WI.

The Mosquito Story (video). Collection of Eric Loveland, RAF (ret.), Orange City, FL. Author's collection.

"NAM—Achievement for Industry in the Year of Victory." 1945 Annual Report. National Association of Manufacturers, New York.

National Defense and Industrial Mobilization. "How—Where—What the Army Buys in Peacetime." *A Special Newsletter Supplement* 1, no. 5 (1940). Washington, D.C.: National Association of Manufacturers. Author's papers.

National Lumber Manufacturers' Association. Organizational Chart. Box 162, Forest History Society Archives, Durham, NC.

National Museum of the United States Air Force, Wright Patterson Air Force Base, OH.

Nelson, Charles. *History of the U.S. Forest Products Laboratory (1910–1963).* Madison, WI: U.S. Forest Products Laboratory Library, 1971.

Nelson, Donald, Chairman of the War Production Board. Letter to Dr. Wilson Compton, National Lumber Manufacturers' Association, May 22, 1942. Forest History Society Archives, Durham, NC.

————. Telegram. Forest History Society Archives, Durham, NC.

————. Telegram to Dr. Wilson Compton, Secretary Manager of the National Lumber Manufacturers' Association, Washington, D.C., July 28, 1942. Box 148, Folder 2. Forest History Society Archives, Durham, NC.

————. Telegram to W.L. Fleishel, Chairman, Lumber and Timber Products War Committee, Washington, D.C., May 5, 1942. Forest History Society Archives, Durham, NC.

New York Times. "WPB Drops Plan for Wood Planes: Contract with Kaiser-Hughes May Be Cancelled as Metal Becomes Available Again." March 2, 1944. Forest History Society Archives, Durham, NC.

Nordine, Tom. Telephone interview by Sara Witter Connor, December 10, 2011.

Northern Hemlock and Hardwood Manufacturers' Association. National Forest Products Association, F-6, Box 38. Forest History Society Archives, Durham, NC.

———. National Forest Products Association, F-6, Box 38, 1941. Forest History Society Archives, Durham, NC.

———. "Reasons Why No Compulsory Unemployment Compensation Measure Should Be Enacted." Oshkosh, WI, November 29, 1931. Forest History Society Archives, Durham, NC.

———. Telegram to the National Lumber Manufacturers' Association, May 27, 1944. Re: MPR-223. Forest History Society Archives, Durham, NC.

———. "Why Hemlock." February 17, 1931. Kilbourn Hall, Milwaukee. Forest History Society Archives—NLMA, Durham, NC.

———. "Wisconsin and Minnesota Wage Adjustments." Oshkosh, WI, August 6, 1943. Forest History Society Archives, Durham, NC.

Office of Price Administration. Advanced Press Release—OPA-5082, December 20, 1944. RE: Distribution of hardwood lumber and price regulations. Forest History Society Archives, Durham, NC.

———. General Box 103. Forest History Society Archives, Durham, NC.

———. Maximum Price Regulation—460, August 31, 1943. Forest History Society Archives, Durham, NC.

———. MPR-223. May 25, 1944. Washington, D.C., U.S. Government Printing Office. Forest History Society Archives, Durham, NC.

———. MPR-348. April 16, 1943. Washington, D.C., U.S. Government Printing Office. Forest History Society Archives, Durham, NC.

———. National Lumber Manufacturers' Association Statements: 1945–1946. Box 103. Forest History Society Archives, Durham, NC.

———. "Notice to Competitive Log or Bolt Buying Plants." Re: MPR 348. Washington, D.C. Forest History Society Archive, Durham, NC.

———. Press release, December 20, 1944. OPA-5082. Forest History Society Archives, Durham, NC.

———. Press release, July 18, 1941. Re: paper supplies. Forest History Society Archives, Durham, NC.

———. Press release, July 24, 1942. Washington, D.C. Box 150: "Truck Requirements." Forest History Society Archives, Durham, NC.

———. Press release, June 18, 1943. Re: MPR-165—Ceilings on contract logging services. Washington, D.C. Forest History Society Archives, Durham, NC.

————. "Tire Rationing Regulations: Establishing a Program for Rationing Tires and Tubes, Retreading and Recapping of Tires and Camelback." Washington, D.C., February 19, 1942. Forest History Society Archives, Durham, NC.

Office of Production Management—Division of Purchases. Press release, February 28, 1941. Re: Stabilizing lumber prices. Forest History Society Archives, Durham, NC.

Office of Production Management. Order No. 15. Conservation of Rubber. E.H. Stettinius Jr., Director of Priorities. Washington, D.C., August 8, 1941. Forest History Society Archives, Durham, NC.

Panshin, A.J., E.S. Harper, J.S. Bethel and W.J. Baker. *Forest Products: Their Sources, Production, and Utilization.* New York: McGraw-Hill Book Company, 1962.

Parker, John. Interview by Norberg. University of Minnesota, Charles Babbage Institute, Center for the History of Information Technology. Minneapolis, MN.

Park Falls Herald. "Roddis Plywood Co. Active Here Since 1903." May 1, 1952. Section 2, 1. Roddis Collection. Wisconsin Historical Society Archives, Madison, WI.

Patterson, Uta. Siempelkamp-USA. E-mail message to Sara Witter Connor, November 23, 2005.

Peterson, Orville. Letter to his daughter Nadine, April 1987. Personal papers of Karen Baumgartner, Phillips, WI.

Phillips, Edward H. *Cessna: A Master's Expression.* Eagan, MN: Flying Books Publishers and Wholesalers, 1985.

Pierce, Dudley W. Telephone interview by Sara Witter Connor, March 4, 2012.

Plywood Doors: The Golden Anniversary Catalogue: 1890–1940: Fifty Years of Service. Handbook Number 50. Roddis Lumber and Veneer Company. Wisconsin Historical Society Archives, Madison, WI.

"Plywood Preferred." *Timber of Canada* 4, no. 9 (May 1944). Roddis Plywood Corporation. Marshfield, WI. Author's papers.

Polivka, Marion Frederick. Interview by Sara Witter Connor, September 2006, Marshfield, WI.

Poster: *Keep 'em Flying—Aviation Cadets Train for Air or Ground Crews. U.S. Army Air Forces.* Personal papers of William H. Roddis II. Marshfield, WI. Wisconsin Historical Society Archives, Madison, WI.

"Pratt-Read Workers Hear of Great Glider Flight." *The Leading Edge.* Pratt, Read & Company. Deep River, WI, October 16, 1943. The Stone House Historical Society Archives, Deep River, CT.

Prazisionwerkzuge fur die mechanische Holzbearbeitung. 1958 Catalogue. Wilhelm Stehle. Memmingen-Bayern.

Prentice People. Special Issue...The Story of Old No. 4. Published by the Employees and Dealers of Hydraulic Materials and Handling Division of Omark Industries. Zebulon, NC (Fall 1974). No. 10.

Press Release. Department of Commerce. Washington, D.C., February 22, 1942. Forest History Society Archives, Durham, NC.

————. War Production Board. WPB-4217. Washington, D.C., September 13, 1943. Forest History Society Archives, Durham, NC.

The Professional Football Hall of Fame. www.profootballhof.com. *USA Today*, January 28, 2004.

"Public Regulation of Private Timber Cutting." Report of a Special Committee of the Wisconsin–Upper Michigan Society of American Foresters. *Journal of Forestry* 40, no. 7 (1942).

Radtke, Bruce, William Blair and Company, Chicago, IL.

Ratcliffe, Ronald. *Steinway*. San Francisco: Chronicle Books, 2002.

Report of Henry Bahr, National Lumber Manufacturers' Association, of his conference with Howard Hopkins of the Timber Production War Project. October 12, 1943. Lumber and Timber Production Defense Conference, Forest History Society Archives, Durham, NC.

The Requisition Number: NM-36833-W for Contract# Nom 43568 was shipped on Car IC-18973. Yawkey-Bissell Lumber Company Invoice #547, December 28, 1944. W.W. Gamble III Collection, White Lake, WI.

Reynolds, R.R. "Timber: A Modern Crop." *U.S. Department of Agriculture— Yearbook of Agriculture: Science in Farming: 1943–1947*. Washington, D.C., U.S. GPO.

Richards, N.E. "Some Structure Temperature Measurements on a Hornet Aircraft." Department of Supply and Development. Aeronautical Research Laboratories. Report SM-139. Commonwealth of Australia, Fisherman's Bend, Melbourne, September 1949. U.S. Forest Products Laboratory Library, Madison, WI.

Richardson, David. Discussion at the Forest History Association Annual Meeting, Sheboygan Falls, MI. Fall 2006.

Roddis, Augusta D. Letter to her great-niece Gillian Bostock for Gillian's school "Grandparents' Project" in 1992. Courtesy of the Lempereur family, whose mother, Ellen Roddis Lempereur, was a sister of Augusta D. Roddis. Author's family papers and Wisconsin Historical Society Archives, Madison, WI.

————. Speech to a civic group in Marshfield, WI. Wisconsin Historical Society Archives, Madison, WI.

Roddis Bulletin. Roddis Plywood Corporation, Marshfield, WI. Wisconsin Historical Society Archives, Madison, WI. January 6, 1944; November 18, 1944; November 25, 1944; December 2, 1944; December 5, 1944; December 9, 1944; December 16, 1944; December 18, 1944; December 23, 1944; December 30, 1944; January 6, 1945; January 15, 1945; January 20, 1945; January 27, 1945; February 3, 1945; February 10, 1945; February 17, 1945; February 24, 1945; March 3, 1945; March 10, 1945; March 17, 1945; March 24, 1945; March 31, 1945; April 14, 1945; April 21, 1945; April 24, 1945; April 28, 1945; May 5, 1945; May 12, 1945; May 19, 1945; June 2, 1945; June 16, 1945; June 30, 1945; July 28, 1945;

Roddiscraft Catalogue. Roddis Lumber and Veneer Company, Marshfield, WI. Wisconsin Historical Society Archives, Madison, WI.

Roddis Plywood Corporation. "Summary of Warehouse Profits." April 30, 1952. Roddis Collection, Wisconsin Historical Society Archives, Madison, WI.

Roddis, William H., II. Interview by Sara Witter Connor, January 28, 2006; July 16, 2006; October 2005; October 2006.

———. Letter to Dan Maurer, January 8, 1997, Marshfield, WI. Wisconsin Historical Society Archives, Madison, WI.

———. Letter to Hamilton Roddis, February 1942. Wisconsin Historical Society Archives, Madison, WI.

———. Speech in Marshfield at the "Wisconsin Flying Trees" exhibit. Opening Reception. University of Wisconsin–Marshfield, Hamilton Roddis Library, 2006. Author's collection.

Royal Aircraft Establishment. Farnborough. Materials (NM) Quarterly Conference. Extracts of Minutes of the 18th Meeting held at RAE on Thursday, January 18, 1945. U.S. Forest Products Laboratory Library, Madison, WI.

Schmoll, Gordie. Interview by Sara Witter Connor, October 7, 2011, Marshfield, WI.

Schroder, Jack (ret.). Alston & Bird. Atlanta. NLRB Board Decision, in Re: Connor Lumber and Land Co., 52 NLRB 641 (1943). www.Bloomberglaw.com.

———. Alston & Bird. Atlanta. Re: Connor Lumber and Land Co., 47 NLRB 867 (1943). Bloomberglaw.com.

Schubert, Dorothy Catlin. Interview by Sara Witter Connor. Marshfield Veterans' Museum, June 3, 2010, Marshfield, WI.

Schug, Mark, PhD. *United States History: Eyes on the Economy. Volume Two: Through the 20th Century.* Economics America: National Council on Economic Education. New York, 1993.

Schug, Mark, PhD, and William C. Wood. *Teaching Economics in Troubled Times: Theory and Practice for Secondary Social Studies.* New York: Routledge, 2011.

Schull, George O. *Curing Time Tests.* Lab Note No. 25. Manuscript. Culver City, CA. Hughes Aircraft Company, May 9, 1941. U.S. Forest Products Laboratory Library, Madison, WI.

————. *Manual of Gluing Techniques*, 1. Hughes Aircraft Company. Copy No. 107. U.S. Forest Products Laboratory Library, Madison, WI.

Seymour, Gertrude A. *The Origin of the Wood Industry in Marshfield and Weyerhaueser.* A History of the Roddis Plywood Corporation. Marshfield, WI, Roddis Collection. Wisconsin Historical Society Archives, Madison, WI.

Sharpe, Grant W., and Clare W. Hendee. *Introduction to Forestry.* New York: McGraw-Hill Book Company, 1976. Fourth Edition.

Sherrill, Lt. Col. F.G. "Lumber Procurement for the War: Our Forest Resources and Contribution to Victory." *Journal of Forestry* 40, no. 12 (1942).

Shull, George D. *Manual of Gluing Techniques.* Hughes Aircraft Company. Copy No. 107. U.S. Forest Products Laboratory Library, Madison, WI.

Siempelkamp, Dieter, President. *Siempelkamp—100 Years of Development.* Krefeld, Germany, December 20, 1983.

Siempelkamp and Company. Krefeld, Germany. Letter to Hamilton Roddis, August 17, 1938. Wisconsin Historical Society, Madison, WI.

Smith, Eldon D., PhD from the University of Wisconsin. Professor Emeritus. University of Kentucky. Letter to Sara Witter Connor, March 18, 2009.

Some Accomplishments of the Forest Products Laboratory. United States Department of Agriculture: Forest Service. February 1, 1937. In cooperation with the University of Wisconsin. Forest Products Laboratory Library, Madison, WI.

Spencer, P.C., President of Sinclair Oil Corporation. "The Significance of Oil Progress Week." Oil Progress Week Dinner. Baltimore, October 12, 1953. Roddis Collection, Wisconsin Historical Society, Madison, WI.

Steinway & Sons Purchase Order No. 10908. LaGuardia & Wagner Archives, CUNY. New York. May 19, 1943; June 10, 1043; July 21, 1943; July 23, 1943.

Steinway, Theodore E. *People and Pianos: A Pictorial History of Steinway & Sons.* Pompton Plains, NJ: Amadeus Press, 2005.

Stevens, J.M. "Problems of Construction and Alternate Substitutions in Wood Aircraft." *Transactions of the American Society of Mechanical Engineers* 66, no 2 (1944). U.S. Forest Products Laboratory Library, Madison, WI.

Stokesbury, James L. A *Short History of World War II.* New York: William Morrow and Company, Incorporated, 1980.

The Stone House Historical Society, Deep River, CT.

Styer, Col. W.S. "Address to the West Coast Lumbermen's Association," quoted in "Editorial: More than Enough Before It Is Needed." *Journal of Forestry* 40, no. 4 (1942).

Summary of Warehouse Profits. Roddis, April 30, 1952. Wisconsin Historical Society, Madison, WI.

Swan, O.T., National Hemlock and Hardwood Manufacturers' Association. Letter to Walter Jones, War Production Board, October 4, 1943. Forest History Society Archives, Durham, NC.

Sweetman, Bill. *Mosquito.* New York: Crown Publishers, 1981.

Sydow, Wes. Interview by Sara Witter Connor, May 4, 2006, Marshfield, WI.

Taylor, Michael J.H., ed. *Jane's Encyclopedia of Aviation.* New York: Crescent Books, 1993.

The Timberman, an International Lumber Journal 47, no. 5 (March 1946). Roddis Collection. Wisconsin Historical Society Archives, Madison, WI.

Timber Producers' Association. *Bulletin* 18, November 18, 1942. Great Lakes Timber Professionals' Association Archives, Rhinelander, WI.

———. *Bulletin* 56, January 1, 1942. Re: Tires. Forest History Society Archives, Durham, NC.

———. *Bulletin* 57, February 1, 1942. Re: Tire. Forest History Society Archives, Durham, NC.

———. *Bulletin* 59, April 1, 1942. Re: Tires and Wages. Forest History Society Archives, Durham, NC.

———. *Bulletin* 60, May 1, 1942. Great Lakes Timber Professionals' Association Archives, Rhinelander, WI.

———. *Bulletin* 61, June 1, 1942. Re: Tires and construction lumber. Forest History Society Archives, Durham, NC.

———. *Bulletin* 62, July 1, 1942. Re: Forest Utilization and OPA Prices. Forest History Society Archives, Durham, NC.

———. *Bulletin* 77, October 1, 1943. Re: Wages. Forest History Society Archives, Durham, NC.

———. *Bulletin* 78, September 1, 1943. Re: Wages. Forest History Society Archives, Durham, NC.

———. *Bulletin* 79, December 1, 1943. POWs. Forest History Society Archives, Durham, NC.

———. *Bulletin* 80, January 1, 1944. Great Lakes Timber Professionals' Association Archives, Rhinelander, WI.

———. *Bulletin* 84, May 1, 1944. Forest History Society Archives, Durham, NC.

———. *Bulletin* 85, June 1, 1944. Forest History Society Archives, Durham, NC.

———. *Bulletin* 88, September 1, 1944. Forest History Society Archives, Durham, NC.

Timblend. *Weyerhaeuser News* 49. Weyerhaeuser Company. Tacoma, WA, April 1962.

Trees: The Yearbook of Agriculture: 1949. Washington, D.C.: United States Department of Agriculture, United States Government Printing Office, 1949.

Trends 12. National Association of Manufacturers. New York: November–December 1945.

Treutel, Leroy. Interview by Sara Witter Connor, September 2007. Stratford, WI.

Truman Commission. Lumber and Timber Products War Committee. Box 149. Forest History Society Archives, Durham, NC.

Uniform insignias of William H. Roddis II during WWII. U.S. Navy. Wisconsin Historical Society Archives, Madison, WI.

Union Brotherhood. Letter to Rudolph Paupl, National War Labor Relations Board, October 14, 1943. Wisconsin Historical Society Archives, Madison, WI.

United States Merchant Marine. www.usmm.org/libertyships.html, www.usmm.org/faq.htm/faqs.

United States Patent Office. Washington, D.C., no. 2,345,025.

———. Washington, D.C., no. 2,384,347.

University of Wisconsin Badgers Athletics. www.uwbadgers.com.

Upson, Arthur. "Lumber and the War Production Board: Our Forest Resources Are Contributing to Victory." *Journal of Forestry* 40, no 12 (1942).

The Use of Prisoners of War in Logging, Pulpwood, and Lumber Industries. United States Department of Agriculture. United States Forest Service. Washington, D.C.: January 4, 1944. Box 78a. Forest History Society Archives, Durham, NC.

"The Use of Wood for Aircraft in the United Kingdom: Report of the Forest Products Mission." U.S. Forest Products Laboratory in cooperation with the University of Wisconsin. No. 1540, June 1944. U.S. Forest Products Laboratory Library, Madison, WI.

U.S. Forest Products Laboratory and the United States Munitions Board Aircraft Committee. *Wood Aircraft Inspection and Fabrication.* January 1951. ANC-19A Bulletin. Washington, D.C. Subcommittee on Air Force–Navy–Civil Aircraft Design Criteria of the Aircraft Committee under the Supervision of the Munitions Board. Forest Products Laboratory Library, Madison, WI.

"Verbatim Record of Proceedings of Senate Committee Investigating National Defense Program—Lumber Testimony. Washington, D.C. November 24–25, 1942." Attached to the letter from C.M. Christiansen to Wilson Compton, National Lumber Manufacturers' Association. Letter from C.M. Christiansen to Senator Harry Truman with a copy to Wilson Compton, National Lumber Manufacturers' Association, December 2, 1942. Lumber and Timber Production of the War Committee. Truman Committee. Box 149. Forest History Society Archives, Durham, NC.

"Wage and Salary Adjustments." ND-169. Lumber and Timber Products War Committee. Washington, D.C., June 8, 1943. Forest History Society Archives–Labor, Durham, NC.

War Department Press Release. "Statement of Secretary of War on Industrial Mobilization Plan," December 10, 1936. Box 109, Forest History Society Archives, Durham, NC.

War Manpower Commission. Advance release, December 9, 1942. Office of War Information. Washington, D.C. Lumber and Timber Products War Commission. Box 78a. Forest History Society Archives, Durham, NC.

"War Manpower Commission Regulation Under Executive Order 932B." Lumber and Timber Products War Committee. Washington, D.C., April 19, 1943. Forest History Society Archives, Durham, NC.

The War Papers. "Part 45: Our Airborne Army Heralds New Phase of Warfare." *Daily Telegraph*, August 26, 1944. Camp 5 Museum/Wisconsin Forestry Museum Archives, Laona, WI.

———. "Part 54: The Daily Sketch." May 9, 1945. Courtesy of Camp 5 Museum, Laona, WI.

War Production Board. Activities and Orders. Forest History Society Archives, Durham, NC.

———. Address by J. Phillip Boyd, Director of Lumber and Lumber Products Division, to the National Hardwood Lumber Association. Chicago, September 28, 1944, WPB. Forest History Society Archives, Durham, NC.

———. Administrative bulletin #2. Washington, D.C., July 1, 1943. Lumber and Lumber Products Division. Box 143. Forest History Society Archives, Durham, NC.

———. Administrative bulletin #3. Washington, D.C., July 15, 1943. Re: TPWP. Lumber and Lumber Products Division. Forest History Society Archives, Durham, NC.

———. Administrative bulletin #4. 2nd Quarter Summary. Washington, D.C., August 1, 1943. Lumber and Lumber Products Division. Box 148, folder 2. Forest History Society Archives, Durham, NC.

———. Administrative bulletin #5. Washington, D.C., August 15, 1943. Lumber and Lumber Products Division. Box 148, folder 2. Forest History Society Archives, Durham, NC.

———. Administrative bulletin #228. Washington, D.C., February 13, 1942. Lumber and Lumber Products Division. Forest History Society Archives, Durham, NC.

———. Advanced press release #5797. Re: Lumber Requirements. Washington, D.C., May 31, 1944. Forest History Society Archives, Durham, NC.

———. Advanced press release #5959. Washington, D.C., June 23, 1944. Forest History Society Archives, Durham, NC.

———. Advanced press release #6012. Re: Lumber Allotments. Washington, D.C., July 1, 1944. Forest History Society Archives, Durham, NC.

———. Advanced press release #6468. Washington, D.C., September 17, 1944. Forest History Society Archives, Durham, NC.

———. Advanced press release #6616. Re: TPWP and production. Washington, D.C., October 6, 1944. Forest History Society Archives, Durham, NC.

———. Advanced press release #6838. Washington, D.C., November 14, 1944. Forest History Society Archives, Durham, NC.

———. Advanced press release #6890. Washington, D.C., November 27, 1944. Forest History Society Archives, Durham, NC.

———. Advanced press release #6970. Washington, D.C., November 12, 1944. Forest History Society Archives, Durham, NC.

———. Advanced press release #7008. Office of War Information. Washington, D.C., December 18, 1944. WPB. Forest History Society Archives, Durham, NC.

———. Box WPB. Forest History Society Archives, Durham, NC.

———. "Field Service Bulletin: Joint PUC No. 15—Urgency Ratings for Logging, Lumbering, and Pulpwood Industries," December 29, 1944, WPB. Forest History Society Archives, Durham, NC.

———. Letter from Leo T. Crowley, May 10, 1945. Box 112—Lumber and Timber War Committee. Forest History Society Archives, Durham, NC.

———. Letter to the Lumber Industry from J. Phillip Boyd, Director of the Lumber and Lumber Products Division, July 25, 1944. Forest History Society Archives, Durham, NC.

———. Letter to the Lumber Industry, January 1, 1945. WPB-#2660. Forest History Society Archives, Durham, NC.

———. Lumber and Timber Products War Committee. General Box 149, folder 1. Forest History Society Archives, Durham, NC.

———. "Lumber for War Purposes Depends on Trucks and Tires." Lumber and Timber Products War Committee. General Box 148, folder 1. Forest History Society Archives, Durham, NC.

———. *Manual of Policy and Procedures: Rules Applicable with Groups and Industry Representatives.* Washington, D.C., January 14, 1944. Forest History Society Archives, Durham, NC.

———. Press release, July 1, 1944. Forest History Society Archives, Durham, NC.

———. Press release, June 29, 1944. Forest History Society Archives, Durham, NC.

———. Press release #91. Division of Industry Operations. Re: Tires. Washington, D.C., January 31, 1942. Forest History Society Archives, Durham, NC.

———. Press release #4217. Re: Woods Workers Status. Washington, D.C., September 17, 1943. Forest History Society Archives, Durham, NC.

———. Press release #5112. Re: Lumber controls. Washington, D.C., March 8, 1944. Forest History Society Archives, Durham, NC.

———. Press release #5139. Washington, D.C., March 4, 1944. Forest History Society Archives, Durham, NC.

———. Press release #5139. Re: Lumber consumption and production. Washington, D.C., March 8, 1944. Forest History Society Archives, Durham, NC.

———. Press release #5722. Re: Wood Workers Selective Service Deferment. Washington, D.C., May 22, 1944. Forest History Society Archives, Durham, NC.

———. Press release #5827. Washington, D.C., June 2, 1944. Re: Estimated lumber production for the first quarter, 1944. Forest History Society Archives, Durham, NC.

———. Press release #5942. Washington, D.C., June 17, 1944. Forest History Society Archives, Durham, NC.

———. Press release #5959. Re: Lumber Controls. Washington, D.C., June 23, 1944. Forest History Society Archives, Durham, NC.

———. Press release #5997. Washington, D.C., May 31, 1944. Forest History Society Archives, Durham, NC.

———. Press release #6006. Re: Lumber Production. Washington, D.C., June 29, 1944. Forest History Society Archives, Durham, NC.

———. Press release #6012. Re: Lumber Allotments. Washington, D.C., July 1, 1944. Forest History Society Archives, Durham, NC.

———. Press release #6128. Washington, D.C., July 20, 1944. Forest History Society Archives, Durham, NC.

———. Press release #6262. Washington, D.C., August 9, 1944. Forest History Society Archives, Durham, NC.

———. Press release #6539. Re: Lumber control Order L-335. Washington, D.C., September 26, 1944. Forest History Society Archives, Durham, NC.

———. Press release #6840. Washington, D.C., November 18, 1944. Forest History Society Archives, Durham, NC.

———. Press release #6890. Washington, D.C., November 27, 1944. Forest History Society Archives, Durham, NC.

———. Press release #6970. Washington, D.C., December 12, 1944. Forest History Society Archives, Durham, NC.

———. Press release #7008. Washington, D.C., December 18, 1944. Forest History Society Archives, Durham, NC.

———. Press release #7056. Re: Manpower Shortages. Washington, D.C., December 21, 1944. Forest History Society Archives, Durham, NC.

———. Press release #7056. Re: Production. Washington, D.C., December 27, 1944. Forest History Society Archives, Durham, NC.

———. Press release #7091. Washington, D.C., January 5, 1945. Forest History Society Archives, Durham, NC.

———. Press release #9031. Washington, D.C., September 11, 1945. Forest History Society Archives, Durham, NC.

———. Press release #9048. Washington, D.C., September 12, 1945. Box 149, folder 1. Forest History Society Archives, Durham, NC.

———. Re: Home Repair. August 8, 1944. Forest History Society Archives, Durham, NC.

———. To Hardwood Plywood and Veneer Manufacturers, from C.P. Settor, Chief of the Veneer and Plywood Distribution Section: Lumber and Lumber Products Division. Subject: Surplus Aircraft Plywood Inventories: Lumber and Timber Products War Committee. January 20, 1944. Box 148, folder 2. Forest History Society Archives, Durham, NC.

———. WPB-2216. Letter to the Lumber Industry from J. Phillip Boyd, July 25, 1944. Forest History Society Archives, Durham, NC.

Warranty deed, March 2, 1943, from Claire Uihlein Trostel to Roddis Lumber and Veneer Company. Vilas County Courthouse.

"Wartime Planning to Meet Postwar Problems." Committee on Postwar Controllership Problems. Controllers Institute of America. New York, 1942.

Weekly Bulletin 25, no. 15. Wisconsin Manufacturers' Association. Madison, WI, October 25, 1945.

A Week of the War. Washington, D.C., Office of Government Reports. March 7, 1942. Box 148, folder 2. Forest History Society Archives, Durham, NC.

Welsh, John D. "Plywood Preferred." *Timber of Canada* 6, no. 9 (May 1944). Ottawa, Canadian Lumbermen's Association. Forest History Society Archives, Durham, NC.

White, Troy. *Moonlight Serenade.* Author's papers.

Winslow, C.P. *Wood Goes to War.* December 1942. United States Department of Agriculture. United States Forest Service. Forest Products Laboratory Archives, Madison, WI.

———. "Wood Goes to War." *Journal of Forestry* 40, no. 12 (1942).

———. "Wood Goes to War." *The Southern Lumberman* 165, no. 2081 (December 15, 1942): 143–47. Forest Products Laboratory Archives, Madison, WI.

Wirsbinski, Jim. Interview by Sara Witter Connor, September 16, 2011. Forest History Association of Wisconsin Conference, Marshfield, WI.

WISCO Airborne Reporter (Winter 2012–13).

Wisconsin and Minnesota Wage Adjustments. Northern Hemlock and Hardwood Manufacturers' Association. Oshkosh, WI, August 6, 1943. Forest History Society Archives, Durham, NC.

Wood, Andrew D., and Thomas Gray Linn. *Plywood: Their Development, Manufacture, and Application.* Edinburgh: W. & A.K. Johnston, Limited, 1942.

Wooden Wonder: The DeHavilland Mosquito Aircraft. Video. Personal collection of Eric Loveland, RAF (Ret.).

Woods, John B., National Lumber Manufacturers' Association. Letter to O.T. Swan, Secretary-Manager, Northern Hemlock and Hardwood Manufacturers' Association, Oshkosh, WI. Washington, D.C., May 6, 1938. Forest History Society Archives, Durham, NC.

WPB—Industry Cooperation Eases Propeller Problem. War Production Board—Lumber and Lumber Products Division. *Administrative Bulletin* 5. Washington, D.C., August 15, 1943. War Production Board, Forest History Society Archives, Durham, NC.

Wunrow, Anna Mancl. Interview by Sara Witter Connor, October 12, 2006, Marshfield, WI.

www.diggerhistory.info/pages-air-support/ww2-allied/mosquito.htm.

www.lancastermuseum.ca/bcatp.html.

www.schallerhardwood.com.

www.2worldwar2.com/mosquito.htm.

Yawkey-Bissell Lumber Company. Adjusted Earnings Statement, 1928–1945. W.W. Gamble II Personal Files. White Lake Historical Society, White Lake, WI.

———. Cash Receipts Journal/Petty Cash. September 1936–April/May 1946. White Lake Historical Society, White Lake, WI.

———. Financial Statement dated September 30, 1940. W.W. Gamble Jr., Personal Files. White Lake Historical Society, White Lake, WI.

———. Financial Statement dated September 30, 1942. W.W. Gamble Jr., Personal Files. White Lake Historical Society, White Lake, WI.

———. Financial Statement dated September 30, 1943. W.W. Gamble Jr., Personal Files. White Lake Historical Society, White Lake, WI.

———. Financial Statement dated September 30, 1944. W.W. Gamble Jr., Personal Files. White Lake Historical Society, White Lake, WI.

———. Financial Statement dated September 30, 1945. W.W. Gamble Jr., Personal Files. White Lake Historical Society, White Lake, WI.

———. Invoice Book, 1942. W.W. Gamble Jr. Personal Files. White Lake Historical Society, White Lake, WI.

———. Invoice Book, 1944. Order #280, Invoice 245. Personal collection W.W. Gamble Jr. White Lake Historical Society, White Lake, WI.

————. Invoice Book, 1944, Order #285-371. White Lake Historical Society, White Lake, WI.

————. Invoice Book, 1944. Order #436-444. Personal collection W.W. Gamble Jr. White Lake Historical Society, White Lake, WI.

————. Invoice Book, 1944. W.W. Gamble III Collection, White Lake Historical Society, White Lake, WI.

————. Invoice #333, August 28, 1945. Yawkey-Bissell Lumber Company Invoice Book, 1945. W.W. Gamble III Collection. White Lake Historical Society, White Lake, WI.

————. Invoice #490, November 11, 1944, U.S. Order# (23-207) 450348. White Lake Historical Society, White Lake, WI.

————. Invoice #508, November 22, 1944. Yawkey-Bissell Invoice Book. W.W. Gamble III Collection. White Lake Historical Society, White Lake, WI.

————. Invoice #543, December 1944. W.W. Gamble III Collection. White Lake Historical Society, White Lake, WI.

————. Invoice, July 5, 1944: U.S. Order #NXsx 61997, Requisition 155/44, Contract #Inq.NA41527-WL U.S. Contract #Inq. NA-43230. Order#NSX-67876, and Order #I-C-15609: Requisition NC-C-582: Contract #Inq., NY 41374-N. Yawkey-Bissell Invoice Book, 1944. W.W. Gamble III Collection. White Lake Historical Society, White Lake, WI.

————. Ledger Journal 5. White Lake Historical Society, White Lake, WI.

————. Ledger Journal 6. White Lake Historical Society, White Lake, WI.

————. Orders and Invoice Book, 1941–1945. W.W. Gamble Jr. Personal Files. White Lake Historical Society, White Lake, WI.

Yearbook of Agriculture: 1943–1947: Science in Farming. United States Department of Agriculture. Washington, D.C.: United States Government Printing Office, 1947.

Young, Col. Charles H. *Into the Valley: The Untold Story of the USAAF Troop Carrier in World War II: From North Africa through Europe.* Dallas: Print Communications, Incorporated, 1995.

INDEX

ABOUT THE AUTHOR

S ara Witter Connor graduated from the Baldwin School in Bryn Mawr, Pennsylvania. She has a BA from San Diego State University and an MS from the University of Wisconsin–Milwaukee. She is a Certified Flight Instructor–Instrument (CFI-I) with a Citation Jet Type pilot. Longtime board member and president of the Forest History Association of Wisconsin, she has also served on the Board of Directors of the Wisconsin Forestry Hall of Fame and Camp 5 Museum Foundation. Connor curated the nationally traveling "Wisconsin's Flying Trees: Wisconsin Plywood Industry's Contribution to World War II" exhibit, which had over 175,000 viewers. She has two sons and five grandchildren and lives in northern Wisconsin.